Twayne's United States Authors Series

EDITOR OF THIS VOLUME

David J. Nordloh

Indiana University, Bloomington

American Literary Criticism, 1800–1860

Volume I

TUSAS 339

AMERICAN LITERARY CRITICISM, 1800–1860

VOLUME I

By JOHN W. RATHBUN

California State University, Los Angeles

TWAYNE PUBLISHERS
A DIVISION OF G. K. HALL & CO., BOSTON

Printed on permanent/durable acid-free paper and bound
in the United States of America

First Printing

Library of Congress Cataloging in Publication Data

Rathbun, John Wilbert, 1924-
American literary criticism.

(Twayne's United States authors series ;
TUSAS 339-341)
Vol. 2 by J. W. Rathbun and H. H. Clark;
v. 3 by A. L. Goldsmith.
Includes bibliographies and indexes.
CONTENTS: v. 1. 1800-1860.—v. 2. 1860-1905.
—v. 3. 1905-1965.
1. Criticism—United States—History. I. Clark,
Harry Hayden, 1901-1971, joint author. II. Gold-
smith, Arnold L., joint author. III. Title.
PN99.U5R37   801'.95'0973   79-9903

ISBN 0-8057-7263-4 (v. 1)

Contents

About the Author

John W. Rathbun is Professor of English at California State University, Los Angeles, where he divides his teaching duties between the Department of English, in which he offers courses in nineteenth-century American literature, and the Department of American Studies, in which he teaches courses in intellectual history and Los Angeles area urban history. Active in professional groups, he has been a member of the National Council of the American Studies Association, President of the College English Association of Southern California, and President of the American Studies Association of Southern California. He has presented papers before various professional associations, has published articles on American literary figures and intellectual movements in such journals as *Modern Fiction Studies, American Quarterly, International Philosophical Quarterly,* and *Nineteenth-Century Fiction,* and has contributed chapters to two books on American culture. He is presently at work on a book on American avant-garde movements.

Dr. Rathbun was born and raised in Sioux City, Iowa, and during World War II served in the Field Artillery and Combat Engineers of the U.S. Army. He received his Ph.B., with twin majors in Philosophy and English, and his M.A. in English from Marquette University in 1951 and 1952 respectively. In 1956 he received his Ph.D. in English from the University of Wisconsin. Between 1969 and 1975 he served as Chairman of the Department of American Studies.

Preface

This book is the first in a three-volume survey of American literary criticism from 1800 to 1960; the other two volumes are *American Literary Criticism, 1860–1905,* by Harry Hayden Clark and John W. Rathbun, and *American Literary Criticism, 1905–1965,* by Arnold L. Goldsmith. Each volume is organized on a plan of chronological development, within which emphasis is placed on the origins and basic principles of critical schools and movements and on the major critics associated with them.

Because the period 1800–1860 has fewer really distinguished figures than in those following the Civil War, this volume differs from the other two in that it concentrates on types of critical principles rather than on schools or critics. The first two chapters provide extracritical as well as critical background for the four chapters that deal with specific critical points of view. The final chapter is devoted to Poe and Emerson, the only two critics who may be considered of the first rank.

While I cite a large number of books published by literary critics, the major effort in literary criticism is to be found in the magazines and journals of the period, of which there were a goodly number. Between 1815 and 1833 alone some one hundred and thirty magazines were launched. These magazines chiefly thought of themselves as annotators of America's new national institutions, an attitude which subtly affected their critical aims and standards. As organs of society, magazines were instrumental in breaking the reverential spell for foreign models and in promoting an "independent tone of criticism" supportive of American writers. In order to assess how well they met these ends, I have completely canvassed the files of sixty-five of these magazines and have consulted the files of many others. The policy in the period was to publish articles anonymously, but I have been able to identify a substantial number of authors.

Politically and socially the period was an immensely troubled one, and bears out Thoreau's point that even states have a confirmed dyspepsia. In 1800 the population of the United States was slightly in excess of five million, the large majority of whom lived east of the mountains. The nation had only one professional writer, Charles Brockden Brown, but it anticipated more. The few books published were laboriously set and printed by hand. A small number of magazines eked out a precarious existence, although the *Portfolio* in Philadelphia, by virtue of Joseph Dennie's editorial discretion and civic support, maintained a fairly good subscription list. Some intellectuals had what we would call today a sophisticated urban view. But the overwhelming view of the country at large was rural. Ideologically, the majority party of Jefferson had a utopian vision of a simple, stable, democratic nation composed of virtuous, self-sufficient citizens.

Even at the time, this vision ignored the built-in energies of westward and economic expansion. By 1860 few vestiges of the old ways remained. The population stood at over twenty-five million; after 1845 three hundred thousand immigrants a year had contributed their numbers to this total. Almost four fifths of the population lived in the North and West. Class identities based on work and income had been established. Confusion, acid controversy, bigotry, and militant prejudice had continually agitated the nation.

In intellectual and literary matters, a basically middle-class perspective prevailed. The general emphasis was on a rational respect for the practical and the objective, despite the occasional hoopla over religious enthusiasm, nature mysticism, and the intuition of truth. Humanitarian paternalism (as illustrated in the McGuffey readers, for instance) and the spirit of reform in general, especially as they aimed at the practical alleviation of established abuses, were also fixed traditions, however much obscured by the intensity of social debate and conflict. The legacies of eighteenth-century moral restraint, ethical idealism, social norms, and picturesqueness were all so deeply engrained in American attitudes that we have only small quantities of romantic pathology and subjective aesthetics to match against comparable movements in Europe. These factors, plus others that might be cited, confirmed Americans in their temperamental loyalty to probability, historical progress, and accepted standards. When Americans went abroad, as they began to do in increasing numbers in the 1820s, the Europeans they sought to meet and with whom they felt at ease were Scott, Southey, Tieck, de Stael, and Thierry. Emerson might make his pilgrimage to Craigenputtock. Most Americans sought more conventional company.

Preface

By the end of the period, American intellectuals, like American society, were confused and drifting. Literary critics, who shared in the uncertainty over the nation's problems, agreed on a few points: the need, for instance, to maintain some semblance of an ethical point of view; the need to integrate literature into the greater life of the country; the need to use literature as a resource in understanding the disturbing complexity which seemed to thwart democratic objectives. Otherwise, critics differed. The most flexible and useful criticism, practiced by E. P. Whipple, George Allen, and others, was an analytical approach based on sympathetic attention to literary structure and the writer's point of view. Its end purpose, not always observed, was evaluation. The impressionistic and eclectic criticism of Henry Giles, John Neal, N. P. Willis, and Henry Tuckerman, usually informed with a cosmopolitan spirit, is interesting but easily dismissed. The criticism of Edward Robinson, W. G. T. Shedd, J. B. Angell, and others, basically historical, was refined and given a secular tone after the Civil War through the vogues of Herbert Spencer and Hippolyte Taine. By then, Poe, Prescott, Irving, and Cooper were dead, and those elements which loosely serve to define the years 1800–1860 as an historical period were scattered.

For my research I have depended on the resources of the University of Wisconsin Memorial Library, the Wisconsin State Historical Library, the Milwaukee Public Library, the Henry E. Huntington Library, and the Library of California State University, Los Angeles. I am grateful to their staffs for the help given me. Expenses were met by grants-in-aid from the Office of Research of California State University, Los Angeles. Several of my colleagues, namely Walter Fisher in Speech Communication and David Laird and John Bushman in American Studies and English, read particular chapters in manuscript and gave helpful advice. Harry Hayden Clark of the University of Wisconsin, Arnold Goldsmith of Wayne State University, and David J. Nordloh of Indiana University read the entire manuscript and offered excellent criticism and suggestions. Nancy Craven and Lyle Waters typed the manuscript and discreetly corrected my errors.

JOHN W. RATHBUN

California State University, Los Angeles

Chronology

1801   Joseph Dennie establishes weekly *Portfolio*.

1803   The Boston *Monthly Anthology* founded. Samuel Miller's *A Brief Retrospect of the Eighteenth Century*.

1806   S. C. Thatcher "On Taste," a statement of conservative associationist theory, appears in the *Monthly Anthology*.

1810   Charles Jared Ingersoll's *Inchiquin, the Jesuit's Letters*.

1811   Robert Walsh establishes the *American Review of History and Politics* as the first quarterly in the United States.

1813   Mme. de Stael's *Germany* and *Influence of Literature upon Society* published in Boston, New York, and Philadelphia. The *Christian Disciple* founded, to become in 1824 the immensely influential and enlightened Unitarian *Christian Examiner*.

1815   De Witt Clinton's *An Introductory Discourse Delivered Before the Literary and Philosophical Society of New York*. *North American Review* founded in Boston.

1819   Irving's *Sketch Book* contains "Mutability of Literature," a defense of harsh criticism. Ticknor begins teaching modern languages at Harvard. E. T. Channing appointed to the Boylston Chair of Rhetoric at Harvard.

1825   Bancroft publishes a laudatory essay on Herder in the *North American*. Bryant and Robert Sands jointly edit the *New-York Review*, an outgrowth of Sands's *Atlantic Magazine*.

1826   Bryant assumes the editorship of *The United States Review and Literary Gazette* and defines a theory of unrestrained romanticism in his Lectures on Poetry before the American Academy of Art. *Graham's Magazine* founded in Philadelphia.

1827   Timothy Flint reflects emerging culture in founding *The Western Magazine* (later *Western Monthly Review*) in Cincinnati. Robert Walsh founds *American Quarterly Review*, known for its intense nationalism. Bancroft begins his influential series on German literature in *American Quarterly Review*.

1828   Cooper defines his social and literary views in *Notions of the*

Americans. Southern Review founded. Noah Webster's *An American Dictionary of the English Language.*

1829   Bryant becomes editor and part owner of the New York *Evening Post.* Samuel Knapp pioneers in writing American literary history in *Lectures on American Literature.* James Marsh's edition of Coleridge's *Aids to Reflection.*

1830   Joseph Worcester's conservative *Comprehensive Pronouncing and Explanatory Dictionary of the English Language* answers Webster. W. E. Channing's "Remarks on National Literature" in the *Christian Examiner.*

1831   Unknown author's "Theory of Association in Matters of Taste" in the *Southern Review.* Edgar Allan Poe's *Poems,* with the prefatory "Letter to B. . . ."

1832   Washington Allston's *Lectures on Art.* Prescott's "English Literature of the Nineteenth Century" in the *North American.* Mrs. Trollope's *Domestic Manners of the Americans.*

1833   *The Knickerbocker Magazine,* soon to be an influential monthly, founded by Lewis Gaylord Clark in New York. James Marsh's edition of Herder's *Spirit of Hebrew Poetry.*

1834   Bancroft begins publication of his monumental *History of the United States.* The *Southern Literary Messenger* founded in Richmond.

1835   *The Western Messenger,* within a year to be edited by J. F. Clarke, begins publication as a spokesman for Western Transcendentalism. G. B. Cheever's defense of Coleridge as poet and philosopher published in *North American.* Ripley precipitates a five-year quarrel with conservative Unitarianism with his review in the *Christian Examiner* of Marsh's edition of Herder.

1836   Emerson supervises first book publication of Carlyle's *Sartor Resartus* and himself publishes *Nature.* Poe reviews the relation between phrenology and literature in his analysis of Drake and Halleck.

1837   *The Democratic Review* founded by J. L. O'Sullivan. Emerson lectures on "The American Scholar" at Harvard. Poe assesses Bryant's poetry in *Southern Literary Messenger.* C. S. Henry edits *The New York Review,* one of the best quarterlies in the entire period, in which appear George Allen's Coleridgean essays, "The Study of Works of Genius" (1837) and "Reproductive Criticism" (1838).

1838   Cooper's *The American Democrat.* The American edition of Tocqueville's *Democracy in America* published. Motley's

"Goethe" in the *New York Review*. Orestes Brownson edits *The Boston Quarterly Review*, which merges with the *Democratic Review* in 1842. Emerson supervises publication of Carlyle's influential *Critical and Miscellaneous Writings* and delivers "Divinity School Address."

1839   Motley publishes his extensive review of "Goethe's Works" in the *New York Review*. Irving's "Desultory Thoughts on Criticism" in the *Knickerbocker*.

1840   Founding of *The Dial*.

1841   Margaret Fuller's "A Short Essay on Critics" in *The Dial*. Emerson's *Essays, First Series*.

1842   *The Southern Quarterly Review* founded, to become under Simms (1849–1855) a leading voice for the Southern position. Poe reviews Hawthorne's *Twice-Told Tales* in *Graham's* and develops his theory of the short story. Rufus Wilmot Griswold's *Poets and Poetry of America*.

1843   Founding of *Bibliotheca Sacra*.

1844   Margaret Fuller's *Women in the Nineteenth Century*. W. A. Jones's "Critics and Criticism of the Nineteenth Century" in *Democratic Review*. Emerson's *Essays, Second Series*.

1845   *The American Whig Review* established in opposition to the *Democratic Review*.

1846   Poe's "The Philosophy of Composition" in *Graham's* and his critical assessments of New York literary figures in *Godey's Lady's Book*.

1847   Motley's "The Novels of Balzac" in the *North American*. Thoreau's "Thomas Carlyle and His Works" in *Graham's*. Founding of *Massachusetts Quarterly Review*.

1850   Poe's "The Poetic Principle" published posthumously in *Home Journal*. Melville's "Hawthorne and His *Mosses*" in *Literary World*.

1854   W. G. White attacks Collier's scholarship in *Shakespeare's Scholar*.

1855   The Duyckincks publish *Cyclopaedia of American Literature*.

1856   George Ripley begins editorship of the book review department of the New York *Tribune*.

1857   Henry Timrod's "The Character and Scope of the Sonnet" in *Russell's*. Lowell assumes the editorship of *The Atlantic Montly*.

1860   William R. Coggeshall's *The Poets and Poetry of the West*.

CHAPTER 1

Growth of a National Literature

IN the first two decades of the nineteenth century an exuberant spirit of nationalism entered almost all aspects of life. Jefferson's inauguration in the new city of Washington, where he democratically walked between his lodgings and the Capitol, dramatized this new self-consciousness. Gradually a complex of symbols began to accrue to the nation. The White House took on additional character. The eagle became the national emblem. President Monroe, the last of the "cocked hats," enjoyed nostalgic respect. The final version of the national flag was established. The Fourth of July became a legal holiday. Uncle Sam replaced Brother Jonathan. Patriotic songs became popular.

Along with these more superficial aspects, there was an extension of economic and cultural nationalism. Despite opposition in the North and South, the American System, which sought to avoid Hamiltonian coercion by basing federal support for sectional trade on enlightened self-interest, was responsible for the protective tariff, a program for internal improvements, and the United States Bank. The Congress, over Jefferson's opposition, initiated an intellectual blockade of foreign books through the imposition of duties. The idea of a national university, proposed by Washington in the first draft of his farewell address and subsequently by Adams, Jefferson, and Madison, led to the establishment by Congress in 1819 of the Columbian Institute for Arts and Sciences as a quasi-national institution.

Traditional restraints on extremes in thought and conduct were complemented by developments within the period itself. The rural nature of the country, sectional diversity, and religious education strongly inhibited tendencies toward emotionalism or romantic sensuality. Writings in theoretical science, as evidenced by American interest in Sir Charles Lyell's three-volume *Principles of Geology* (1830–1833), focused attention on the orderly, intelligible principles of natural change. Utilitarian movements in science, documented in

15

Benjamin Silliman's *American Journal of Science* (founded in 1818), did much the same. Cooper, Emerson, and many others read the numerous government publications, marveled at the expansion of the railroads and S. F. B. Morse's invention of the telegraph, both of them aids to communication, and welcomed the establishment of *Scientific American* in 1845 and the American Association for the Advancement of Science in 1848.

The educated clergy were a significant element in promoting this sober intellectualism. Since secular liberalism did not become a force in American thought until the 1840s, it fell to the clergy to profess reason, humanitarianism, progress, and culture. The absence of church-state ties (the reform action of Massachusetts in 1833 was one of the last) encouraged the clergy to develop their intellectual rather than their political muscle. Conditioned to a new world view by, among other things, the turn from physics to the biological sciences, even conservative Congregationalists, Presbyterians, and neo-Calvinists fostered a changing intellectual and emotional atmosphere, which reached fruition by the 1840s. But they consistently maintained sturdy objective criteria in social organization and literature.

I   American Magazines

By the 1830s American publishers were vigorously meeting the expanding literacy of the country on practically all levels. Benjamin Day's New York *Sun*, established in 1833, was the first mass-circulation paper to sell for a penny. It was followed by James Gordon Bennett's New York *Herald* in 1835 and Horace Greeley's New York *Tribune* in 1841. The needs of more literate readers were met by the *Knickerbocker, Graham's,* the New York *Mirror,* and *Godey's Lady's Book,* among others, all of which printed original poetry and fiction and supported, often precariously, a rising professional class of writers. A notch above these were learned quarterlies like the *North American Review,* the formidable representative of New England intellectualism, and the *Christian Examiner* and *American Quarterly Review.*

As early as 1796 the *Massachusetts Magazine or Monthly Museum* described itself as a "kind of thermometer" for ascertaining new movements in literature, history, politics, art, manners, and improvements. This kind of intellectual range was prized even then. The periodicals, said the *Southern Quarterly Review,* "constitute our native learning, and . . . if learning and scholarship are sought for, they are to be found in these works, which are an evidence, and a fair one, of our literary pretensions and our national character."[1] And when Cornelius Mathews and Evert A. Duyckinck established the *Arcturus* in 1840, their editorial statement declared that the magazine would range from the fine arts, architecture, painting, music, religion, and drama to fashions. "Whatever is an index to the habits of thinking of a people, fairly falls within the attention of the critic."

Supporters of a national literature in those early years especially sought to liberalize critical thinking. The lack of "formal criticism" in his review of Irving's *Sketch Book*, said Verplanck, was due to the fact that the "public law of literature" absolved periodical critics from conforming to the standards of "ordinary critical tribunals."[2] Faced with a dearth of good work and sensitive to the still fresh memory of European derision, early nationalists simply eschewed formal criticism in hopes of creating a sympathetic environment for native writers. For this seemingly lax attitude, both broad-minded cosmopolites and backward-looking conservatives attacked them as "impetuous chemists" trying to promote a national literature like a hothouse plant. But nationalists took the emergence of Irving, and shortly later of Bryant and Cooper, as at least a partial vindication of their method.

II *Popular Democracy and Literary Ideas*

Early nationalists had stressed picturesqueness, patriotic tradition, and mild, broadly based principles of social and moral authority.[3] After 1830, such simple expectations carried little weight. A new tone of militancy in promoting national progress appeared. The franchise, especially in the North and West, was broadened to include almost all white male citizens, and property qualifications for officeholding were eased. Reform movements of every imaginable kind strove between 1830 and 1860 to incorporate principles of social justice and democratic equality into the national life. Utilitarian secular reform began to supersede the traditional Christian movement. Francis Lieber and Samuel Gridley Howe worked effectively for penal reforms. A substantial peace movement began through the efforts of such men as William Ladd, William Lloyd Garrison, and the indefatigable Elihu Burritt. Women battled for the franchise and against demon rum. Utopian communities, especially those under the auspices of Fourierite socialists, spread from Massachusetts to Illinois. Antislavery agitation, often fettered by an extremist fringe, gradually became so significant as to constitute one of the key issues in national politics. Revivalism, Millerism, Mormonism, and Transcendentalism all testified in their various ways to rebellion against the "pale negations" of religious orthodoxy.

This complex movement in dynamic popular democracy, often described in shorthand fashion as the age of Jackson, had its analogues in thought and art. The so-called sensationist materialism of Locke and the Scots, the reliance on conventional formulae for thought and creativity, the trust in "associations" as a means for fostering the imaginative use of physical details—these were either rejected or incorporated into a broader intellectual scheme. The new issues that engrossed men's reflection until the Civil War were the result of developments on three fronts.

A. *The Writer as Seer and Leader*

The first of these—certainly the most fruitful in terms of perennial influence on the theory and criticism of literature—was the romantic idealism of yea and nay sayers like Emerson, Whitman, and Melville. Its most significant attribute is a deep subjectivism, in which individual expression is equivalent to the universal. Romantic idealism was foremost a democracy of spirit, prompting men to reject all demands that writers accommodate themselves to traditional forms and ideas. The American tendency to lean too heavily on England had resulted, said Emerson, in an "enormous paper currency of Words" that spelled the death of the imagination. It was no better to rely on American scenery or American types. Hawthorne might relax into the old view of Irving and complain about the lack of associations in American culture, but his best work was thought to illustrate the principle that personal vision rather than patriotic antiquarianism made for literary achievement. The attempt to write like an Englishman or a Frenchman or to "cleave to nationality" was wrong, said Melville in his review of Hawthorne's *Mosses;* "let him write like a man, for then he will be sure to write like an American."

These men recognized that literary culture is rooted in place and time, but they wished to startle society out of its fur-lined ruts of convention, custom, and habit. Society must be persuaded to honor wisdom over knowledge, imagination over talent, vision over circumstance. Thus their apotheosis of the artist, whose main objective was to break up old habits of perception in order that we all might see better. "The maker of a sentence," Emerson wrote in his journal, "like the other artist, launches out into the infinite and builds a road into Chaos and old Night, and is followed by those who hear him with something of a wild, creative delight." The militantly democratic Whitman celebrated the writer as seer and leader. And Melville said that critics might "intuit" a writer's artistry, but they would never be able to "ring" it or test it through the mind.

This elevation of the artist in romantic idealism has its links with the older view of genius. But there is a significant difference. Melville's description of Hawthorne as "a great, deep intellect, which drops down into the universe like a plummet," was couched in an image that would scarcely have been thought appropriate twenty-five years earlier. The difference lies in the later concept of symbolic expression. A literary work should transcend its empirical reality, suggest a range of reality not ordinarily encountered in everyday life, or radiate a spiritual power beyond its conceptual nature. Ideally, there should be a supreme fusion of form and expression. "Ask the fact for the form," said Emerson. Out of all this came a view of the writer as oracle, who shows us what is spiritually distinctive about human life, and who in his passionate intensity creates a perfect synthesis of aesthetic aim and spiritual achievement.

B. *Cultural Cosmopolitanism*

The second major front, cultural cosmopolitanism, is also anchored in romantic idealism. Its expectations, when one looks at such representative figures as Irving and Longfellow, were modest and its aims were tame. Because of its close ties to Europe, cultural cosmopolitanism will be discussed at greater length in the next chapter. But it needs to be noticed here because it was in sturdy opposition to the strident clack and clutter that disturbed the American scene in these years. Two points characterize cultural cosmopolitanism: a nostalgic memory for older European art forms, and a sense of world community. The first led to a wide and on the whole nerveless critical toleration, and the second performed a real service by placing art outside the context of national progress or Manifest Destiny.

Theoretically, cultural cosmopolitanism was based on what Lowell described in his preface to the *Pioneer* as "the eternal and unchanging laws of beauty which are a part of the soul's divine nature."

Fortunately Lowell, whose criticism is muscular and flexible, had the will to bring out the particulars embedded in such a generalization. And so to a lesser extent did Ticknor, Prescott, and on occasion Longfellow. But in the main, criticism was genteel, vague, and slight.

A thin critical view is especially true of those men who revered Italy, a country most Americans regarded as the culture center of the world, and which almost all travelers made the penultimate stop on their grand tours. Following in the footsteps of Washington Allston, large numbers of American artists, including Hiram Powers, Horatio Greenough (whose prose was thought superior to his sculpture even in his own day), and Harriet Hosmer, settled there in the 1830s and after. Charles Eliot Norton, who later published his notes on Italy, hobnobbed with these American expatriates, as did Henry Tuckerman, whose mild *Artist Life* (1847) is representative of the amiable lack of definition of artistic purpose in the group. All these people saw Italy through the muzzy folds of the past. Inspired by Renaissance art, they extolled a cultural fusion of literature, painting, sculpture, and philosophy. Kenyon's spiritless self-doubt in Hawthorne's *The Marble Faun* suggests that the fusion lacked substance. Yet the work of the cosmopolites did loosen the grip of parochial concerns and did help to broaden American cultural awareness.

C. National Character

The third frontier is a quickened interest in concretely defining national character—a problem that at one time or another caught the attention of every critic. Almost alone Edward Everett thought it would be more rewarding to study the pluralistic nature of societal structures. The vast majority of his contemporaries viewed society as a culturally integrated whole moving progressively according to some dominant spiritual law lodged in the society itself. Thus all sectors of a society were assumed to be organically interdependent.

In one form or another Emerson's dictum that "America is a poem in our eyes" was ratified by every nationalist. But how to analyze the poem? Verplanck spoke for the common view when he said in 1818 that American intellectual power must grow "in conformity to the general system of our institutions and manners." Consequently men must look not to individuals but to "aggregate results" to understand national character.[4]

To Brownson, in his radical period, this meant study of economic conflict. To the political activists identified as Young America, it meant study of the progressive movement toward social equality. But the majority of critics thought that the "internal law of [American] organic and spirititual life" lay in the nation's Anglo-Saxon heritage. In simpler terms, the people through their institutions would develop a character within the context of Protestantism and political freedom. Reviewers struck on the point over and over, with all the moral fervor of present-day Soviet critics decreeing "social realism."

After 1830 American periodicals were full of the idea that American national character would be an improvement over the original racial stock. Men spoke of the dominant Anglo-Saxon element and the "providential balance" of other races who were expected to contribute their best characteristics. The "destiny" of America, Margaret Fuller pointed out, was to "accomplish great things for human nature, and be the mother of a nobler race than the world has yet known."[5] Longfellow noted in his journal in 1847 that the American race would be a blend of the French, Spanish, Irish, English, Scotch, and German, and said that a national writer would represent the best of all these, a view he repeated in *Kavanagh*. Simms likewise agreed that the Anglo-Saxon strain would achieve its greatest glory in a "modified American form."

Concern for national character had its effect on the attitude taken toward the writer. Practically every critic acknowledged that God directed the events of the world. But God worked through the "agency of natural causes" in impressing "distinctive moral and intellectual traits" on a people. In the realms of mind and matter, nature was the efficient cause. Speaking of the history of thought, Daniel Webster said that there was a "fixed relation between cause and effect," so that "the most transient idea, that passes in the brain, may be traced to some determinate circumstance of intellectual education."[6] Lowell ridiculed those phrenologists who felt that the form of art is determined by the shape of the author's head, which in turn is shaped by "the peculiar configuration of his native territory," but even he admitted that literature had its "pedigree," so that American literature would be a "true reflection of our social, political, and household life."[7]

Few critics subscribed to the radical freedom of Emerson, who thought that the autonomy of the individual, the universality of moral law, and voluntary acceptance of the law guaranteed individual perfection. Practically everyone felt that the individual, including the writer, should voluntarily submit to the gentle constraints of national character, itself subject to universally valid natural law. Sometimes this view had strong political underpinnings, as James Mulqueen has pointed out in his study of Whig attitudes in *The American Review*.[8] At any rate, the idea of national character prompted men to speak of freedom in collective rather than individual terms. Here, however, they attached a substantial reservation: society has a circumstantial ability to translate desire into action in order to realize its good. In a slightly backhanded fashion, the reservation granted society self-forming powers.

Thus the writer was supposed to draw his literary sustenance from the national vitality. Lowell celebrated individual creativity, but in the larger view writers were the product of "some genetic principle in the character of the people and the age which produce them."[9] Whipple was of similar view, and so was a whole galaxy of critics. Even Emerson, whose views on consistency are well-known, admitted that literature was the best "illustration of the laws by which the world is governed," and like Brownson said that this was not a matter of "luck" but of "Fate."[10]

III   The Study of the American Past

As a consequence of these general political and philosophical ideas, some critics were prompted to literary history as a means for pinpointing aspects of the national character. The venture was thought a novel one. Early in the century Joseph Buckminster, reviewing Samuel Miller's pioneering *Brief Retrospect of the Eighteenth Century*, pointed out that none of the ancients had written a "formal retrospect" of their literatures. It was only in modern times, he said, that "the history of literature" could become a "distinct branch of knowledge."[11] The view was repeated in 1827 by a critic writing for the *American Quarterly Review*. Previous to the nineteenth century, he said, "no investigations were made to search out the almost forgotten memorials of former efforts, and trace the culture of the country to its origin." As American literature had come to assume "high rank," interest in the past increased and its literary and social characteristics were being established.[12]

Most lengthy studies were unsatisfactory. Samuel Knapp's *Lectures on American Literature* (1829), one of the first full-length studies in nationalist terms, is deficient in scope and analysis. William Dunlap's *History of the American Theatre* (1832) still provides rich source material, but, while Dunlap thought of himself as an historian, the book is primarily a defense of the theater against rigid moralists.

The literary and intellectual history that Verplanck once contemplated never got written, but *The Adventures and the Dangers of the American Scholar* (1836) is based on his idea that the momentum of American society was carrying every institution and discipline in its train.

Among shorter studies, George Tucker's discourse before the Lyceum at Charlottesville enumerated writers and events in American literary history from Edwards to the present and argued that the periodicals best reflected "national talent and taste."[13] Samuel Osgood, trying to ascertain how Puritanism had imperceptibly shaded into Emersonian idealism, argued that the genius of Puritanism was in the "graphic imagery" and spiritual depth of its prose.[14] Dexter Clapp, who adapted the theories of G. P. Marsh and George Bancroft to a survey of the fine arts in America, corroborated Osgood's finding. The Puritan character, in its origins cold, uniform, strong, and judicial like the English, had responded to its relocation in America by developing new institutions, new principles of political and religious freedom, and a new identity.[15] Such views were emphasized for English eyes in the articles of N. P. Willis and Timothy Flint for the London *Athanaeum.*

IV *Language and the National Mind*

With the appointment in 1819 of George Ticknor to a professorship of modern languages at Harvard, and with increased interest in language as a means of ethnological and cultural investigation, study of the relationship between language and literature was greatly spurred. Periodicals published reviews of dictionaries and books on Americanisms, and contracted for articles on idiom, language structure, and histories of languages.

Critics differed on the extent to which changes in language should be sanctioned. William Tudor, a staunch advocate of a national literature as the early editor of the *North American Review*, nevertheless wished to preserve the energy and beauty of the language in its "original purity," and he therefore attacked all "innovation and false taste."[16] The cause of purism was a losing one, however. More realistic than Tudor, Joseph Dennie admitted there existed no *a priori* principles for controlling changes in the language. Nevertheless, he sought to restrict change as much as possible, and he was absolutely opposed to Americanisms.[17] Earlier a defender of the purity of the language and hostile to innovation, Edward Everett abandoned this position while abroad to adopt the view that language grew out of situation in order to "keep progress with the changes in literature and manners."[18] Lowell's preface to the second series of the *Biglow Papers*, which began to appear in 1846, contains a long defense of language as a cultural phenomenon which sucks up vigor from the native soil. And N. P. Willis consciously used Americanisms and new coinages in his writing, provided that they were "conformable to American taste, customs, climate, or scenery."[19]

The net result of this thinking was to make language an index to the national mind. Peter Duponceau, writing in the *Transactions* of the American Philosophical Society, ascribed differences of articulation to accent, national tone of voice, and variations in elementary sounds, particularly vowels. Both Samuel Knapp and Jared Sparks maintained that geographical differences assured "equally varied and peculiar" languages. This close connection between national character and language caused scholars to advocate their mutual study to gain a full knowledge of the culture. For if a national language was the "mould in which the mind of a nation is cast," it followed that speakers of the language should have the "same mental identity."[20]

While these ideas were generally accepted among scholars, dictionaries were the authoritative means of disseminating them throughout intellectual circles. The big three of American lexicographers were John Pickering, Joseph Worcester, and Noah Webster. Pickering was a purist who recommended the "standard authors" of the eighteenth century as a guide to American English. He maintained that American speech was more uniform than the English and asserted that Americanisms were largely English provincialisms diffused over the country at the time of immigration. This view was upheld by John Russell Bartlett's *Dictionary of Americanisms* (1848), which noted that approximately nine tenths of the New England colloquial peculiarities were inherited from England. Bartlett's work in particular reinforced interest in the colloquial and in the national origins of expression, especially since he was well known as corresponding secretary of the American Ethnological Society and foreign corresponding secretary of the New York Historical Society.[21] Worcester, more liberal, said that differences in language resulting from "different institutions and the different circumstances and employments of the people" could hardly be overlooked by the lexicographer.[22]

As early as 1773 Webster had foreseen the time when America would have a national character commensurate with its civil and

ecclesiastical institutions. About the time of the Revolution he
founded the Philological Society, which fostered a literal attitude
toward language. Webster definitively stated his views in *An American Dictionary of the English Language* (1828). His long introduction
dealt with language from Adam to the present, the affinity of
language, the Saxon and Gothic languages, changes in the language in
both sound and signification, orthography, pronunciation, etymology, and a host of other subjects. The book's influence was pervasive.
Through its publication the cause of purism declined and usage
became established as the criterion of good language. And it put the
mantle of authority on the contention that language represented the
group mind of a nation. This in turn provided for a literature
illustrative of national psychology.[23]

Webster's influence on attitudes toward new idioms and provincialisms can be found in almost any random study of articles on
language. Noah Porter, in response to Webster, attributed new
words to the progress of thought, the extension of education, the
influence of new writers of "peculiar education, habits of thought,
sources of illustration," and the new liberty of creation.[24] Authoritative critics like Prescott, George Ellis, and the Reverend S. F. Smith
all argued for discretion in encouraging innovations in the language.
Others commented favorably on Webster's idea that while Anglo-
Saxon roots predominated, the language tended to merge foreign
idioms with main stems. Pointing out that etymology opened a "vast
career to true criticism," a writer in the *Southern Review* called for
etymological study in terms of the progress of language, national
history, and analogical conjectures and resemblances in structure and
pronunciation.[25]

One of the main contentions of students of language was that
philology was a tool in the scientific classification of racial origins.
Operating exclusively according to "historical principles," scholars
had given "an impulse to comparative philology which has re-
volutionized all previous methods and theories concerning language,
and made it a department of positive science. . . ."[26] Study of the
cases of the Indo-European languages, for instance, revealed a single
system of cases whose variations followed the "actual developments"
of the Western mind. The influential and scholarly Benjamin Barton
of the American Philosophical Society did not argue positively for the
unity of man as a species as did Blumenbach and Camper, but he
thought that, on the basis of language, it was probably true. He
included the Indians of North America as offshoots of the original

species in Asia. Such evidence of wide scholarly background and acquaintance with authorities is by no means uncommon in the period. It tends to corroborate the idea that, as elements of diversity multiplied to undercut old views of stability, corresponding attempts to find a basic underlying unity were also undertaken.

Once language was accepted as an index to the national mind and literature viewed as the legitimate product of a national language, philology became an integral part of critical theory. Language and literature were mutually dependent, went the refrain. In studying national literature, scholars made intensive research into language to establish chronology, the state of society, authorship, indebtedness to foreign countries. Ardent nationalists extolled the beginnings of peculiarities of American speech, and indirectly sanctioned pioneer attempts at the vernacular like Robert Montgomery Bird's *Nick of the Woods* (1837) and W. T. Porter's publishing of native humor in *The Spirit of the Times* (1831–1858). Thus G. P. Marsh's *Lectures on the English Language* (1860), a collection of thirty lectures delivered at Columbia College, was a militant call for a national speech and literature, which, he felt, could best be promoted by the liberal view which philology took of language change.

There can be no doubt that philology proved a useful critical tool to true students of language and literature. One of the distinguishing traits of Verplanck's edition of Shakespeare is his study of the connection between Elizabethan dialects and American speech and of the different growth of English in America. The appendix to Ticknor's *History of Spanish Literature* contained a long essay on "The Origins of the Spanish Language" which analyzes in detail "those idiomatic phrases, those unobtrusive particles, those racy combinations" which Ticknor had praised in *Lecture on the Best Methods of Teaching the Living Languages* (1832). B. W. Dwight, whose views on race are similar to Prichard's, wrote an impressive study of the Indo-European languages for *Bibliotheca Sacra* in which he developed an historical view based on "true, positive, philosophic, divinely ordained materialism."[27] In his inaugural address as professor of modern languages at Bowdoin (1830), Longfellow suggested that language was not an object in itself but a means to familiarize oneself with literature, trace the progress of the national mind, and "become a citizen of the world." Like G. P. Marsh, Longfellow deliberately chose historical over analytical criticism in his teaching at Bowdoin and Harvard and in his public lectures and articles, and at one point confessed to a "natural antipathy" to "censorious criti-cism."[28]

V *Balladry*

Ballad literature was also much valued in showing how varying manners and customs were signposts toward understanding the national mind. Antiquarian interest in national origins had its genesis in the eighteenth century, and Percy's *Reliques of Ancient English Poetry* (1765) especially recurs in nineteenth-century discussions of ballad literature. Americans found a real scholar among themselves in the Chaucerian F. J. Child, who published between 1857 and 1859 a series of eight volumes on *English and Scottish Ballads*. A revised edition was published in 1860. Influenced by Grimm and Herder, Therese Robinson (wife of the biblical critic Edward Robinson) published a two-volume edition of Servian popular poetry in 1826 designed to depict its development and relation to its country and people. Besides these better known editions, there was a host of collections and translations of ballad literature, the great majority of which reflected the current interest in relating ballads to social history.

The developmental thesis held that a national literature had its origins in ballad poetry, which undercut pleas for a distinctive American literature. But proponents of a national literature main-tained that the United States could rely on English tradition, and cited Robert Burns and Walter Scott as prime examples of the late expression of the ballad spirit. Whittier's *Lays of My Home* (1843) and *Ballads and Other Poems* (1841) and Longfellow's *Ballads and Other Poems* (1841) reflect their belief that modern balladry could still express the national spirit. And many scholars, viewing folklore as an index to group psychological attitudes, encouraged the folklore movement typified by Joel Chandler Harris as a means for focusing interest on the peculiar and diverse.

As might be expected, the ballad literatures of Spain and Scotland were the most conspicuous fields cultivated, though attention was also given to Teutonic and French balladry. English balladry was studied within the limits set by English scholars like Percy and Ritson. Discussing various anthologies of Scottish and English bal-lads, a writer in the *Southern Literary Journal* said that Scotland "far surpassed" England in indigenous balladry directly reflecting Scottish character and language. The Scot balladists were "of the people," whereas the work of Gay, Raleigh, Marlowe, and others was too self-conscious and lacked community of feeling.[29] The idea is echoed in the criticism of Prescott, Henry Reed, Lowell, and Longfellow.

VI   Sir Walter Scott

Through his poetry, novels, and criticism, Scott was a powerful force in the genesis of new critical attitudes. He also enjoyed a reputation as a scholar; he edited Dryden's *Works* and wrote a life of Dryden, edited Herbert of Cherbury's autobiography, the *Works of Jonathan Swift* and *English Minstrelsy*, and wrote many articles for the *Quarterly*. As a border balladist and chronicler he vastly encouraged the historical poem and novel in the United States. Simms, for instance, found his own views on the relation of literature and history easier to promulgate because of Scott, whom he praised repeatedly in *Views and Reviews*.[30]

It was through his novels, however, that Scott attained his greatest popularity and most influenced the turn taken by American literary theory. Once Scott began writing novels the attitude toward him was little short of idolatry. The historical novel in Scott's hands was compared to the soap bubble in the hands of Newton; it was an instrument of educative value. In an excellent article on American novels, Jared Sparks summed up the characteristics of the Waverly books which influenced American writers. The novels were historical, an advantage to the novelist because sympathetic associations were called forth in the reader. The novels used the variety and beauty of national scenery. And they used a large amount of dramatic dialogue, which provided point of view and revealed the actors as national and often provincial characters.[31]

Gradually three critical points of interest evolved: Scott's place in the history of the novel; his novels as repositories of antiquarian lore; and Scotland as a determinant in Scott's genius. Scott held "the throne and pinnacle" among writers. His work was a new venture in fiction. It did not hurt Scott's reputation that his position in English literature was exemplary, bearing on the best interests of society, and amusing and morally instructive. No one, said a writer in the *Southern Quarterly Review*, "capable of reading English at all, can be so utterly destitute of critical sagacity as not to have perceived that the novel became, in the hands of Scott, essentially different from any thing which it had previously been."[32]

Critics viewed Scott as an historian as well as a fictionist, and this attitude led to a queer suspension of critical principles in the analysis of his work. A critic for the *Southern Review* confessed that he was unfamiliar with the time and setting of *The Fair Maid of Perth* and so had consulted Buchanan's work on Scottish history to check Scott's facts.[33] Scott was a true antiquarian, said A. P. Peabody, and the reader could trust his "authentic information" just as much as that of the historian or traveler.[34] And the usually judicial W. B. O. Peabody excused Scott from lack of plot and unity because no unity existed in the "history of common life." This review, in fact, was one of the most liberal to come from Peabody's pen.[35] Even after one admits the influence of Byronism, German Gothicism, anthropological investigations by men like Heckewelder and Catlin, and historical incidents such as Tecumseh's rebellion, the metrical and prose romance of Scott must be reckoned the primary factor in both the theory and mechanics of the form.

VII   *The Anthology*

In the 1820s and after, the anthology became a favorite means of exploring the resources of a national literature.[36] Anthologies of foreign literature were intended to inform readers of the philosophy, history, and literature of people living under different institutions and modes of thought. Anthologists of American literature were inevitably literary nationalists. Here, as Henry Tuckerman pointed out, the "great object" of an anthology was to give a "candid and authentic presentation" of the standard of education and authorship in the United States in order to illustrate "past achievements and actual tendencies of the American mind as exhibited in literature."[37]

In terms of American response, Charles Cleveland's *Compendium of English Literature* (1856) and Longfellow's *Poets and Poetry of Europe* (1847) were two of the more popular anthologies of English and European literature. Cleveland's book was intended to show the "progress" of the English language and literature from Mandeville, Wycliffe, and Chaucer to the present. Longfellow's book, different from the hack job he did in *Prose Writers of America,* was explicitly based on historical principles and consisted of introductions, biographical notices, and criticism that related the literature to national manners and customs.[38] Among other anthologies, George Bethune's *The British Female Poets* (1848) is illustrative of a vagrant tendency at this time to extoll women as poets of the sensibilities, and

J. W. Jenks's *Rural Poetry of the English Language* (1856) reflects the interest in untutored and "plain" poetry.

American literature anthologies commonly included selections from Puritan writers, but there was some question about whether a distinctively American literature could have existed before political independence. Usually length won out. In his *Compendium of American Literature* (1858), Charles D. Cleveland raised two questions: what is American literature, and when did it begin? He answered the first question inadequately, and concluded that the "native growth" began in the Revolutionary period. His anthology, however, starts with Edwards, whom Cleveland pictured as a true American who had been "nurtured, trained, developed, matured, on our own soil, by the manners, habits, scenery, circumstances, and institutions peculiar to ourselves." John Keese's *The Poets of America* (Boston, n.d.) found most American poetry occasional and fugitive and its writers too busy in government, but he also discovered that it had a "true spirit" (which he left undefined). G. B. Cheever's immensely popular *American Commonplace Book of Poetry* (1831) was exclusively composed of modern American poems, because Cheever felt that a distinctive literature had not begun until after the political controversies with England. Cheever was particularly concerned with the religious attitude of American poetry, and his *The Poets of America* (1849) stressed the religious element in the national character.[39]

One of the more popular anthologies was the three-volume *Specimens of American Poetry* (1829) edited by Samuel Kettell. Robert Walsh viciously attacked Kettell's anthology in the *American Quarterly Review* largely because Kettell was a hack writer for S. G. Goodrich ("Peter Parley"), and others complained that Kettell lacked a sense of discrimination. But these men failed to see that Kettell's purpose was primarily historical. All of American letters, he said in his preface, were of "some value" if simply to afford insight into the American past and "the degree of social and mental improvement" of the nation. Complaining that there was "no where . . . even a tolerably accurate list of American authors," he set himself to trace "the general history of letters, and their connexion with the development of the moral and intellectual character of a people."

The best known, if not the best loved, anthologist was Rufus Wilmot Griswold. His numerous anthologies of American literature indicate the appetite of the American public for such books even in the face of almost unanimously adverse criticism. Griswold's critical principles, while not complex, are fairly sound. But his application of them is another matter. He was a Baptist and a predestinarian and a political conservative, and these features of his thinking have a tendency to creep into his writing and critical selections. His failure to adequately represent the West led to William Gallagher's *Selections from the Poetical Literature of the West* (1841) and W. T. Coggeshall's *Poets and Poetry of the West* (1860) and *Protective Policy in Literature* (1859). Many critics, especially the Young Americans, held that "a good history" of American letters was desirable, but felt Griswold was unable to distinguish elements of the national character or to note the literary contributions that had been made.[40] Yet Griswold does adequately reflect many of the root attitudes of American romantics. He was opposed to the "mechanist" philosophy of Locke and others. He was a militant nationalist. He believed passionately in copyright. He repeated the view of many that a national literature was the result of "an incidental consequence of energetic and well directed action for the moral and spiritual liberation and elevation of man." And he believed that poetry eternally progressed at a rate commensurate with the progress of ideas.[41]

VIII *Sectionalism*

From one point of view, critics believed that literature should be true to general nature. Yet they also recognized that literature was modified by the mediation of time and place, so that, as Simms said, critics had to deal with how writers "embody and represent the spirit of the age."[42] It was but natural, then, especially since sectional divisions had always been prominent in American political life, for literary activity to be closely related to geographical divisions. By the 1840s there was marked interest in sectional literatures as segments of an overall American literature. The *Literary World* said in 1847 that it desired a time when every state and section would find "its peculiar painter and historian."[43]

One reason for the rise of sectional sentiment was the tendency of New England to confuse its interests with those of the country at large. In her New York *Herald Tribune* review of Emerson's *Essays* (second series), Margaret Fuller praised New England as the "chief mental focus to the New World" and said that New England led America intellectually just as the heart, lungs, and nervous system lead the body.[44] Samuel Osgood noted that New England poetry breathed the spirit of America by a sort of "instinctive" law, and cited Alcott, Emerson, Thoreau, Bryant, Whittier, and Longfellow who best represented American virtues of independence, manly faith, devotion to nature, reverence for women, love of country and home, passion for liberty.[45]

Such smug conclusions irritated the other sections of the country. Educated Westerners, aspiring to the ease and decorum of culture, complained that the East failed to appreciate them or to properly understand them, and they frequently deplored, out of their own feelings of inferiority, the pendanticism, obscurity, and lack of commonsense values that seemed to characterize Eastern thought. Yet Westerners wistfully emulated the culture of the East, employed New England textbooks in their classrooms, and subscribed to Eastern and British periodicals in such numbers as to unfavorably handicap Western editors.[46]

Western periodicals invariably prefaced their way into existence with a call for sectional loyalty. But loyalty, fine in the abstract, seldom translated into the tangible rewards of financial support. As much as possible the magazines published Western poetry, stories, articles, and reviews of Western books in the belief that these would reflect a distinctive Western "tone." Sometimes they did. Timothy Flint was quite correct in stating that his *Western Monthly Review*, which was equal in quality to James Hall's *Western Monthly Magazine*, would serve as a synopsis for future historians of Western literary activity. But actually the best magazine to be published in the West during the period looked to the East rather than to its own region. This was the *Western Messenger*, which counted in J. F. Clarke and W. H. Channing two capable editors of strong critical intelligence. These men, while observing the amenities of Western concerns, reviewed European and Eastern scholarly books, and published articles by Margaret Fuller and poems by Keats, Emerson, and Jones Very.

New York criticism reveals many of the criteria accepted by the country at large: social obligation as against individual self-indulgence; moral rectitude as opposed to idiosyncrasy; American wholesomeness in contrast to European skepticism; national optimism and progress versus feudally derived traditionalism. Yet in its metropolitan spirit and a certain socially pragmatic tone, it had qualities of character all its own. From almost the very beginning, New York criticism was distinguished by a flair for humor, an admiration for ready wit, and a town spirit that felt uneasy before the heavy ethical philosophizing of New England. By the 1830s and following, factional disputes disturbed the literary scene.[47]

New York criticism was fairly slim before 1830. The most lively magazine was the New York *Mirror* (1823–1832), a weekly established by Samuel Woodward and George P. Morris, for which Fay, Cox, and Willis published genial and tolerant criticism in the manner of Lamb. Paulding, Samuel Woodworth, Robert Sands, and Verplanck were the prominent critics. Their contributions are markedly different. Both Paulding and Woodworth were versatile men of sturdy good humor who tackled practically all literary forms. Their concern for common sense, metrical decorum, and congruity places them firmly in the neoclassical tradition. Sands and Bryant made their contribution as editors; under their respective editorships the *Atlantic Magazine* and *United States Literary Gazette*, although short-lived, were the two best magazines in the city. Both men championed Wordsworth and were instrumental in moving New Yorkers to an acceptance of a moderate romantic literature. Sands died at an early age, but Bryant, even after assuming the editorship of the *Evening Post*, continued a major influence in New York politics and literature.

Irving and Verplanck both testify, in their development as critics, to shifting critical approaches to literature. Irving's drift from the neoclassical satire of *The Knickerbocker History* and the judicial essays on Holland and R. T. Paine to his later urbane sentimentalism and impressionism illustrates a changing temper which anticipates the relaxed tones of younger critics like Cox and Willis. The early criticism of Verplanck is almost exclusively appreciative, his reviews of Irving and Hunt being among the first examples of sympathetic impressionism. He had a more forceful intellect than Irving, and as he matured and laid more knowledge under contribution, his critical attitudes took on a scholarly aspect that owed much to contemporary German ideas on history.

The social, political, and intellectual ferment which agitated the country after 1830, especially intense in New York by virtue of its central commercial and political position, considerably altered the literary temper of that city. Lewis Gaylord Clark's *Knickerbocker*, established in 1833, tried to maintain the traditional tone of New York *savoir-faire* in its various departments, but the attempt was strained and on occasion lost grace altogether under the goading of the rival *Democratic Review* and other periodicals of Young America. The Establishment and the Movement, as John Stafford has characterized the Whigs and Young America, engaged in an aggressive and sometimes vengeful campaign for opposing views.[48]

The *Democratic Review*, established in Washington and later moved to New York by Hawthorne's friend, J. L. O'Sullivan, was designed to express and support the doctrines of the Jackson administration. While not precisely an organ for Young America, the magazine often reflected Young American views on class conflict, the immediate need for political and social equality, the labor movement, and the banking interests. O'Sullivan managed to bring together an impressive list of contributors in the Duyckinck brothers, Parke Godwin, W. A. Jones, Cornelius Mathews, and Hawthorne and Melville. Its leading critic was certainly Jones, who adapted the critical theory of Hazlitt to a strong democratic social consciousness. The general run of criticism in the magazine reflects the criteria with which we are already familiar. But in its emphasis on a democratic literature based on social equality, social justice, and the common people, in its hostility to all literature reflecting an acceptance of class and rank, and in its often unquestioning praise of writers if only they were "national," the magazine was bound to irritate its more conservative rivals.

Those rivals, in addition to Clark's *Knickerbocker*, included the *American (Whig) Review*, a handsomely edited periodical that published a good deal of solid criticism, especially in the area of theory, where such men as E. P. Whipple and Henry Norman Hudson presented their semi-Germanic and Coleridgean views. The magazine also had its fair game in Cooper and Cornelius Mathews, but its tone was not so vitriolic or vituperative as Clark's raking of Evert Duyckinck, Simms, Poe, and others.

The New Yorkers were cordial to such transplanted New Englanders as Margaret Fuller and George Ripley, both of whom wrote for Horace Greeley's *Tribune*, but they were uniformly opposed to Transcendentalism. The Episcopal beliefs of Duyckinck and Jones, coupled with their faith in the efficacy of reform legislation, made them chary of Emerson even after 1850, by which time Gaylord Clark had begun to participate in what ultimately became the national pastime of rehabilitating Emerson to a more acceptable image. The *New York Review*, a high-class Episcopalian magazine founded in 1837 which published excellent criticism under the capable editorships of C. S. Henry and J. G. Cogswell, also opposed New England Transcendentalism. Writers for the magazine, such as George Allen, who had been tutored by James Marsh, shared with the Transcendentalists a reverence for Coleridge, a respect for German scholarship, and belief in the moral sentiment and the intuitive reason. But these views, as John McVickar demonstrated in his preface to the 1839 edition of Coleridge's *Aids to Reflection,* were all safely tucked within the doctrinal precincts of the established church, much in the manner of Coleridge's later period.

The shift from sectionalism to regional nationalism distinguishes the South from the rest of the country. Even though politically the South was having difficulties with the Union throughout the period, it was not till nearly mid-century that its literature and criticism became divisive. Like the other regions, the South early hoped to promote a literature representative of Southern culture, and this led in time to a number of good magazines dedicated to improving the Southern position. "A southern book is both southern and American, as Charleston is both a southern and an American city," said *Whitaker's Magazine* in 1850, "and literature, in general, but does not lose its sectional character because it is national, nor its national character because it is sectional."[49]

Before reaction to Northern provocation resulted in critical sclerosis, Southern criticism was quite as complex and diverse as that elsewhere.[50] Most Southern critics ignored the German distinction between *Vernunft* and *Verstand,* extolled Scott as almost the sole arbiter of form and idea in the romance, and in general tended to defend caste, a strange blend of cosmopolitan and regional interests, and conventional literary forms broad enough to include the lyric and Poe's special kind of gothic tale. This is about as ideologically close as Southern critics got to one another, however. The old order was represented by William Grayson, staunchly neoclassical in his devotion to Horace and Johnson. Superior to Grayson in intellect and judgment was Hugh Swinton Legaré, a Charleston man of complex sympathies who preferred German to French scholarship and Greek models to the modern. His criticism, indebted to A. W. Schlegel, was on the whole moderate, with taste—as Edd Parks has recently pointed out—the final arbiter. The aesthetic view was upheld by Henry Timrod, who shared Poe's concern for beauty and imagination but left a place for truth as well.

The most energetic and capable critic next to Poe was William Gilmore Simms. Simms was a critic of catholic sympathies. His views tended to shift with added experience, but he was temperamentally an analytical critic who softened his judgments by reference to social and intellectual factors. "Neither to praise nor to blame," he said, "is the object of true criticism. Justly to discriminate, firmly to establish, wisely to prescribe and honestly to award—these are the true aims and criteria of criticism."[51] Until politics caused a break, Simms was on easy terms with many of the New York literati, and for a considerable time he was counted among the Democratic liberals hoping to promote a national literature. Later, as his review of *Uncle Tom's Cabin* indicates, Simms defended the South in as shrill a manner as any of his Southern contemporaries.

In the early decades, Baltimore, where John P. Kennedy, John Neal, John Pierpont, and William Wirt were especially active, was almost alone as a Southern literary center. It was here that Poe realized his first success, and it was due to Kennedy's recommendation that Poe became associated in 1835 with the *Southern Literary Messenger*. Later Charleston became a leading center; Gregory Paine cites sixty-three magazines published there before 1860.[52] After 1830, the chief magazines in the South were Legaré's *Southern Review*, Thomas White's *Southern Literary Messenger*, Simms's *Southern Quarterly Review*, and John Russell's *Russell's Magazine*.

In the 1850s the Southern position, aggravated by such matters as the Dred Scott decision, the troubles in Kansas, the panic of 1857, and the tariff controversies, became increasingly reactionary and isolationist. The abolition issue prompted both Northern and Southern critics to introduce extraneous matter into their critical articles. Antiabolitionism was not strictly a Southern position; such respectable periodicals as the *American (Whig) Review* were opposed to what was considered the radical position of men like Lowell and Whittier. Even Whitman in 1847 spoke of abolitionists as dangerous fanatics. But the South was forced to look for a propanganda medium of its own to counter books like *Uncle Tom's Cabin* or the preface to *Dred* in order to present the "truth" of the Southern position. Southern magazines uniformly maintained that American literature had been "corrupted by the turbid waters of Abolition." In the various Southern conventions of 1854 and after, as Benjamin Spencer has shown, respected Southerners like Charles Cayarré and Longstreet joined together to find ways to exclude Northern writings, to see that only those books favorable to the Southern position were adopted in the schools, and to generally promote what has been described in our time as "the closed society."[53]

CHAPTER 2

Continental Influences

AMERICAN interest in Europe in the nineteenth century is amazingly complex and diverse, as such monumentally thorough studies as Howard Mumford Jones's *America and French Culture,* Stanley Williams's *The Spanish Background of American Literature,* and Henry Pochmann's *German Culture in America* have demonstrated. Despite a vast ocean, irksome travel conditions, and tediously slow schedules, so many Americans increasingly visited the continent that their criss-crossing reminds one of a pedestrian scramble at a busy intersection. The motive was the pursuit of culture. Agents for rich but inexperienced lovers of art ransacked Paris and the Italian cities in search of "old masters." Scholars and scholar-amateurs made their pilgrimages to the great names of Europe and worked industriously in the European libraries. European expatriates, especially unsuccessful revolutionaries, were welcomed into the various American academies, seminaries, and colleges, whose curricula were expanded to include modern languages and literatures. European books, the French early and the German somewhat later, were reviewed and commented on at length in American periodicals. In time, translation took on aspects of an industry.

Yet the English tradition throughout the period remained the most compatible with American attitudes, as the discussion in the following chapters will suggest. English letters were simply more familiar, more comfortable, less radical, a sort of fatherland to the American mind. There were "arguments," of course. Yet everyone could love Sir Walter Scott, sympathize with William Cowper, marvel over Shakespeare, argue with John Locke and Thomas Reid, all in stimulating fashion. Compared to the English, European thought occupies a minor although important place in American critical theory.

The heady eighteenth-century French *philosophe* tradition found few American advocates. But French historians and the French eclectic school, led by Cousin, enlisted supporters and eventually

37

achieved a minor popularity. Their practical emphasis on both moral and secular issues, so at odds with the previous period of strife in France, was comforting and attractive to Americans. Interest in Italian culture was widespread, but except for Dante scholarship it remained largely unfocused. Why this was so is difficult to understand, but in general must be attributed to an uncritical nostalgia for past grandeur. Spain also presents problems, as Stanley Williams has indicated. Again it was largely an emotional rather than a reasoned respect for the past, although contemporary scholars like Conde and Saavedra were appreciated. The Spanish grandeur to which Irving, Ticknor, Longfellow, and others reacted was a past "poetry" in which the names of Lope, Cervantes, and Calderon loomed large.

The clue to German influence is in its concern with eternal truths, its sweeping philosophical statements, its passionate idealism. The Germans had developed a systematic, wide-ranging description of historicism and genius, which appealed to intellectuals increasingly aware of their period as "an age of history." Where English theory looked to empirical corroboration, and where the French tried for an uneasy reconciliation of empiricism on the one hand and objective idealism on the other, the Germans addressed themselves to the totality of being. Their philosophical principles, especially in the cases of Schelling and Hegel, resolved all contradictions. Existence was consistent and complete, its sources the realm of spirit.

Two aspects of European thought bore directly on American literary and critical theory. One was a cultural tradition rooted strongly in the past and evidenced primarily in the arts. The other was a happy blend of social character and individual genius that had its inception in the new romanticism. Scholar historians like George Ticknor and W. H. Prescott managed to bring these two aspects into fruitful relation, and even a relative amateur at history like Irving succeeded in making his Spanish work something more than a sentimental excursion into the past. But these were rare men. For the most part, the two aspects seem to have commanded separate loyalties, or at least to have occupied separate compartments within the same minds.

I   *Cultural Tradition*

A. *Interest in Italy*

Americans were infatuated with Italy. To many it was the *arbiter elegantiarum* for all attitudes toward art. There Jefferson had become enamored of Roman architecture and subsequently introduced into American public building a tradition that has never really been absent since. Washington Irving made his pilgrimage in 1805, and Washington Allston about the same time became the chief model of the American expatriate and the friend of Coleridge, who told him never to judge works of art harshly. In time Rome and Florence literally teemed with artists—such as W. W. Story and his circle, described in detail in Paul Baker's *The Fortunate Pilgrims* (1964)—all of them passionately involved in coming to terms with beauty and most of them hopeful of converting their countrymen at home to higher views.

Thus Thomas Cole, who arrived in Italy in 1831 for a four-year stay, published articles on Sicilian scenery and Italian antiquities in New York journals like the *American Monthly Magazine* and the *Knickerbocker*. Ticknor managed the acquaintance of Count Cicognara in Venice, the president of the Academy of Fine Arts, who presided over that city's society and was presently bringing out the third volume of his *History of Modern Sculpture*. Cooper, versed in painting and sculpture, advised S. F. B. Morse on how to paint in the Louvre and recorded his travel impressions in *Gleanings in Europe: Italy*. The eccentric art collector, James Jackson Jarves, published *Art Hints* (1855) and *The Art Idea* (1864), both of which show the influence of Ruskin's ideas. Emerson, traveling in Italy, was uneasy before the filagreed cathedrals, overdone architecture (which he thought imitative), and the self-conscious awe that Italy evoked in his friends; and in St. Peter's his manly sympathies were extended to "those mutilated wretches [who] sing so well it is pitiful to hear them." But while he reacted adversely to the continual drumming on his senses of the "rococo joy" offered by Italy, he could say, in walking through the museum on Capitoline Hill, that it contained "the wealth of the civilized world."[1]

This interest in Italian art led naturally to interest in the literature. Through Italians like Antonio Gallenga Mariotti, who lectured in New England and produced books written in Italian, such names as Monti, Foscolo, and Manzoni became more familiar and less exotic. Periodical articles increased and deepened. According to Angelina La Piana, more articles were published in the *North American Review* and the *American Quarterly Review* on Italian art, literature, and history than on any other European country.[2] Dante elicited attention. Reverently passive toward the great Italian poet, Americans regarded him as a man of profound morality and vaulting imagination, a noble poet whose works were a cornerstone of modern Western literature. New England was in the vanguard. "The New Englanders set his shrine next to those of Shakespeare and Milton," says La Piana, "and to them Dante became almost a symbol of a new cultural cosmopolitanism cherished as the ideal to be attained by all America in the not distant future."[3]

By the 1830s Dante's popularity was widespread. Southern magazines were publishing articles on Italian literature. Simms even translated sections of *The Divine Comedy*. Richard Henry Wilde, with the assistance of the young Charles Sumner, pursued Dante research in Roman archives. In New York, Lorenzo da Ponte, previously Mozart's librettist, was teaching the Italian language and literature at Columbia, and at Harvard Pietro Bachi was making his contribution to excellent programs in modern languages.

Still, the men who popularized Dante scholarship were Ticknor, Longfellow, Lowell, and Norton, all New Englanders. The first three, tenured in the Smith Professorship of Modern Languages and Literature at Harvard, regularly lectured on Dante. All four had both an historical and an aesthetic interest in Dante which found expression in teaching, translation, articles, and scholarly work. Margaret Fuller might complain of the "pedantic style" in which Dante was approached, but the fact is that these men did some fine exploratory work in the Italian's artistry and symbolism. Longfellow's complete translation, published in 1867, was excitedly discussed in American periodicals; and it was even commended by the duke of Sermoneta's Centennial Committee after a copy was received from the noted Scandinavian philologist, George Perkins Marsh, then American minister to Italy. Norton translated both the *Vita Nuova* (Emerson had tried his hand at a private translation about 1843) and the *Divine Comedy*, and serialized in the *Atlantic Monthly* a biography of Dante which he published as a book in 1859.

Norton was also one of the early defenders of his close friend Ruskin and of the Pre-Raphaelites, as was the New Yorker, William J. Stillman. But Ruskin and the Pre-Raphaelites were at best but moderately influential on American theory. There was simply nothing in America similar to the tradition against which the Pre-Raphaelites rebelled, although Pre-Raphaelite sympathy with the German Nazarene painters should have given them a foothold with Americans favorably inclined to religiosity and medievalism in art. Americans encountered some Nazarenes in Italy, where these

Catholic converts from Protestantism had moved to reverently study true painters like Fra Angelico and Martini. But the Nazarenes naturally tended to congregate in German art centers, and there they had to compete with the greater popularity of the Dusseldorf school.

B. *The Dusseldorf Influence*

The Dusseldorf influence on American art still needs extensive documentation, but enough is known to indicate that it was a formidable rival to such American movements as the Hudson River school. Albert Bierstadt, George Caleb Bingham, John Ehninger, and James MacDougal Hart were only four of great numbers of Americans who swarmed into Dusseldorf to study under Friedrich Schadow and Karl Lessing. These two were superb teachers of draftmanship and landscape painting. But the work often verged on the two extremes of melodrama and sentimentality, and it is likely that these kinds of theatricality proved irresistibly attractive to Americans. The Dusseldorf school's moral restraint in handling the human figure was also a factor in American acceptance. Americans were chary of nudity in art, just as they were nervous about public expression of sexuality in any context. William Rimmer, alone in depicting nude males (generally in engravings), omitted the genitalia. William Page and others rendered the female nude, but they relied on history, classical references, and precedent to avoid disapproval. At any rate, so influential was the German school that the Dusseldorf Gallery was a remarkable success in New York, where it competed with such other centers as the New York Gallery of Fine Arts, the American Art-Union, the Free Gallery, and the Cosmopolitan Art Association. Its genre approach was most popular, T. S. Noble's borrowings from Irving's *Knickerbocker History* and Ehninger's "Yankee Peddler" being representative of the regional humor and attention to detail that characterizes much of the Dusseldorf school. Even after Thomas Couture began to attract Americans to Paris in the 1850s, the Dusseldorf school remained a heavy influence on American painting and theories of art.[4]

C. *Cosmopolitanism*

In general, this taste for antiquities, traditional art forms, and sprawling canvasses of melodramatic landscapes or charming genre studies, all of which reinforced, as Lowell said, "the sense of permanence, unchangeableness and repose," nourished a cultural cosmopolitanism that played along the genteel surface of the emotions. It was not limited to Americans. Bryant noted that he had heard four thousand Englishmen visited Italy each year, and even then the Germans were indefatigable travelers. Regardless of the nationality of the travelers, veneration was their chief emotion, conventional content and attitude rather than freshly perceptive art their chief concerns.

As a result, cosmopolitanism partly accounts for the uncritical acceptance of a great deal of art that made little pretense to intellectual rigor. Shakespeare might lie on the shelves, but he was embalmed in gilt covers. Americans read Chateaubriand and Lamartine, cherished "polite authors" like Novalis and Jean-Paul, presented gift books like *The White Veil* and *The Cypress Wreath*, overpraised female writers like Mrs. Hemans, Mrs. Sigourney, and Hannah More, attended plays like Boker's *Francesca de Rimini* and Willis's *Bianca Visconti*, and attempted novels like William Ware's *Zenobia*, Allston's *Monaldi*, and Motley's *Morton's Hope*, not to mention Hawthorne's *Marble Faun*. Americans adored Jenny Lind, swamped the concerts of the prodigy, Adelina Patti, and reacted in fragile tenderness to the waves of musical elegies that have been described as the school of "Weal and Woe." Cosmopolitanism betrayed Thomas Cole into his grandiosely allegorical *Course of Empire* and *The Voyage of Life;* architects into such "specimen" designs as Gothic, classic, and Egyptian; and Greenough into his "monumental" seminude Washington, which even the Congress, scarcely composed of sophisticated lovers of art, could not accept. It was perhaps no different then than today, when washed-out Van Gogh prints have been domesticated to living room walls and the Hollywood Bowl serves as the scene for a collaboration between the Los Angeles Philharmonic and Zappa's Mothers of Invention. The point is simply that cosmopolitanism very easily became a program of cultural "uplift," with criticism at best an uneasy accomplice.

II   *The Collective Mind*

The second major European influence on American aesthetic theory, the accommodation of individual genius to social character, enjoyed considerable prestige after 1830. Such eighteenth-century figures as Jefferson, Crèvecoeur, William Stanhope Smith, and Franklin, because of their involvement in the great democratic experiment, had anticipated this development. But its later systematic elaboration by French, English, and German intellectuals made the work of American critics easier. For what Europeans such as Herder did was to systematize the elements composing a collective consciousness existing in community, and then to give the whole a broad philosophical base.

What emerged was a view of the "electorate" as a vast undifferentiated mass moved by obscure (often irrational) impulses buried deep in the mass psychology. Today most intellectuals view such a theory with dismay. But the nineteenth century saw it as the bedrock of democracy. Precisely because the theory involved a substratum of social compulsions that inconspicuously affected the expression of ideas, it was of immense value to the budding institutions of American culture. The "people" (especially as envisaged by George Bancroft) were the best hope for an emerging democracy. In the equation the people equal society, the people were antecedent to the individual and transcended him in importance. Later, radicals like Arthur Brisbane and Parke Godwin established a vigorous native socialist movement by translating this doctrine into a form of group organization which they called association. But whatever their social aims, many intellectuals addressed themselves to a mythical community of men possessed of a common language, one dominant racial heritage, and a singularly uniform group mind.

A. *French Criticism*

This view helps to explain American interest in Thierry, Sismondi, Guizot, de Stael, and the eclectics, and the relative obscurity of strictly literary figures like Stendhal and Sainte-Beuve. Prior to 1860 there are only three references to Stendhal in American periodicals.[5] Some Americans knew and appreciated Sainte-Beuve. But outside of a few unimportant book notices, there was no periodical discussion of his work. Longfellow, Ticknor, G. H. Calvert, Tuckerman, and Emerson all knew Sainte-Beuve and mentioned him in their journals and letters. Sainte-Beuve wrote Calvert to praise him for his sophisticated use of Sainte-Beuve's critical principles in presenting the man behind the book. In time Emerson read nearly all of Sainte-Beuve's work and lamented his death in 1869: "He was for me the best of his nation in the late years."[6]

American appreciation of French literary movements was restrained. There was the vague suspicion of infidelity, a carry-over from earlier days, and Americans were skeptical of the *savoir-faire* of the salons. Besides, the French were Celtic and therefore volatile, gracious but irregular, and untidy in their domestic relations. Not till Taine would French thought appreciably influence American criticism.[7] Francis Bowen's views are probably representative of the majority. He found the literary scene in France since 1830 gloomy and discontented, reflective of a temporarily lawless "state of manners." Quoting Dumas that "a revolution in letters is the necessary consequence of a political revolution," Bowen said that the defeat of the "pedantic school" of criticism had resulted in a violent and excessive romantic "anarchy" that sapped the strength of promising young writers.[8]

Defenders of French criticism, as one might expect, avoided such easy and specious generalizations through familiarity with the cause. A. R. Spofford noted that a "vast amount of unjust and ignorant criticism" was published in American reviews because of the influence of English periodicals, and he pointed out that Thierry, Guizot, Thiers, Sismondi, D'aubigné, and Lamartine (all of them social theorists) were "familiar and indispensable companions to our studies." F. W. Palfrey confessed that he preferred Guizot's criticism to that of A. W. Schlegel. And J. B. Angell, whose Nordic sympathies did not hinder a wide-ranging literary taste, did yeoman service for the French cause in editing Chambers' *Handbook of French Literature* (1857) and in defending French literature in several long articles in *Bibliotheca Sacra*. The *North American* also did its part when it published an energetic and perspicuous series of articles on French literature and criticism. Their author, Countess de Bury, was a follower of Cousin and applied his method of blending elements of moral philosophy with historical "periods."[9]

The influence of the eclectics, of whom Victor Cousin was the acknowledged leader, was brief but intense. If frequency of translation is an index, Cousin and Jouffroy were the most popular. George Ripley, W. H. Channing, R. N. Tappan, and C. S. Henry all translated and commented on them. In time, as Howard Mumford Jones has established, eclectic doctrine spread as far west as Ohio and Wisconsin, and in the East became so popular that it stirred a decade of solid discussion and debate.[10]

Cousin's most militant exponent was Orestes Brownson. In a series of articles in the *Christian Examiner*, he sharply defended eclecticism from the attacks of those who sought to link it with German metaphysics. Cousin, he argued, was in the philosophical tradition of

Locke, Bacon, and Descartes. His philosophy was empirical, based on psychology rather than ontology, a point also maintained by C. S. Henry, another American disciple and popularizer.[11] But most American reviewers were prone to see Cousin's philosophy as a synthesis of Scottish realism and German idealism buttressed by an historical point of view. They duly noted that Cousin's first principle was the idea of universal Providence. Then came the ideas of order, purpose, and eternal progress toward perfection. The order in which these occurred was learned analytically and confirmed historically. In some fashion, then, truth was a matter of historical development. Its segments were elaborated by various nations and expressed in languages which modified the universality of these segments by placing them in the context of the national psychology. As a writer for the *Boston Quarterly Review* remarked in reviewing Ripley's edition of the *Philosophical Miscellanies* of Cousin, Jouffroy, and Constant, every nation had its own mode of perception, a "special manner of viewing things in general" that brought into prominence some aspect of the whole which had never before been perceived. Here was matter for the literary critic, for study of diverse literatures could help to identify national contributions to the universal spirit of mankind.[12]

B. *German Criticism*

Interest in German criticism can be detected as early as 1803, when Samuel Miller published his *Retrospect of the Eighteenth Century*, but its period of influence dates from the 1830s. By then, critics were referring slightingly to the "old ways" of judging literature according to absolute critical standards, party loyalties, or individual whims. Conservative critics, unwilling to abandon traditional modes of critical judgment, had argued that the vogue of German ideas was little more than a coterie movement—full of "misty speculations and fine-spun theories," as Francis Bowen said. By 1860, when German influence was extensive, this position was no longer defensible. The German method had supported the movement away from the doctrine of kinds. It had encouraged sympathetic appreciation and an orderly critical approach through a determination of the author's purpose. It had discounted caprice or harsh critical condemnation. And it had proved invaluable in systematizing many romantic principles already nascent in American thought.

Americans were introduced to German criticism along many fronts. English periodicals began to discuss it in the 1820s. Men like

Peter Will and Bentley published their pioneering work. Many Americans returned from study at German universities filled with a new zeal. German expatriates like Follen and Beck popularized German study in American colleges. German literary histories were translated and anthologies of German writing published.

Through these various channels, Americans encountered concepts of perpetual progress and organic change, analogies drawn from natural laws discovered by the sciences, and the unconscious group mind, a substratum of general emotional currents and habits subtly affecting the national intellect. The primacy of genius as opposed to talent was acknowledged, as well as the durability and invariability of man's moral nature. The organic and ontological integrity of literary works was stressed, so that they could be studied both in terms of relations and of universal principles, much as in Coleridge and Carlyle. Content was universal. But its mode of expression was indigenous. Hence literature was both national *and* cosmopolitan. Sympathetic reading in national literatures enriched the sensibilities of readers and led to a sense of brotherhood through realizing the universality of experience on the level of the feelings.[13]

Singly or together, these features were adopted and applied by many Americans. Henry E. Dwight, whose *Travels in the North of Germany* (1829) extolled German methods of scholarship, stressed the new latitude given the critic by the Germans, and led the *Southern Review* to assign formidable objectives to the literary scholar:

He must become thoroughly acquainted with the geography, the antiquities, the physical character of the country, whose literature he is perusing, before he enters upon this mode of studying. In pursuing it as an exeget [sic], he must study, most intimately, the character of the people, as moral, intellectual, and physical beings; be able to trace every custom and every image to its source; become acquainted with their mythology and philosophy; ascertain whether their opinions on these subjects were introduced by their intercourse with surrounding nations, or had their origin in their own peculiar character . . . examine the circumstances under which the writer wrote his book, and of the nation at the time it was written.

These were well-formulated critical tools, even anticipating the method of modern "American Studies," and they excited attention. Earlier a conservative associationist, W. H. Prescott, by 1839 was admiring the way the "reconciling spirit" of German criticism introduced unity into "the elements of discord." Theodore Parker and Emerson were of like mind. Parker's letters are full of pleas for the "new" criticism, which gave "depth, philosophy, all-sidedness, and geniality" to the study of literature. Citing Wolf, Niebuhr, Goethe, Pestalozzi, Coleridge, and German philosophers like Kant and Schelling, Emerson felt that the "bold and systematic criticism" being promulgated was fertilizing all departments of intellectual inquiry.[14] Emerson's *Representative Man* reflects in part these broader critical methods.

From Francis Dana Channing's "A Brief Review of the Progress of Literature in Germany" (1804) to George Bancroft's essays on German literature and philosophy in the late 1820s, the cause of German criticism was increasingly favored. Edward Everett, temperamentally conservative, with his taste formed largely by the Greek and Roman classics, nevertheless vigorously championed German criticism both as an early editor of the *North American* and as a prolific writer. His essay on Orphic poetry, a puff for the book of Georgio Bode—the German scholar who had recently begun to teach at Bancroft and Cogswell's Round-Hill school—typically reveals a thorough knowledge of German scholars and methods, although Everett mainly relies on Hermann's philological efforts to establish the date of composition of the poems and their probable origin. Bancroft's thoroughgoing philosophical determinism, which he acquired through his reading in Jonathan Edwards, provided him with a solid base for the theories of continuity, organic development, unlimited progress, and cultural relativism which he absorbed from his study in Germany. The articles on German letters that he published in the decade following his return to the United States show less interest in exploring a literary work in terms of its own structures than in placing it in its social context. In a world in which the "certainty of change" was the only fixed principle, literature was but another institution of a people; it could, therefore, be studied for the light that it shed on history as a whole.[15]

Yet Bancroft's determinism placed him in the minority. Americans were prepared to admit, through long acquaintance with Locke's theory that human nature is plastic, that physical conditions were important in defining human nature. But they were not prepared to ascribe absolute priority to physical causation. Their refuge has since become the classic American position. Men are hedged about by necessity. But within its limits they act freely. This was the position held by Lowell, Parker, G. H. Calvert, W. H. Hurlbut, and many others, and is reflected in their criticism. Frederic Hedge, taking a different tack, referred to the Leibnitzian doctrine of preestablished harmony to resolve the question of free will versus necessity, an echo of which can also be found in Carlyle. Hedge's edition of *Prose Writers of Germany* (1848) has long biographical introductions analyzing such things as how Fichte was "genetically related" to Kant, how Johann Zschokke arrived at his historical principles, how Schelling's philosophy mirrored his intellectual growth. Similarly, W. H. Hurlbut sought to capture the peculiar spirit of German literature by bringing it all under the primary racial characteristic of religious feeling. One solemn power brooded over Germany, reflected in the "wonderful architectural poems" of its Gothic churches (the phrase is borrowed from Coleridge) and the devotional aspirations of its people.[16]

Much of the reason for the excitement over German criticism was due to the wish of Americans to hone into shape their own critical abilities. The "uncontested superiority" of the "existing laws of criticism"—by which Americans usually meant the "laws" of historical criticism—which the Germans had promulgated made that country the only one in which a genuine "science of criticism" was practiced. Jefferson and his many followers had adumbrated most of these assumptions, which had developed along other lines in America before the German vogue. It was not difficult, therefore, for enthusiasts of things German to make the adaptation. What particularly impressed Americans was the "organic view of history" that had been developed in "the recent historiography of the Germans."

For this view, Americans relied heavily on German interpretations in their articles on German literary achievements. G. W. Haven's translation of Heine's *Letters Auxiliary to the History of Modern Polite Literature* in Germany (1836), C. C. Felton's translation of Menzel's *German Literature* (1840), and Gervinus's *History of German Poetry* (1844) were widely reviewed in American periodicals and even more widely echoed. Americans occasionally had reservations—Menzel's and Heine's views on Goethe were controverted in a number of periodicals—but they liked the tack the German literary historians took, especially Gervinus, who was "purely historical."

German criticism was chiefly valued as a tool for overcoming "the barrier of national peculiarities." In a long essay on Italian drama, Mme. C. de la Barca used German critical principles (she continually cites German critics, especially the Schlegels) to trace the growth of drama from its origins to the present, settling finally on the distinctive qualities of Italian drama. While not so theoretical as Mme. de la Barca, the essays of J. B. Angell reveal a better application of German critical methods. He knew not only the German critics, but Frenchmen like Sainte-Beuve, Stendhal, Destouches, Montesquieu, Constant, de Staël, and Guizot. Professor of modern languages at Brown, later editor of the Providence *Journal* and after 1871 president of the University of Michigan, Angell was a Teutonist interested mainly in the cross-fertilization of national literatures. He felt that attention to cultural relations would strengthen the bond between the "great families of the Teutonic race in which the hopes of humanity are centered."[17]

The first sustained application of German critical theory to a national literature is George Ticknor's three-volume *History of Spanish Literature* (1849). Antedating Taine's more secular study of English literature by five years, the book reveals Ticknor as a monogenist with a pronounced Anglo-Saxon bias and teleological views that link him with the earlier part of the century. Immediately upon his appointment by Harvard as Smith Professor of the French and Spanish Languages and Literature in 1816, Ticknor had left for study in Germany. He was to become the first of a long line of German-trained scholars. In Germany he worked under men like Blumenbach (revered by Marx), Bouterwek, and Eichhorn, all of them in one way or another advocates of the new critical method. Eichhorn was widely known as a biblical critic and as the initiator of the project to write a collaborative history of the arts and sciences, which had resulted in his two-volume introduction to the series and Bouterwek's *History of Spanish Literature.* In time, Ticknor came to know a large number of scholars—Tieck, Wolf, Moratín, Fauriel— who encouraged him to deal with literature in historical terms. The key to his history is his concept of Spanish national character (typified by loyalty and religious devotion), but one discovers too the postulates of universal history, progress, the sequential order and unity of phenomena, and the nineteenth-century blend of mechanistic and genetic causality.[18]

1. *Mme. de Staël and the Schlegel Brothers*

Americans could find in de Staël and the Schlegels all those elements which in the early nineteenth century constituted a theory of the "new" criticism. De Staël and the Schlegels stressed perfectibility (by which they meant indefinite progress); the primacy of

morality; the importance of genius as an intuitive force commenting
on the eternal moral truths; the effects of religion, laws, and climate
in molding national character; the relation of democracy and literary
progress; race, especially as independence and loyalty characterize
the Teutonic nations; and the need for universality of appreciation in
order to comprehend and appropriate the diverse productions of
nations. Their works constantly endeavored to show the relationship
between forms of religion and government, the folk imagination, and
above all the events of history—all of which combine to produce those
cultural diversities which the critical mind must understand. Mme. de
Staël also stressed changes in manners and the status of women,
important points in nineteenth-century thought. Practically every
American abroad made it a prime objective to meet her.[19]

The verdict of the *Southern Quarterly Review*, that she was the
"most exquisite of critics," typifies the general tone of American
appreciation. Numerous biographical sketches and extracts from her
literary, biographical, and historical work appeared early in American periodicals. More sophisticated readers echoed Carlyle's remark
that she was somewhat too enthusiastic and uncritical, but everyone
acknowledged that her work was seminal in encouraging acquaintance with German literature and in breaking down "the trammels of
the French code of criticism." *A Treatise on Ancient and Modern
Literature*, *Reflections on Suicide*, and *Germany* all had London
editions in 1813. In the same year New York and Boston editions
appeared of *De la Littérature*, the latter including Boileau's
"Memoir," which praised de Staël's ideas on "perfectibility" and her
attention to such factors as climate in influencing art. Later *De la
littérature* was incorporated into the 1844 edition of George Combe's
influential book, *The Constitution of Man* (1829). *De l'Allemagne* was
generally thought her greatest work, although by the 1830s, with the
growth of knowledge of German literature, it was regarded as
inadequate for anything more than an introduction to the renaissance
of letters in Germany.

Early notices of Mme. de Staël's work were mostly reprints of
English reviews, while the later American articles in the 1820s and
1830s were general biographical essays that assumed an intimate
knowledge of her work. Francis Jeffrey's review of *Sur la littérature*
(1813) could have been read either in the *Edinburgh Review*, which
enjoyed a wide readership among American intellectuals—Emerson
testifying that a new issue was practically a literary event—or its
American reprint in the *Analectic Review*. The *Analectic* also re-

printed Sir James Mackintosh's article on *De l'Allemagne* in 1814, the same year in which a long laudatory article on de Staël appeared in the New York edition of the *Quarterly Review*. These articles had reservations about her ideas of perfectibility and beauty, and they attached more value to utility and self-interest than did de Staël, but they praised her "harmonious system", which transcended the "apparent chaos of human affairs." In spite of its occasional diffuseness, Mme. C. de la Barca's article in the *North American* is the most important American commentary on de Staël's philosophy and method. Mme. de la Barca herself used de Staël's method in tracing the patterns and growth of de Staël's intellectual powers. The method visibly enlarged one's intellectual and moral outlook, said Mme. de la Barca, and therefore put one in a position to judge competently of diverse national literatures.[20]

August Schlegel was much more popular with American critics than his brother. His *Lectures on Dramatic Art*, his friendship with Mme. de Staël, and Friedrich's Catholicism were all factors. G. H. Calvert, Margaret Fuller, Ticknor, and Prescott especially had a high regard for his critical method. Prescott's admiration for August's work did much to swerve Prescott from his early critical conservatism. But while Prescott agreed that the "first principles" of the brothers' critical theory were correct, he was sufficiently independent to argue with their conclusions, and at one time called August a "dogmatic critic," scarcely a complimentary term in Prescott's sense.[21]

The *Portfolio* was one of the early American periodicals to call attention to August Schlegel. In 1817, the magazine printed an extract from *Lectures on Dramatic Art* and another article, apparently by an American writer, which tried to formulate a liberal theory of criticism. This second article urged critics to drop the fettering spirirt of arbitrarily established rules in order to adopt principles developed by Sulzer, Herder, and Lessing and systematized by August Schlegel. These principles, the author said, formed "an epoch in the history of criticism." The 1833 Philadelphia edition of *Lectures on Dramatic Art* prompted a brief flurry of articles that paid tribute to the Schlegels as the founders of "the nobly liberal school of criticism" having "the fixedness of a science." The *American Monthly Magazine* called their method "reproductive criticism," using the same phrase George Allen borrowed from Heine to describe Coleridge's approach; and indeed, the Schlegels and Coleridge differ only on the relative importance that they assign to matter as a determinant in literature.[22]

By the 1830s, as the *American Monthly* said, the Schlegels had become a "household ministry," though their influence was perhaps not deep. Hannah-Beate Schilling argues that the Schlegels failed to enlist support when they seemed to run counter to the "Scottish tradition," so that Americans were willing to follow them only when they "reinforced certain tendencies inherent in that critical tradition—for example, the stirrings of a historical sense."[23] They did not cut so dramatic a figure as de Staël, whose tribulations with the hostile Napoleon and whose defense of liberty proved so attractive to Americans. But they stimulated many American critics to examine the literature of the Middle Ages and of ancient Greece and Rome in terms of their legacies to modern literature. And by emphasizing the need for adopting the author's perspective, they performed a genuine service to American critics interested in formulating new critical attitudes.

2. *The Influence of Herder*

Johann Gottfried Herder was the recognized founder of the historical method in Germany. His critical theory was important in swinging Americans toward the idea of examining literature in terms of feelings, sympathy, necessity, geography, and the institutional and psychological revelations of *das Volk*. Incidental references to Herder indicate a greater familiarity with his writings than the relatively few articles devoted to him would seem to indicate. Those Americans who lacked a reading knowledge of German had to wait for James Marsh's edition of *Spirit of Hebrew Poetry* in 1833, although *Outlines of a Philosophy of Man* and *Oriental Dialogues* had appeared in London editions in 1800 and 1801 respectively.[24]

The fact that Herder had a reputation as a religious liberal, even a radical, partially accounts for his relatively late and narrow influence in America. He enjoyed his greatest prestige with liberal New Englanders. The *Western Messenger* was the only Western periodical to mention him, and then in a detached manner. The *Southern Quarterly Review* published an article on Herder's philosophy of history in 1844 which sought to measure Herder "by his own scale," but promptly forgot the principle in order to warn against this "false guide and dangerous monitor." In New England, it was George Ripley's review of Marsh's edition of Herder that touched off the great Unitarian-Transcendentalist theological debate of the late 1830s, as Perry Miller has shown in *The Transcendentalists*. Ripley, who saw Herder as a "connecting link" between the school of Luther and the "modern school" of rational divines, consistently championed Herder's critical theory, perhaps to greater effect in the field of religion than of literature.

Marsh's translation of *The Spirit of Hebrew Poetry*, with a long appreciative preface, marks a sort of transition point in American acceptance of German critical theory. Reared in a strict Calvinist household and taught according to the principles of Locke and the Scottish philosophy, Marsh revolted against his early training and became one of the group of Vermont religionists championing Coleridge's epistemology and German methodology. Marsh accepts Herder's genetic point of view as the most promising critical strategy. Bishop Lowth's "mode of critical comparison" was valuable in cultivating interest in diverse national literatures, but, Marsh maintains, judging a work by the conceptions of one's own time prevents a critic from imbibing the "genuine spirit" and "simple power" of foreign literature. Criticism should be capable of the higher power of divesting itself of habitual patterns of thought in order to adopt an unfamiliar perspective aware of different historical facts, modes of life, and antiquarian lore.

Marsh's preface is a useful reduction of Herder's theories: how climate and custom affect literature and the idiomatic richness of language; how nationality and milieu and the individual self are imperceptibly revealed in literature; how richly varied folk literatures can still contain universal emotional content; how scholarly historical research can lead to increased understanding and sensibility. At the same time, Marsh (following Coleridge) stresses even more than Herder the belief that the moral order is constant and enduring. Good and evil have existed from the beginning, and their relation, as Bancroft said, is unalterable. This was one of the major points of difference between Coleridge and Herder, and Marsh, who knew Coleridge's work intimately, elected the more conservative position of Coleridge.

Longfellow, George Bancroft, and Alexander Everett also paid tribute to Herder as the pioneer of a truly indigenous German literature and criticism. Bancroft was attracted to Herder's idea that continuity gave vitality to history. Hostility to the concept of a static world, Bancroft felt, was an effective curb to the impulse to reason "coldly" on "matters of taste," while continuity encouraged men to explore "the national feelings of different ages and race" in order to show the underlying psychological "identity" of all. Alexander

Everett, who possessed a remarkably incisive and wide-ranging mind, felt that Herder was one of the most important critics in Germany, the founder of a "new national school" which patiently and persistently attempted to fathom the tastes of people in order to appreciate the diverse creations of genius. His praise of Herder as a "uniformly earnest and serious" scholar was not calculated to represent him as a dry-as-dust antiquarian. To New Englanders, earnestness was almost the eighth cardinal virtue, as Baudelaire was to make ennui the eighth cardinal sin.[25]

In 1857 Littell's *Living Age* observed that there had been such an "accession of knowledge" since Herder that he had been largely forgotten: "Yet he is rarely named without respect and admiration. It is felt that if his ideas attract less attention now, the reason is that they have become commonplace through universal reception."[26] Outside of Hillebrand's later article on Herder in the *North American*, critical attention was limited after 1857 to occasional citations and quotations that indicate it was still to some purpose to read him.

3. *The Influence of Goethe*

Many more Americans were interested in Goethe, who himself admitted to the profound influence of Herder. Except for a few experts in reading German, Americans were unfamiliar with Goethe's critical principles until the translation and publication of his critical work in the 1830s and 1840s. Prior to that time, critical attention to Goethe was of necessity preliminary and largely preoccupied with a definition of his character. Scholars reviewed his various novels and poems and the London edition of *Dichtung und Wahreit* (1824), commented unfavorably on his "unscrupulous" moral attitudes, and, while recognizing his artistic ability and his place in the forefront of modern German literature, condemned his lack of moral tone and "uplift." Margaret Fuller's translation of Eckermann's *Conversations with Goethe*, published in 1839, was the first domestic edition to concentrate on Goethe as critic rather than Goethe as artist or man. G. H. Calvert published his translation of Goethe's correspondence with Schiller in 1845, and in 1872 his biography of Goethe, based on Lewes's account. Readers of Samuel Ward's translation of Goethe's *Essays on Art* (1845) could have read Goethe's acceptance of the ancients over the moderns, his praise of organic and plastic art, his advice to follow multifarious nature, and his conclusion that criticism should be primarily biographical. These, plus the spurt in interest in all things German, drew attention to Goethe's critical philosophy and stimulated its study.

Throughout his career Goethe dwelt on the need for the artist to accommodate himself to the emotional and intellectual character of his time to achieve literary greatness. A true work of art was a natural growth out of the conditions in which the writer found himself. Influenced by Herder in his early career, Goethe conceived of nature and art as organic forms having their due place in the totality of being. This conception led him, in his early work, to emphasize feeling, and to some extent antiintellectuality, since reason alone could not encompass successfully the organic wholeness present in the art work. But later Goethe was influenced by Kant and Ficthe on the reason and evolved a more sophisticated position in which reason was dominant.

Goethe's theory of "productive criticism" was designed to ascertain the degree to which the artist had utilized tradition in creating his art and the extent and value of his achievement. A critic could judge art works by comparison with some literary ideal (destructive criticism), or, more ideally, he could enter sympathetically into the work, discover its inner form, and note how idea dictated organic expression. The door is obviously left open for evaluation, however much Goethe himself tended to slight it in his own criticism. He also believed in the possibility of a world or universal literature—he called it *Weltliteratur*—that would retain the flavor of nationality and yet be a blend of all national literatures. This strongly impressed Americans like Lowell, Fuller, Calvert, and possibly Longfellow. The artist pursued the good, the noble, the beautiful. These values, however, were modified in expression by unconscious, irrationally conceived "inward traits."[27]

American critics generally had no difficulty in accepting this view that the writer and his work bore the imprint of time and culture. Alexander Everett's address on German literature, delivered at Dartmouth in 1839, argued at length that both Schiller and Goethe were the "exact reflexion" of political and literary events in Europe. Critics as diverse as F. Cunningham and John S. Dwight repeated the attitude. But they could not accept Goethe's picture of himself as a man completely subject to passing events. Edward Everett—who wrote the first article to seriously consider Goethe—and five years later the *New Monthly Magazine* both rejected *Dichtung und Wahreit* as a descriptive title and praised Goethe for transcending his time in establishing a leading position in German literature. And

Leonard Woods, Jr., a very fine critic, differed with men like George Bancroft and Robert Walsh who regarded Goethe as antidemocratic and antireligious. The liberal views which Woods expressed in his essay, one of the best of its kind published in the period, were based on the idea that Goethe had identified himself with the interests and feelings of his countrymen and yet had so written as to belong "not to an age or nation, but to the race."[28]

Many critics also sympathized with Goethe's notion of the community of nations. In the preface to his translation of *Hermann and Dorothea* (Richmond, 1805), Thomas Holcroft, the English friend of Godwin, spoke of the separateness of peoples in terms of "moral sentiments, poetical feelings, and idioms of speech." Yet the "grand characteristics" of men were much the same and made possible a world pool of knowledge. The *Democratic Review* echoed Holcroft's statements forty-three years later in running a five-installment translation of *Hermann and Dorothea*. Both the *Democratic Review* and the *Literary World* introduced a note of racism, which had been absent in Holcroft, in asserting that the American temperament possessed a "certain eclecticism of character" which could encourage adaptation of foreign materials to the dominant Saxon element.[29]

Reluctant at first to engage in his circle's current enthusiasm for things German, Emerson came in time to appreciate the significance of Goethe. In *Representative Men*—the title is significant, when compared with Carlyle's comparable book on heroes—Goethe becomes "the writer," an expression of the age if not of the universal mind. To Emerson, the nineteenth century was the century of multiplicity, Goethe its philosopher, the second part of *Faust* its book. Discerning readers could have seen the care with which Emerson developed his picture of the age in order to place Goethe in historical perspective. Hermann Grimm, reading Emerson's essay, exclaimed that for the first time he could see Goethe's position in history.

Like Emerson, George Bancroft had his reservations about Goethe's morality. For this reason he sided with Follen and others in elevating Schiller over Goethe, an attitude first assumed by Mme. de Staël. In 1819 and again in 1821 Bancroft visited with Goethe, talking on America, Kant, the English poets, and Bancroft's doctoral studies at the University of Göttingen. Returned to American, Bancroft over the years wrote considerably about Goethe, all of it based on the idea that "the literary history of Goethe is explained by his private life."

The essay of 1839 is a vitriolic attack on Goethe's lack of principles; the others are more even-tempered if still unfavorable. Recasting these essays for *Literary and Historical Miscellanies*, Bancroft remained displeased with Goethe's "disgraceful" immorality, but he did note the German's "extensive and lasting popularity."[30]

Bancroft's method was to depict the larger picture of the growth of German literature and Goethe's relation to it. John Lothrop Motley's two fine essays in the *New-York Review*, landmarks of Goethe criticism in America, illustrate a method closer to Goethe's practice. Motley explored the biographical elements to find the point of unity beneath the changing surface of character. It is obvious, however, that Motley was especially attracted to Goethe's critical theory. Like so many of his contemporaries, Motley was interested in laying the comparative method to rest once and for all. He needed a precise and accurate critical theory to take the measure of the individual writer. Goethe's theory, in which criticism became "an art of almost physical investigation," struck Motley as ideal. It avoided "narrow systems of criticism, which would bring all men to one standard." It never indulged in the unprofitable comparison of writers or works. It simply tried, on just and catholic grounds, to resolve the mass of particulars surrounding a writer and his work to a few orderly principles. The theory prompted Motley to proclaim Goethe "the greatest critic of modern times; and in a country so eminently distinguished for proficiency in a branch of literature, which they [the Germans] were the first to make a science, he is decidedly the first."[31]

By the 1840s, it was the rare critic who did not know Goethe. James Russell Lowell read Goethe during his college days, and came eventually to the position of calling him "the most widely receptive of critics." Parke Godwin, a leading Fourierite in the United States, translated *Dichtung und Wahreit* and later wrote an extravagant review of Lewes's *Life and Works of Goethe*. Godwin touted the whole series of Goethe's work as "a complete bodying forth of the successive steps of progress in the mighty struggle." Reviewers of Godwin's translation also put Goethe in historical perspective. An anonymous writer for the *Democratic Review* pointed out that Goethe had seen the futility of "perscriptive principles" of criticism, and a reviewer for the *Southern Quarterly Review* argued that one cannot "judge fairly" of an author until local circumstances and intentions have been thoroughly ascertained.[32]

Of all Goethe's disciples in America, Margaret Fuller was the most forthright and militant in urging the acceptance of his critical principles. She was at the center of popular interest in Goethe. In chronicling the days of New England Transcendentalism, Frothingham calls her "the critic," a sentiment repeated by a recent biographer, who says that she "was one of the best of the earlier American critics, and did much to shape our critical tradition.[33] Much of her power came from her obvious enthusiasm for Goethe, whom she called "my parent." Emerson, who had previously felt the impact of her ardent enthusiasm and self-consciously backed away, noted that when she turned to Goethe "the effect . . . was complete."

Throughout her short career she made it her chief duty to advance the cause of Goethe, noting all the translations and reports of him, and endeavoring to inculcate his principles of sympathy and perspective. She bitterly attacked those men who sat "intrenched" behind the infallible We, and who sought, as "judicious" men of the world, to legislate literary opinion. The critic, she thought, forgetful of her own preaching about Goethe as "king and lord," should not presume to be an infallible adviser to his reader. Nor should he be "subjective," registering merely his own impression of a work. Such critical views were out of fashion. The "new" criticism, she wrote, enters "into the natural history of every thing that breathes and lives . . . believes no impulse to be entirely in vain . . . scrutinizes circumstances, motive and object before it condemns, and believes there is a beauty in each natural form if its law and purposes be understood."[34]

When once Americans ceased to judge Goethe on moral grounds, the process of appreciation began. They interpreted him as he himself had, in the light of immediate purposes and the general nature of the culture in which he found himself. At the center of this method was the doctrine of sympathy. For it was by sympathy, rather than rational effort, that one discovered the inner meaning or "spirit" of a work and thereby the key to interpreting that work. Following this, the critic could relate the artist and work, not according to a received moral code or agreed upon literary conventions, but according to the author's nation, environment, and history. This done, there still remained the work of art, but now transfigured and translucent. Coming at a time when many American had come to view judicial criticism as mechanical and rigid and often motivated by party and personal malice, Goethe and attempts to interpret him provided a well-formulated critical method that promised a more enlightened and objective means of literary study.

4. *The German Effect*

If quantity of critical notices is any criterion, German critical theory was most important in advancing romantic criticism in America. While it might be necessary to make minor adjustments in relation to individual writers, in general German criticism held to a few fundamental points, most of which had been expressed briefly as theories by earlier American writers such as Jefferson, not to mention the English. But the Germans elaborated and applied these theories in greater detail. They held that genius cannot be confined by rules. They believed that imagination and feeling triumph over reason. They praised the spontaneous and unstudied poetry of the people as being the most sincere and hence the best gauge to the national character. They were cognizant of cultural change as affected by external circumstances and national psychology. They based cultural change itself on theories of continuity, progress, and organic development. They believed that since literature was an index to the national mind, the study of many diverse national literatures could best acquaint the scholar with the complexities of foreign cultures. Such study could weld into one whole what was fundamentally diverse and unique, and thus root cosmopolitanism itself in the very truth of things.

Beginning with the early reviews of de Staël and the Schlegels, these principles took hold until in the late 1830s and early 1840s they had become part of a literary credo, especially of the radical portion of the Boston-Concord coterie. It is difficult to evaluate the comparative influence of individual German critics. Bancroft was thoroughly acquainted with de Staël, Schlegel, Herder, and Goethe, and he knew Coleridge and Carlyle. Prescott knew de Staël and Schlegel, and read desultorily in the others. C. S. Henry had a scholar's knowledge of Carlyle, Schlegel, and Goethe, and an intimate knowledge of the French eclectic philosophers, who espoused much the same critical method. And so one could go on with Lowell and others. Through Herder, Americans were shown concretely how to write literary history. The Schlegels and de Staël, in additon to literary history, encouraged what came to be known as "reproductive" criticism. Goethe synthesized biographical and reproductive criticism and avoided the haphazard collection and putting together of data, and he saw the individual as subject to law, both physical and spiritual. With its emphasis on sympathetic understanding, which was supposed to lead to universality and comsmopolitanism, it was almost inevitable that German criticism should prove attractive to American scholars, still caught up in the discussion over a national literature.

III   The Continent and Native Ideas

Continental attitudes were a part of the intellectual crosscurrents of the period and were helpful to Americans in elaborating a broader more liberal criticism. Yet often foreign ideas were little more than elaborately stated principles of doctrines already known in America. The two key points in the American romantic theory of literature— race and nationalism—were both given indigenous expression long before their importation from Europe in more detailed form. And the English were pervasively influential in diverse ways. Scott's vogue, for instance, was helpful to literary nationalists in showing how nationalism could be an essential part of literature. His celebration of the Scottish countryside and folk made Americans aware of difference as a positive value. This subtly influenced their literary criticism. Scottish associationism, almost the official philosophy in American colleges at the time, gave psychological and philosophical grounds for many root concepts of romantic criticism. Coleridge and Carlyle taught Americans how to successfully combine history, universal principles, and sympathy to "reproduce" a literary work for wider comprehension. The sometimes extreme enthusiasm of disciples of German theory, plus philosophical differences between empiricists and idealists, were largely responsible for the hostility of a number of Americans toward the Germans. But the internal consistency of German theory undoubtedly contributed to its appeal, and to many American followers it became almost a shibboleth.

American intellectuals, as these first two chapters suggest, were not original thinkers, but they were emotionally and morally committed to the great democratic experiment initiated by the American Revolution. They thus pursued social and political theory with such passionate intensity that the relative poverty of their intellectual inventiveness does not seem so important. Their one unquestioned principle was that the various branches of knowledge, including literature, were subordinate in capacity and function to the needs of the country. Literary nationalism thus served to meld the diverse population into one people. And European theories which described the uniform structural character of a culture were used to validate the association of literature with national purpose. The critical theories to which we now turn represent different ways that literature might advance that association.

CHAPTER 3

Rhetorical Criticism

I *Foundations*

RHETORICAL criticism, dominant in the first quarter of the nineteenth century, had to be specially adapted to literature, because rhetoric commonly includes only expository writing and public speaking. Further, whatever power and importance it possessed were due in part to its clearly identifiable critical principles, its connection with a durable literary traditon, its serious and conventional moral orientation, and the qualities of mind possessed by its practitioners.

In the early years of the century, criticism was not a profession. Persons of a mind to practice it were usually associated with the law, the ministry, or the academy, disciplines which emphasized rhetorical training and which provided some leisure for avocational pursuits. It was only natural that rhetoric would provide the footing and method for writing literary criticism. There was also the example of English periodicals, which, as E. T. Channing pointed out, led the way in printing "elaborate investigations of the subjects of works, of the genius of authors, the principles of criticism, the faults and beauties of style and language." The entire culture seems to have thought that literature should be useful, edifying, and eloquent. Eloquence, in fact, was esteemed most of all, and served for public entertainment. The Lyceum movement enlisted such popular public speakers as Emerson, Lowell, Edward Everett, Daniel Webster, and Charles Sumner. People took notes on Sunday sermons, listened critically to orators and lawyers, and read with sharp eyes and knowledgeable minds the many anthologies of addresses printed as bread and butter books (like our cookbooks today) by enterprising publishers.[1]

A. *Curricula in Rhetoric*

Prior to general acceptance of Richard Whately's *Elements of Rhetoric* (1828), which sharply distinguished between rhetoric and literature, the tendency was to include under rhetoric, as he himself observed, "all composition in prose." In actual fact, poetry was also included. A strong though limited connection was thus maintained between classical rhetorical theories of invention, disposition, and style on the one hand and belles-lettres on the other. In *A Grammar of Composition* (1823), William Russell argued that the addition of rhetoric to "the course of English literature" would do much to raise the critical level of the students and to promote a "liberal education." As students moved beyond the lower forms of grammar, dialectic, and disputation, they were introduced to Latin authors and the writers of the English Augustan period. These were analyzed not only for elements of literary enjoyment but for instruction in how to appreciate great men and to understand human nature. Thus literature was thought to point beyond itself to subjects which it was the business of literature to clearly define. Critics approached literature possessed of one strategy and one objective: the strategy was to apply rhetorical theory to literature in the manner counseled by J. Q. Adams and Joseph McKean at Harvard, the prolific and scholarly Charles Anthon at Columbia, Ebenezer Porter at Andover, and Chauncey Goodrich at Yale; the objective was to fix the world in its place, and thus become better citizens, through the good graces of literature.

To support the relationship between rhetoric and literature, grammars and studies of Greek and Roman antiquities were published by such influential teachers as Peter Bullions, Charles Knapp Dillaway, John Smith, and James Luce Kingsley. These published materials were incorporated into college curricula both in grammar and composition and in the programs of pulpit eloquence, where they helped to mold the tastes and critical methods of large numbers of students. Some of these editions were models of scholarship. Benjamin Apthorp Gould, principal of the Latin Grammar School, began to publish annotated editions of Latin authors as early as 1827. His edition of Horace (1828) was superseded in 1830 by Charles Anthon's critical edition of *Horatti Poemata*, which ran over a thousand pages. Anthon, Jay Professor of the Greek Language and Literature at Columbia, was excellently schooled in German scholarship and gained a considerable reputation among American scholars. His editions of Greek and Roman authors, heavy with exegetical and critical notes and commentary, became staples in the teaching programs of colleges throughout the East.

Before 1800, training in rhetoric invariably had as its immediate aim the preparation of students for the ministry. But with the increasing number of professions from which the student might choose, and with the increasing self-consciousness of the nation and the consequent emphasis on cultural growth, rhetorical training moved steadily in the direction of a secular program in writing and criticism.[2] The program was reinforced during the first quarter of the century by the establishment of a number of chairs in rhetoric and oratory. Their occupants were given a dual charge. Students were to be taught in grammar and composition and introduced to the excellencies of classical literature. A considerable drain of time and energy was involved in meeting this charge, with the result that training in elocution was necessarily curtailed. While bad for the platform performer, the advantage to the critically minded student was immense, for it meant not only considerable practice in writing but an expansion of the course beyond the drab mechanics of essay preparation to include instruction in philosophy and art.

The philosophical views of rhetoricians holding chairs of rhetoric varied widely. Men like Adams and McKean were staunchly classical, but most seem to have preferred, according to their orientation, the associationism of Kames, the faculty psychology of John Ogilvie or Hugh Blair, or the commonsense view of Thomas Reid. These attitudes can be found in such American rhetoricians as E. T. Channing at Harvard, Samuel Phillips Newman at Bowdoin, John McVickar at Columbia, S. G. Brown at Dartmouth, and E. A. Park at Andover. On the whole, the rhetorical theory of these men tends to be less prescriptive than classical theory, because it is based on a more "scientific" view of the relation between human psychology and literary purpose.

B. *Classical Influence*

The inclusion of classical literature in the rhetoric program in the early years, however, encouraged greater uniformity in the practical approach to writing and literature than differences in theory would seem to allow. And when one looks closely at the work of Blair and Campbell, the two most influential English rhetoricians on American thought, it too reveals a solidly classical arrangement and methods of interpretation.[3] The result is that all these men, despite philosophical differences, were quite certain about the characteristics of good literature and how those characteristics might be identified in particular literary works. On many counts the most liberal professor of rhetoric, E. T. Channing always maintained his faith in universal principles of beauty, correctness and perspicuity of style, and critical gauges for the assessment of literature. His teaching between 1819 and 1852 as Boylston Professor of Rhetoric at Harvard incalculably influenced several generations of students. At Bowdoin, Samuel Newman exerted the same kind of influence on students like Longfellow and Hawthorne. Elected to the chair of rhetoric and oratory in 1824, Newman published *A Practical System of Rhetoric, or the Principles and Rules of Style* (1827), a widely adopted text that eventually reached sixty editions. It defined taste in terms of "refinement, delicacy, and correctness," defended purity and decorum in vocabulary and sentences, praised Johnson's dictionary, and on the whole was conservative in terms of language, judgment, and taste.

Many professors of rhetoric continued to teach well into the second quarter of the century. Goodrich was at Yale until 1839, and Channing taught at Harvard until 1852. But rhetoric as a viable form of criticism steadily declined after 1830. One of the immediate causes of the decline was the movement to separate instruction in classical literature from the rhetoric curriculum. Classical study came into its own in departments of classical languages and literature, but departments of rhetoric felt the pinch of a lack of content. Some rhetoricians, notably E. T. Channing and W. G. T. Shedd, initiated research into English literature that paved the way for F. J. Child's work and for his eventual appointment as a professor of English. But by this time the various forms of romantic criticism had almost completely preempted the field of literary criticism.

II *Principles*

A. *Social Orientation*

Rhetorical criticism was almost totally unconcerned with an epistemology of literature. Following the lead of Latin and English rhetoricians, American teachers of rhetoric made poetry, style, and such matters part of a general social orientation.[4] The end of rhetoric was construed as the maintenance of order in public affairs. Since it was assumed that rheotric subsumed literature, this end was regarded as common to the two disciplines. Thus Aristotle's *Poetics*, the classical statement of the epistemology of literature, was seen as little more than a treatise on tragedy concerned with problems of character, narrative continuity, and thought (*dianoia*). Literature was not a self-contained imaginative discipline. It was a practical, socially communicative tool for promoting social norms.

Such a view had been traditional for centuries, upheld by such men as Horace and Sir Philip Sidney. Henry Day expressed the views of American critics when he said that rhetoric "represents moral states, implies moral aims, and consequently proceeds in conformity to moral principles."[5] The popularity of this view in the early part of the nineteenth century, apart from such obvious reasons as the need for a recently born nation to establish its own form of social organization, was intensified by two conditions. First, educators (as well as men in public life) were prone to celebrations of the speculative intellect. Consequently their favorite rhetorician was Quintilian, who recommended the mutual accommodation of philosophy and rhetoric. Their ideal orator fitted Quintilian's concept of the good man, firm in virtuous action, his morality soundly reflected in his art. Second, the century was witness to a progressive breakdown of the relatively simple eighteenth-century ideas of social communication and social order. If literature under the aegis of rhetoric could relate author, subject, and audience as all part of one complex whole, it would be useful to men increasingly absorbed in problems of communication.

Such a rhetorical view of the function of literature encouraged critics to move beyond "mere issues of art" (generally defined as ornament and ostentation) to focus on problems relevant to social needs or social theory. According to the *Monthly Anthology*, eloquence was not a small matter but "the glorious talent of improving all the treasures of art and of science, of history and of nature to the illumination, conviction and subjugation of the hearts of men. It is the dome of the temple, the perfection of human powers, the action of mind on mind, the lightening of the moral world." Twenty-one years later the *Portfolio* put it more succinctly if less elegantly: we all "owe something to society," the magazine said, and if we disregard societal claims our learning and literature become "effeminate."[6]

As a mode of social intercourse, literature in its broadest sense was given institutional status. This effectively proscribed any tendency to unduly exalt its position or any tendency to subvert the recognized standards of the society. The function of literature was to move men to solidarity, rectitude, and good actions by combining, as Samuel Newman said, "instruction with amusement." Here rhetoric was an aid to literature. It taught an "art of superadded ornament," said Adams, that embellished the basic communication of ideas as taught in grammar. "To delight the imagination, or to move the passions, you must have recourse to rhetoric." Several years later Channing, himself an occupant of the Boylston Chair of Rhetoric and Oratory, made much the same case for rhetoric to his Harvard seniors: "It does not ask whether a man is to be a speaker or writer,—a poet, philosopher, or debater; but simply,—is it his wish to be put in the right way of communicating his mind with power to others, by words spoken or written."[7]

B. *The Matter of Truth*

Rhetorical formulas included, along with social relevance, the determination and communication of truth. Strictly speaking, the determination of truth was the province of the philosopher, the advocacy of truth the province of the rhetorician. But as almost all rhetoricians admitted, logic and rhetoric were inseparable. The question then became one of how to determine the form of the particular truth and how best to state it. The case was particularly poignant in literature, for on the one hand the communication of truth subordinated literature to rhetoric by including literature in the forms of persuasion, and on the other hand literature was often viewed as a "tributary" to rhetoric. Matthew Boyd Hope argued in *The Princeton Textbook of Rhetoric* (1859) that some arguments are not fully conclusive even though the "laws" of human nature are invariable, and hence conviction must rely on general belief or probability. Here literature was functional:

The caused agency in such a case is assumed, or invented, or imagined, and the only limits imposed on the invention of causes, in such a case, are 1, that they shall not be improbable; i.e., they shall be causes, not unlikely to occur in the circumstances supposed; and then, 2, that the consequences following from them shall be such, as those causes would produce, if they were actual. Within these limits, fiction commands our *general belief,* sufficiently to induce our human interest in the events. If the causes feigned, strike us as unlikely to occur, we condemn the fiction as *unnatural,* or *improbable;* and refuse to become interested in it accordingly. (16)

E. T. Channing also acknowledged that human nature was always the same and that there were fixed principles of taste and canons of criticism. But he was more disposed to recognize the importance of such variables as nationality, individuality, and circumstance in a man's moral character. Consequently literature was valuable not only in clarifying human existence but in recognizing its complexity.[8]

On grounds analogous to these Emerson looked to eloquence (the practical application of rhetoric) to "wash the ears into which it flows." Emerson, who took the Boylston prize for declamation while a Harvard student, had three standards for oratory: moral purpose, communication rather than exhibitionism, and the conveying of "new truths in incandescent phrases." Beauty was the equivalent of truth, presented through the "collocation" of words, and the result was the universal spoken with conviction. It is no wonder, given this position, that Emerson should speak slightingly of Poe as "the jingle man." Beyond these matters, he depended on talent to build an original persuasive force in which the rich figurative language, the epigrams and elaborations and apposite diction, served conviction and sentiment. Emerson's contemporaries knew exactly what he was about, and many were appreciative. "The delight and the benefit were," Lowell later wrote, "that he put us in communication with a larger style of thought, sharpened our wits with a more pungent phrase, gave us ravishing glimpses of an ideal under the dry husk of our New England; made us conscious of the supreme and everlasting originality of whatever bit of soul might be in any of us; freed us, in short, from the stocks of prose in which we had sat so long that we had grown wellnigh contented in our cramps."[9]

Most rhetorical critics associated truth with social relevance in their discussion of truth as one of the goals of literature. In arguing that literature should be rooted in the human temperament, critics believed, as Matthew Hope said in his *Princeton Textbook in Rhetoric* (1859), that literature should be consistent with "general experience and popular opinion." Such a view demands in effect that conflict be contained within the frame of the nation's general beliefs and commitments. But who is to say what those beliefs and commitments are? Hope's argument, or ones similar to it, was often used to exclude theories of social atomism as preached by the Utilitarians or tendencies toward polarizing the individual and the group such as are found in Emerson's early essays.[10] The major reasons in this period for faulting books seem to lie in the fact that the books were considered subversive of social hegemony, that they lacked moral fervor or noble sentiment, or that they lay outside the context of values of the Christian order. It is possible to see these reasons as cary-overs of the moral earnestness of Puritanism and as evidences of the current belief in the moral destiny of America. But they are nevertheless extrinsic to the body of general principles that serves to define a work of art.

The hortatory tone of early nineteenth-century literature and criticism is directly related to these literary aims of social concern and truth. As a functional part of the art of persuasion, literature was a social tool for perfecting the citizen as a moral and social individual. Accordingly, literature was expected to employ argument and disposition, the latter meaning little more than the method of arrangement or adaptation of material. Thus rhetorical critics consistently looked for clear exposition and unity of design in the books they reviewed, while logical imprecision, confusion in organization, or inattention in continuity and development were thought to be imperfections. "Obscurity is an author's worst sin," said a writer in the *Democratic Review,* "and one for the commission of which the critics (though literary popes) can give no absolution." The properties of literature, said Henry Day, were clarity, energy, and elegance; among these clarity was the most important, for literature was a means of communication.[11]

C. *The "Nature" of Literature*

Yet in some fundamental sense literature was thought to have its own nature. Ideas unfolded through the interplay of human beings and dramatic situations, and not entirely through argumentation or disposition. According to the Reverend James R. Boyd, all literature displayed "great readiness of invention," imagination, sympathy, taste, and perceptivity. Beyond these, the requirements of the different forms called for more specific considerations. Writing in the *Portfolio,* another critic observed that it was a "canon of criticism" to maintain point of view in an epic poem in order to capture imaginative illusion and at the same time to capitalize on what has been invested in characterization. Centuries earlier Aristarchus had made the same point in reference to Homer's heroes. Narration, an important consideration to rhetorical critics, was defined as a special kind of invention that dealt with events, and included the presentation of facts or incidents which unfolded in a continuous sequence. In the aggregate the facts or incidents were so shaped that the narrative culminated in a solution that was credible, significant, and morally sound. And while narration supposed a "penetrating insight" into causal relations, it was an art that could be studied and acquired.[12]

While authors were granted narrative inventiveness, they were nevertheless expected to obey the "literary law" of verisimilitude, or of probability as it was sometimes called. Critics schooled in rhetoric looked for plausibility rather than photographic reproduction. The view had its ground in two concepts thought to govern literary composition: the need to maintain some correspondence with the natural and social order, and the need to employ established literary conventions in order for the imagination to illuminate the rules and principles governing the natural and social order. The first was restrictive, the second liberalizing, and together they served to countenance verisimilitude.[13]

A writer should be given "wider scope" than the really existent, said *The United States Literary Gazette* in speaking of Cooper, and he should be able to "avail himself not only of all probable, but even of all possible combinations." Yet the tendency of authors to move beyond the range of experience of the ordinary human was a constant worry to rhetorical critics. Writers who "too violently" opposed "obvious probabilities" ran the risk of falling into the freakish, the monstrous, the incongruous. A frequent complaint against Cooper, often warranted, was that his incidents and characters were improbable. W. H. Gardiner felt that the "invention of the machinery" in *The Pioneers* made up for a lack of argument and kept the novel "within the narrowed limits of modern probability." But the view of Willard Phillips that *The Pilot* showed "poverty of invention" was shared by critics in regard to most of Cooper's novels. As the improbable shaded into the exceptional it became destructive of art.[14]

This preoccupation with the probable explains the continual critical concern with the "romance," which, within reason, was thought to indulge writers in their wish to invest characters and scenes with picturesque qualities, and to tolerate their inclinations to see our lives and our world in poetic terms. A few unreconstructed conservatives thought that "A modern Romance must, in its very inception, be a sin against good taste." But the majority hoped to make the romance the literary equivalent of the verities of human nature and social organization. Traditional forms of the romance—the historical, the gothic, the Indian—were tolerated and reviewed. But more and more the emphasis was on maintaining balance and a sense of realism in character, setting, and action. It was not so much that critics called for unswerving optimism, moral sweetness, and evasive delicacy—although this indeed did sometimes happen—as that they rejected philosophical cynicism, social and political radicalism, inordinate attention to the immoral, or soft and affected sentimentality.[15]

D. *The Social Role of the Writer*

Throughout the process of criticism, the rhetorical critic was mindful of the work's possible beneficial or deleterious effect on the reading public. Hence he looked for *sincerity* in the writer, which sometimes became simply moral earnestness, as well as elements of honesty, integrity, and imaginative ability. Genius could not hope to win "continued and universal admiration," said the *American Quarterly Review*, except in "alliance with virtue."[16] The writer, as a more responsive and imaginative man, should establish a "delightful intimacy" with his admirers and render all that interested him "deeply interesting" to them. He is not to antagonize the public, nor to besiege it with importunities nor pit himself against it, but as a citizen among citizens to develop truth and beauty through the techniques of his craft.

If the writer met these conditions, he produced literature that corresponded to truths discovered by common sense and acknowledged by general consent and practice. This was too abstract, however, to be a truly functional principle, and rhetorical critics were frequently misled into narrow, unimaginative positions. It was surely too illiberal a construction of social interest that led Adams to repeat Rymer's view that *Othello* represents the "violation of the law of nature" by linking a "thick-lipped, wooly-headed Moor" and a woman who "discards all female delicacy," and that led the *Democratic Review* into a similar statement some years later.[17] Writers for the Federalist *Monthly Anthology* (1803–1811), dedicated to guarding "the seats of taste and morals at home," attacked the "moral and political conduct" of Milton, admired the "propriety" and "utility" of Johnson's moral imagination, and praised Adams's "regular and scientifick study of rhetorick" the more because his "pure and exalted morality" was "always sanctioned and impressed by the authority of the gospel." Much of the early praise for Maria Edgeworth's novels was prompted simply by the belief that they were beneficial to public and private morality.

But as institutions, customs, and concepts of polish and refinement came to be seen as quite different things at various times in history, even though their ends may remain the same, a more liberal attitude toward the role of literature began to prevail. Commonly accepted criteria of conduct and morality still guided rhetorical critics. But by 1820 many were reviewing books in terms of sentiments, sympathies, and interests evocative of man's common identity. In reviewing Charles Brockden Brown's novels, E. T. Channing called for novels that would "shew us some peculiar operation of familiar principles, in men who received their natures from our common author, and their distinctive characters from limited external influences."[18] Books were no longer "models" useful in the readers' regimen for self-improvement. They were rather modes for acquainting readers with the varieties of human conduct. Thus the emphasis was still on purposiveness, only now more broadly conceived and less sternly applied.

III   Rhetorical Analysis Applied

The value of rhetoric lay in the workable guidelines for creative writing and evaluation that it provided. These guidelines were based on three principles. First, writing should be classified in terms of ends. Second, a major distinction should be maintained between conviction (logical argument) and persuasion (psychological appeal), even though they might be blended in literary works. And third, the writer should always be aware of his audience as a factor in the communication process. James Boyd's *Elements of Rhetoric and Literary Criticism* (1847), a popular rhetoric exclusively concerned with writing, illustrates how these principles could be refined into a useful critical method. Boyd engages in the usual analysis of sentence patterns and language elements (diction and syntax), discusses literary types and the well-made plot in the traditional manner, reasons that taste resides in emotion, explores the utility of imagination and judgment, and brings invention into close relation to style so that the two can work together to marshal all available support for persuasion. He also uses contemporary magazine literature for a short discussion of English and American literary history.

Looked at from one angle, the three principles of ends, conviction and persuasion, and audience, have reference to one matter: the question of effect. Rhetoric thus anticipates Poe's preoccupation with the problem of effect, but in quite different fashion. In the hands of a conservative rhetorician like William Russell, effect meant the clear imparting of an idea. Russell warned against imitating the "ambitious, high-wrought manner of writing" that he found about him in his own day, which sought effect through a "perpetual affectation of sublimity or of beauty" or an "extravagant cast of expression," and he recommended Addison and Franklin as models for students of style and effect, since these two men "expressed themselves with that chaste simplicity and plainness which are natural to a clear and correct mind." A more liberal rhetorician, such as Matthew Boyd Hope, sought to link effect to the rhetorical concern with persuasion. According to Hope, the "actual effect" of persuasion is to kindle the passions to a higher degree than the matter can possibly achieve. Thus there is a disparity between the ground of excitement and the excitement felt. The difference is explained as the difference between the actual and the ideal. Imagination is responsible for the difference, and the result is art which is a "genuine human product" rather than a slavish imitation of the forms of nature.[19]

While it was honored more in theory than practice, rhetorical criticism did provide a means for analyzing the constituent parts of literary works (their diction, narration, tone, and so forth) in some detail. Rhetorics consistently emphasized the need for students to apply the tools of criticism to specific works. The vocabulary sounds archaic to twentieth-century ears, consisting as it does of such words as "figure," "ornament," "trope," "sublime," but it was useful to the critics in assessing, sometimes very lucidly, particular aspects of a work. Indeed, our reaction to the language can obscure the flexibility with which these terms were sometimes used. The analyses of poems in part 3 of Boyd's *Elements of Rhetoric and Literary Criticism* are sometimes sharply focused. A good review of Bulwer's *The Disowned*, by Hugh Swinton Legaré, although it quotes excessively, first touches on the species, here defined as the Beau-Brummel school; discusses the nature and manners of the society depicted; considers the tone of the novel in terms of conception and style; evaluates the moral tendencies of the novel; and ends by discussing some of the novel's characters in terms of plot and subplot.[20]

A. The Stress on Unity

Mostly, however, critics were cavalier in examining the particulars of a work. But they were obviously interested in and talked a good deal about the next step, that of examining the total relationships of the parts and drawing conclusions about its unity and effect. Analysis enabled the critic to reduce a piece of writing to its component parts and to ascertain their nature and use. Criticism, on the other hand, was a guide in forming a judgment of "the individual correctness of every part, and of its adaptation to the whole."[21]

Rhetoric texts constantly stress the need for a work to be congruous, although often enough the analogy is to the "manufacturing" of a discourse. Congruity is usually estimated in terms of what rhetorical critics call the "artistry" of a work. That is, a literary work at a minimum should possess an elevated artistic tone. Once the tonal key is established, and therefore the "type" of the work identified, the various criteria having to do with lyricism, satire, and such are brought to bear on the piece.

In the hands of rhetorical critics, analytical procedures tended to be mechanical and prosaic, mostly, I think, because the often flat and labored expositons of the rhetoric texts were not very inspirational. And frequently literary works themselves failed to rouse critics to enthusiasm. Percival's "Prometheus," one critic remarked, was exalted enough in some of its passages. But it left no "distinct impression upon the mind" because it lacked unity and design. W. H. Gardiner made much the same remark about the novel, *Hobomok*, which he termed flat and uninteresting and devoid of unified plot. For congruity to become a significant working principle, there were needed outstanding contemporary writers and such critical concepts as Coleridge's shaping powers of the imagination.[22]

B. *Style*

In matters of style, rhetoric again offered critics a consistent and well-articulated theory. Channing, Newman, and many others distinguished between logical discourse and imaginative writing by emphasizing the "elevated" style of the latter. In its belletristic sense, writing was characterized by the "heightened language" in which the inspiration of the writer was apparent. Sometimes rhetoricians appealed for a style having many of the qualities Aristotle assigned to the epideictic as the proper mode for imaginative literature. But such appeals had their real base in something akin to the English rhetoricians' views that the reason must be supplemented by the "affections" if general tendencies to good ends are to be encouraged. At any rate, good sense animated by exalted language was a major critical criterion drawn from the rhetoric textbooks. Translated into criticism, it became the association of purity and perspicuity as elements of reason with elements of style like propriety, dignity, and fancy. James Kirke Paulding put it perfectly: "I believe the perfection of a work of genius to consist in the symmetry and harmony of its parts, the purity of the design, the chastity of its embellishments, and the nice judgment with which the whole is put together."[23]

Each American rhetorician phrased it differently, but in general a good style was composed of four factors: fancy, good usage, contemporaneity, and reputability. Sometimes nationality was added as a fifth factor.[24] Porter, Channing, and even Adams thought—as had Francis Bacon—that the fancy was appropriate for all forms of communication except mathematics. Fancy was directly related to literary eloquence as a means for adapting the work to its end. This view undoubtedly derives from Blair and Campbell, the two most influential English rhetoricians on American theories of belles-lettres. Campbell thought that the fancy was useful in "ravishing" the reader's soul by adding feeling to knowledge. The American theory of style, especially that associated with faculty psychology rhetoric, envisioned a clear progression of intention. The movement was from knowledge to fancy, to the stimulation of passion, to a movement of will in the reader. Throughout the entire movement, all the reader's faculties were engaged. Each genre might have its object in moving some particular emotion (tragedy, for instance, evoked pity and fear), but the very excitation of that emotion stirred secondary responses in others.

It was only for the practical purpose of exposition and study that style could in any way be separated from thought. American rhetoricians constantly took pains to point out that writing is much more than thoughts tricked out with various tropes and figures. Adams maintained that only when argument and persuasion are indissolubly joined would action result.[25] The same view was held by W. E. Channing, William Russell, W. G. T. Shedd, and many others.

Still, the matter of style does present some knotty problems, largely because the theory seems inconsistent with the rhetoricians' illustrative material or with the style as actually found in the prose and poetry of the period. Rhetoricians spoke for such virtues as earnest simplicity, but it is clear that sonorousness had an unspoken but esteemed place. James Boyd, for example, counted perspicuity first in the elements of style, but immediately added that the next most important quality was ornament or elegance. This continuing infatuation with a "high" style is probably responsible for more bad writing at this time than any other cause. The complaint that Alexis Eustaphieve (author of the epic poem *Demetrius*) failed to reach "the magnificient and sublime" because he lacked the resources for sustaining the high style is representative of such a critical attitude.[26] Partly too the concern for sonorousness is simply literary fashion falling into inept hands. Much of the adulation of Hannah More as an American Shakespeare, for instance, is based on a surface correspondence to the rhythms and flourishes of the Shakespearian style. The swelling periods, the bombast, and the sheer turgidity of the greater part of the poetry go unrecognized and unacknowledged. Finally, part of this concern for sonorousness is due to the fact that critical vocabulary does not necessarily coincide with trenchant criticism.

Rhetoric offered at least three ways to analyze the appropriateness of a writer's style. First of all, the critic could examine the adjustment of style to thought. In pointing to ten lines of Addison as fruitful lines for analysis and criticism, William Russell argued that good style was consistently modeled on thought.[27] By having cultivated his taste, the critic acquired what amounted almost to an instinct for spotting the phony, the overly declamatory, or the insincere. He became sensitive to tonalities of language, spotting the flats and sharps of particular passages and forming in his own mind a sense of the writer's attitude toward his material.

Next, and quite as important, the critic could look to the way that the writer adjusted his style to the capacities of his audience. Strictly speaking, adaptation to audience is not any more an aspect of style than it is of invention, disposition, or delivery. But American rhetoricians from Adams to Henry N. Day (*Elements of the Art of Rhetoric*, 1850) obviously thought it important. Audience was defined broadly; it was not divided into certain segments and these addressed exclusively. Consequently there was a greater emphasis on readability, organization, and simplicity than we might expect today. It was also felt that the writer was a servant to the public, and that it was his responsibility to assure complete communication. The poet, said a writer in the *American Quarterly Review*, "must show a respect for [his readers], and understand their feelings."[28]

As a result, writers were asked to immerse themselves so completely in the general cuture that its characteristics—the habitual frames for looking at things—were second nature; and secondly, writers were expected to have studied men so carefully that they were absolutely familiar with the broad aspects of "human nature."[29] Such knowledge guarded against the expression of eccentric views or of "talking down" to the audience. And it assured an easy alliance of author and reader which advanced, as the *North American* said, "the confidence which ought to exist between man and man."

Finally, the critic could look at style as revealing the author.[30] Here one could observe the writer's mastery of his craft. An apprenticeship immediately revealed itself, and so could years of devoted attention to precision. With precision gained, language became the servant of its master, and the full rich temper of a thoughtful mind could be found in writing to which one might respond.

IV Rhetoric and Romantic Views

Rhetoric as a critical tool steadily declined after about 1830 as romantic literary theory became popular. There were, however, sporadic attempts to adapt rhetoric to the changing times. In 1833, John McVickar in his annual report to the trustees of Columbia College complained that his students were ill prepared in classical rhetoric due to the separation of classical study and rhetoric.[31] But a few years later McVickar, who bore the imposing title of Professor of Moral and Intellectual Philosophy, Belleslettres, Political Economy, and the Evidences (he joined Columbia at a time when there were but three professors, one adjunct professor, and a president), was leavening his teaching of literature by frequent reference to Coleridge, although the precise extent is difficult to assess. In 1839 he wrote a controversial preliminary essay for the New York edition of *Aids to Reflection,* in which he rehabilitated Coleridge to Episcopalianism by attacking James Marsh's essay in an 1829 edition of the same book.

An intense but relatively narrow German influence also linked rhetoric and the romantic theory of the imagination. C. C. Felton, who held the Eliot Professorship of Greek Literature at Harvard from 1834 to 1860, adapted German theories of linguistics and philology to all modes of expression of a language. In 1843 he published with Barnas Sears and B. B. Edwards *Classical Studies: Essays on Ancient Literature and Art,* which stressed the relation between imagination and language. The book included a chapter on schools of German philology. And in 1844 Barnas Sears, at the time president of Newton Theological Institution, published *The Ciceronian: or the Prussian Method of Teaching the Elements of the Latin Language.* Weak on many points, the book did, however, emphasize the originality and freshness that results from a close relation between language and national character.

The best illustration of the "new" rhetoric is to be found in W. G. T.

Shedd's translation of Francis Theremin's *Eloquence a Virtue: or, Outlines of a Systematic Rhetoric* (New York, 1850). American rhetoricians, in their criticism, had generally begun by assuming the moral nature of the American national character. Rhetoric, with its attention to invention and argument and to concepts of finish, taste, and originality, was an analytical tool for explicating the expression of the national character. Theremin's book, as Shedd stated it, moved beyond the "mere collection of rules respecting the structure of sentences and the garnish of expression" to blend thought and expression into one organic form. Theremin's book is weak as a teaching manual, however, for while it has the admirable aim of organically consolidating idea and expression, the means to be used to achieve this aim are made a matter of "impulsive genius" rather than "practice and experience."

Theremin and Shedd relate rhetoric to literature in terms of two basic principles. First, rhetoric is defined as the science of organic form. The starting point and guiding principle of art is an idea. This idea then evolves and establishes the general pattern of the argument. Second, rhetoric has a moral function. That is, rhetoric is immediately associated with the area of man's freedom rather than man's necessity. It has, says Shedd in his introduction, a "moral origin, moral means and improvement, and a moral end." Theremin's views are obviously closely related to Emerson's theory of art. Rhetoric is totally removed from social and sectarian attitudes in order to address the private moral self of the individual, that sphere which Kant had placed outside the causal influences of space and time. The end of rhetoric, and of art, was to stimulate innate ideas of duty, virtue, and happiness in the reader that he might freely choose better "sentiments and conduct."

These few attempts to reconcile rhetoric and the romantic aesthetic constitute a passing and largely unsuccessful phase. A random look at such later editions as Adam Sherman Hill's *Principles of Rhetoric* (1878) and James De Mille's *The Elements of Rhetoric* (1882) confirms the suspicion that invention, argumentation, and the principles of persuasion continued to be the organizing categories of rhetoric textbooks. At least in its literary character, romanticism simply encouraged the development of different, more congenial modes of critical analysis.

Consequently, rhetorical criticism tended to be relatively conservative of established literary forms and of the relation between literature and social values.[32] Its period of strength was the first quarter of the century, before the general acceptance of romantic writers. By the very nature of its standards, rhetorical criticism leaned strongly toward judgment and the legislation of literary opinion. There has been a tendency in some scholarship to view rhetorical critics as members of an "upper class" self-consciously interested in perpetuating a social hierarchy in which they remained the arbiters of social, moral, and literary conduct. But really the issue is more complex. Men like Joseph Stevens Buckminster, E. T. Channing, and the many anonymous rhetorical critics of the periodicals were overwhelmingly interested, according to their various fashions, in establishing a harmonious, composite society. They were naturally opposed to any form of individualism which threatened to make a virtue of nonconformity—that of Bulwer, for instance, or Byron. In their eyes literature was a very practical means for helping to fix and to refine the American character. When one considers the fact that in the first quarter century the republic was scarcely out of infancy, this concern for a stable society built on proven values becomes understandable. Thus rhetorical critics had their programs. They also had their forums. If writers set themselves in opposition, they were in danger of being read out of the club.

CHAPTER 4

Judicial Criticism

JUDICIAL critics held that their function was to pass judgment on individual works of literature and to rank them according to conventional or universal standards. Their choice of criteria often involved a veiled subjectivity and partisanship which peeps through apparently rational intellectual comments on literary works. They were socially conservative, frequently paternalistic in their judgments, and rather more abrasive in their responses to literature than they would have wanted known. These characteristics lay them open to the charge of being pedestrianly narrow, bigoted, and unimaginative, and sometimes they were. There is little charm in the work of a "gentleman of leisure and inquiry" like James McHenry, whose querulous dislike for any sort of innovation led him into sweeping condemnations of some of the best writers of the century. Nor is it easy to react favorably to Irving's early Malthusian image in "The Mutability of Literature" (1819), which he used to argue that destructive judicial criticism is "one of those salutary checks on population spoken of by economists." A few judicial critics were simply unintelligent and insensitive. Their writing is superficial, and as Arthur Edwin Jones says of an earlier period in American criticism, "a pontifical seriousness clothes naive generalizations."[1]

Yet there is also much on the positive side. Judicial critics drew on a large body of critical theory and opinion, and often exercised it with discretion and taste. Many possessed real imagination and insight and an almost Arnoldian passion for the best that has been thought and said. Faced with third-raters like Bulwer, they felt it a dereliction of duty to avoid censuring what was obviously shallow. In a sense, criticism today is relieved of this task of dealing with bad writing because of the general recognition that it is intended for popular consumption and makes little pretense to complexity and seriousness. A critic can make a fine reputation, provided he has the intellectual equipment, when he limits himself to literature of significant stature. But the nineteenth century did not easily distinguish between "two cultures." As a result, critics often expended energy on writing that in no way could contribute to their reputations.

I *Neoclassical Premises*

Judicial critics generally got their theories from a medley of five sources: ancient classicism (Aristotle and Plato), neoclassicism, rhetoric, aesthetic of taste, and associationist psychology. Ancient classicism is a ground swell in the period, to be marked in college instruction in ancient literature, the frequent references to Aristotle and Horace, and the better parts of the criticism of Hugh Swinton Legaré. Neoclassicism, which bases its critical standards on tradition and authority, seems to have been a significant force in the early part of the period, as Merrill Heiser has shown in opposition to the earlier objections of Robert Spiller and Howard Mumford Jones that it had no existence and no followers.[2] The insistence of critics like Paulding, Grayson, Kirkland and others on principles of decorum, judgment, balance, objective standards of a moral and social nature, and universality, would seem to indicate a relatively straight line of descent from Franklin and John Adams through Samuel Miller, Joseph Stanbury, and the younger Adams to these men. And the considerable amount of scholarship on the influence of English neoclassicists in America (Swift, Pope, Addison, Johnson), plus what can be mined from contemporary periodicals, all point to an early but extensive preoccupation with neoclassical attitudes.

While judicial critics of a neoclassical bent sometimes shared in the eighteenth-century tendency to melt before sentiment and to sigh over graveyards, their critical views exalted diligence, good sense, and sober realism to an uncommon degree. A poet had no special equipment exclusive of other men. He was, said William Grayson, simply a man plying a trade just like "any other intellectual laborer."[3] The most characteristic quality of the good poet was his exceptional judgment. This feature is mentioned continually by critics like James McHenry, for a time coeditor with Robert Walsh of the *American Quarterly Review* and violently neoclassical in his taste; Stephen Simpson, one of the most important reviewers for the Baltimore *Portico* and a rock-ribbed conservative; E. W. Johnson of the *American Whig Review;* and Richard Hildreth, the American historian who wrote occasionally for the *American Monthly Magazine.*

One of the stranger positions, but in some respects a clue to the attitudes of these men, can be found in W. B. O. Peabody. His criticism reveals a general uneasiness with commonly accepted authors like Cowper, whose writings were unquestionably orthodox but whose tones verged on the romantic. Peabody simply felt more comfortable with Addison, who although not a "true genius" reflected a sturdy moderation that never exposed the reader to disquieting feelings.[4]

Neoclassical critics also continued the eighteenth-century veneration of particular authors. Of the ancients, Homer, Virgil, and Horace were especially popular; Shakespeare was still the "untutored genius" of his period; and following him came Milton, Addison, Cowper, Burns, and a few others. Pope's position was ambiguous simply because he stirred such deep controversy.[5] J. S. Gardiner, a defender of Pope, praised the finish and vitality of Pope's work and attacked his detractors for championing a volatile and gross originality.[6] Gardiner's own "deadly absolutism," syas Lewis Simpson, results from taking as "unalterable values" the statements of a "decadent neoclassic authority."[7]

Neoclassicists located the standard of taste in the great works of the Age of Reason, less often in classical writing. "In every language," said Willard Phillips, "there is a small number of authors, whose claims upon posterity are not to be disputed. From these the critick draws his rules, and these it is the first business of the student to learn to admire."[8] J. C. Gray maintained that careful reading in English literature and criticism provided the "permanent rules of good taste" and critical strategy. Even so liberal a critic as Samuel Knapp, whose *Advice in the Pursuits of Literature* (1837) differentiates between the truly historical and the merely chronological, thought that readers should begin with the English eighteenth century ("an age of taste and pure English") and from there work back to Anglo-Saxon literature before attempting the modern. Such views generally recognized authority more than grounded principles, although it is difficult to discriminate between the two. The typical view is exemplified in an article in the *Portico*, which proclaimed that "legitimate criticism" began with Dryden, flourished under Pope and Burke, and was then tapped by Blair and Campbell. Three results followed. Criticism established a "standard of taste"; it justified writings by appealing to experience; and it analyzed the "sterling productions of established character" for precepts or "precedents for censure."[9]

One last point, the theory of imitation, needs to be made in discussing neoclassical doctrine. The "standard writers of the old school" were often cited for their "intrinsic utility" for budding writers.[10] Older established authors were thought to help writers forge their judgment, control the imagination in its tendency to excess, and maintain sound morality and common sense.[11] The anonymous author of the introductory biography to the *Sermons of Samuel Stanhope Smith* asserted that Smith's adherence to neoclassical models had promoted "uniform perspicuity, strength and elegance" in the writing.[12] As a matter of fact, many of the early American writers first went to school under eighteenth-century English writers, especially the satirists, so that the fledgling efforts of Irving, Bryant, Paulding, and many others reveal the influence of such models as Fielding, Swift, Sterne, and Goldsmith. The purpose, of course, was to use satire as a corrective of nonconformity to group attitudes. The obituary notice of Nathaniel Ames, a militant neoclassicist, in *Manufacturer's and Farmer's Journal* called Ames the "Spectator of the Age" and described his "melodius fluency" and satirical "keenness" as comparable to Addison's. O. W. Holmes as late as 1836 pointed out that he had been educated in "the schools of classical English verse," and described himself as "his own Boswell" who represented standard social norms through satirical verse.

II *The "Watchdog" Role of Criticism*

Whether their loyalty was to neoclassicism, rhetoric, taste, or associationism, judicial critics felt they had a "trust" to provide "faithful criticism" that would guard against any attempt to "corrupt public taste and sentiment." "Misplaced indulgence to the offender becomes, in this case, an act of treachery to the public."[13] Sometimes this role provided militant conservatives a sanction for their theory of social stratification as modified by Christian attitudes. Reviewing Catherine Sedgwick's *The Poor Rich Man*, the *American Quarterly Review* maintained that literature could acquaint the "poorer and humbler classes" with their proper role in the "social economy." "In them a spirit of contentment, not of ambitions, should be fostered."[14] Taking a somewhat different tack, Fisher Ames argued that society by nature tended toward social inequality. Once class strata were established, the aristocracy could develop a literature consonant with its needs.[15]

But most judicial criticism was based on the view that superior critics have such "force of intellect" and such "authority of nature" that their opinions spring axiomlike from their pens and are the "ratios of truth."[16] Such sentiments continued well into the period, although their frequency declined. In 1834 an article in the *American Monthly Magazine* defended judicial criticism and denied the popular view that adverse criticism had harmed Chatterton, Burns, Keats, Shelley, and Byron.[17] And Charles Card Smith, reviewing Edwin Whipple's *Essays and Reviews*, warned that Whipple sometimes forgot the motto of the *Edinburgh Reivew—Judex damnatur cum nocene absolvitur* ("Judgment is damned when it is absolved from evil")—and said that this "sententious maxim of critical jurisprudence" was needed if the true cause of literature was to be advanced.[18]

This "watchdog" role of the critic, as William Charvat has termed it, was in its largest sense exercised in terms of strict moral views based on the Christian virtues and conservative ideals of social conduct. "The best songs," said William J. Grayson, "are the crackling of thorns under a pot compared with the interests of truth and virtue."[19] Reviewers admitted that writers should draw from the imagination. Thus there should be few restrictions on the manner in which writers chose to address their audience. But at the same time, writers had an obligation to the community and should be aware of "the general concerns of society."[20] Man was moral by character. Part of the "utility of art" was ministering to this moral character.[21] When writers seemed to ignore this duty they were angrily brought to heel. Reviewing Coleridge's *Christabel,* the *American Monthly Magazine* exclaimed: "It is time for the professed guardians of morals and arbiters of taste, to interpose the authority with which they are invested, to shield the one, and to rescue the other, from the rude attacks of a wantonness of innovation, that has attempted the violation of both."[22]

Aspects of this concern for the moral relevance of literature can be seen in the critical debate over the relative importance of primary and secondary associations. Primary associations described those ideas traceable to the structure of man's mind, whereas secondary associations described ideas attributable to familial inheritance or environmental influences. Conservative critics became alarmed at a growing tendency to place all associations on the same moral level. Accidental or secondary associations, it was argued, could result as much from "the indulgence of our evil propensities" as from the good side of our natures. Tendencies to evil associations should be firmly checked.[23] Nor were conservatives inclined to the position of Sir James Mackintosh, who held that conscience was a "secondary formation" created by associated ideas resulting from the acquisition of social feelings. They preferred instead the position of the Scottish philosophers Thomas Reid and Dugald Stewart, who held that conscience was original in human nature and simply needed to be strengthened through acquiring virtuous actions.

III   The Quest for Universal Criteria: Scottish Philosophy

As Poe observed, judicial critics were often culpable of large generalizations and extraneous considerations. But much of this distraction is due to preoccupation with establishing a firmer ground for a uniform critical and literary theory than had obtained in the eighteenth century. Many critics of the judicial frame of mind distrusted the neoclassical tendency to categorical judgment. They sought instead a firm, empirically stated ground on which true critical judgments might be based. Dogma would be replaced by law. The search for such law carried critics far beyond mere concern with literary matters and into areas of philosophy, science, and history, so that the critical "wars" that were fought were primarily conflicts of religious, political, economic, and philosophical differences.

What men sought were universals or constants in human nature, ethics, and art as these could be empirically demonstrated. In 1821 Samuel Gilman wrote that "Edwards on the Will is still the principal rallying point of our orthodoxy, and Locke is a general classic among our colleges."[24] Conservative Lockeans like Frederick Beasley, professor and provost at the University of Pennsylvania, Francis Bowen, professor of moral philosophy at Harvard, and A. H. Everett, were engaged in publishing texts like Beasley's *A Search for Truth in the Science of the Human Mind* (1822) which provided standards for judicial critics.

Scottish philosophy, sometimes thought of as an extension of Locke but more often as a correction of aspects of his teaching, was also popular and in many colleges triumphant. Samuel Miller as early as 1803, while praising Locke and Hartley, had listed Reid, Stewart, Beattie, Oswald, Kames, and Ferguson as in the ascendancy.[25] The work of Hutcheson and Hume was also attractive to men of a conservative mind, for both strongly defended older forms of litera-ture on the basis of the uniformity of the mind.[26] By insisting on "laws" of mental action, the workings of the mind could be mechanically plotted, as A. P. Peabody suggested.[27] The best way to prevent "corruptions in literature," said John Kirkland, was to seek authority for "laws of composition" in "nature, in reason, and in experience."[28] Everything depended on applying "right methods" to the philosophical or literary process, and this involved a "scientific acquaintance" with the processes of thought themselves.[29]

The rules for judging literature were thus codified in terms of human nature. Abraham Mills claimed that Kames had been among the first to discard "all the arbitrary rules of literary criticism derived from authority" in order to seek "new and appropriate ones in the fundamental principles of human nature itself."[30] And Theodore Dehon nearly a half century earlier had pointed out that "perpetual experiment" was as inimical to literature as to government. The principles of both were "fixed"; "They spring from sources and have relations, which are unchangeable and eternal."[31] Stating his poetic principles from this point of view, Andrews Norton said that "a correct and refined moral taste" should dominate poetry in which three lesser elements were also necessary: "truth of imagination"; "possible and consistent" combinations of "qualities"; and "a conformity and taste of the writer, to the laws of the moral universe in their numberless bearings."[32] Such principles could easily serve the judicial purpose. When judgment was withheld, it gave critics reasons for explaining the lack of universal popularity of such a poet as Percival: he simply did not appeal to "the common feelings" of mankind.

A. *Taste in Scottish Thought*

Ideas on taste also supported traditional principles of Christian ethics. The Scot Francis Jeffrey, for instance, while admitting that the tastes of all men were "equally just and true," denied that they were "equally good or desirable." The best taste, he maintained, depended on cultivated "affections and sympathies" proportionate to the degree of individual sensibility and social sympathy. Jeffrey thus emphasized the close connection between the social and moral natures of good taste.[33] The conservative F. W. Winthrop, in commenting on Jeffrey's views, thought even this too liberal. He appealed to the sense of universal taste discovered and established by the best writers of the past. Anything that showed a "want of conformity to the taste of others" might be "powerful and interesting," he admitted, but he thought such productions would be ephemeral. In effect, Winthrop was abiding by the old dictum that the *consensus gentium* was the best guide and criterion of good taste. "If we wish to gain reputation by the publick display of any liberal accomplishment, we must throw off every thing, that is particular and accidental in this part of our constitution."[34]

Following such English theorists as Beattie, judicial critics commonly held that a literary work should adhere to an absolute standard of taste, but that a subtle admixture of individuality enhanced its freshness and originality. The criterion of worth would be the extent to which the work might "engage the attention and extort the praises of the publick."[35] Keeping this criterion in mind, the critic had three alternatives for evaluating a work. He could refer to literary judgments of the past, to established "canons of criticism," or to the "more enlarged knowledge of human nature."

But in their efforts to be inclusive, judicial critics left a weak spot which was increasingly exploited by the romantic opposition. While they emphasized standards, they also admitted that, in terms of personal reactions, a work might be natural or eccentric. As the individual grew in importance during the period and obvious diversities of taste became more noticeable, the relativistic views of men like Jeffrey and Archibald Alison enlisted more recruits. As early as 1813 the *General Repository and Review* had noted that Alison had produced a "standard work" which should be read by all "desirous of obtaining just notions of taste, or correct principles of criticism."[36] By 1830 an article in the *American Quarterly Review* openly condoned the relativity of taste, arguing that differences in taste between English and French drama completely exonerated the French from being subject to English standards and therefore English criticism.[37]

B. *Beauty in Scottish Thought*

On the subject of beauty, critics were almost evenly divided. Some followed the early position of Thomas Reid and Sir George Mackenzie, both of whom held that beauty was intrinsic in nature, varying only in quality according to the object. Others held with men like Thomas Brown that the sense of beauty distinguished between objects, but that secondary associations were sufficiently powerful to alter or subtly affect our sense of beauty. This latter group argued that while association cannot confer beauty upon objects it could invest them with such interest that we are pleased. All kinds of modifications were rung on this second attitude. Thomas Cogswell

Upham, the teacher of Longfellow and Hawthorne, wrote that beauty was an emotion. Hence objects in themselves do not possess intrinsic beauty. But he retreated somewhat from this position when he admitted that objects did have some trait or quality which caused the emotion of beauty. Not all objects equally pleased. In this he was following the main outline of the position taken by Dugald Stewart.[38] Stewart's *Philosophical Essays* were also used by F. W. Winthrop in the latter's disagreement with Jeffrey. Jeffrey said that objects had something in common if they were termed beautiful. But Winthrop held that this was simply an unfounded philological assumption. Jeffrey's idea of association, said Winthrop, is not nearly so important as a one-to-one correspondence between some characteristic in the object and a universal sense of beauty in man.[39]

Lines do tend to blur, however. Both Alison and Jeffrey made beauty dependent on the imagination and attempted to prove it a subjective emotion. Many American critics rejected the theory of Alison and Jeffrey that beauty consists in a succession of harmonious images, but were themselves partly subjectivist in arguing after Brown that beauty is one instantaneous absorbing feeling or in following Stewart's view that our sense of beauty is modified by association.[40]

C. *Sympathy in Scottish Thought*

Judicial critics were also conservative in defining their theory of sympathy. Jeffrey had made sympathy the basis for the appreciation of beauty. But American conservatives urged that things appeal because they address some elements of human character common to all men. The *Southern Review*, in a striking survey of the entire controversy, linked sympathy to secondary associations. Thus sympathy might enhance the original beauty possessed by an object, or it might lessen the original ugliness of an object. In this sense, sympathy could be termed a "relative beauty," or, in Stewart's phrase, "the doctrine of felt relations." It provided a feeling of interest, but it frequently attached to objects having little or no beautiful qualities.[41] Sympathy, then, could easily be confused with enthusiasm, and it was precisely to guard against this possibility that judicial critics emphasized the primacy of judgment.

One result of this whole controversy regarding taste, beauty, and sympathy could have been a relaxation of the doctrine of kinds (literary types or models), although other factors are certainly more important. Lord Kames had noted very early (1762) that beauty was not wholly intrinsic in the object but was dependent on the observer also. This had led him to be distrustful of the doctrine of kinds, feeling that literary models shaded imperceptibly into one another. Winthrop, in opposing Jeffrey's contention that everything outside man owes its interest to accidental connections with man's thoughts and feelings, pushed Kames's position a little further. In wondering how "dissimilar and distinct" elements could be resolved under the one principle of beauty, Winthrop saw the only solution in an elaborate classification and arrangement of all forms of gratification. From this it might be possible to determine what intrinsically pleases and what pleases only through its situation and relation. "To pursue our inquiries into the nature of beauty we must examine individual objects, a single poem, or a painting, or a building, and discover what it is that pleases; and everything which does afford pleasure, enters into the composition of the beautiful."[42] Here there is a complete isolation of the individual work and a resolute (if unconscious) rejection of models.

IV   *Literary Cosmopolitanism*

Judicial critics thought of themselves more as conservators of value than as opponents of the new. Their position seemed reasonable enough. If literature had endured, then it must reasonably have something to offer. In their eyes, fancy, imagination, and wit were the "lighter faculties" that need to be controlled by a masculine and logical "sound judgment." Imagination by itself was "enthusiastic," and so judicial critics tended to distrust it, although they left room for the "passions" (following Blair) as a legitimate element in literature. Legaré represented the attitude well when he championed study of the ancient classics as a discipline of genius, a refinement of taste, an elevation of decorum and propriety, and a perfecting of moral sentiments. These were the values offered by good literature, and a thorough grounding in them would be the best possible thing for promoters of a national literature, whom Legaré suspected of championing utility at the expense of worth.[43]

In the debate over a national literature that followed the War of 1812, judicial critics, while not always precisely antinationalistic, tended to justify the universal and cosmopolitan side of literature. Their main positon was that a nation's literature could not afford to be isolationist. While some critics felt that America was simply not rich enough in history to warrant a national literature,[44] most looked to English racial, political, and literary antecedents as positive assets. The *Southern Review* listed four reasons for opposing a national literature: English literature was good enough for the present; nothing existed from which a national literature might be formed; the frontier spirit was too gloomy and depressing; and continuous emigration to the West was siphoning off talent that might otherwise rise.[45] Similarly, an article in the *Southern Quarterly Review* thought it "suicidal folly" to turn from the cosmopolitan heritage of English literature to the inevitably provincial character a national literature would possess. All literatures in the past had been influenced in their development by neighboring literatures, and while American characteristics of freedom, intrepidity, and inventiveness should be prized, the "accidental imperfections" resulting from narrowness should be avoided.[46]

Southern critics seem to have stressed more than the North the nation's heritage from the past as opposed to radical demands for a national literature, although some thought that eventually the nation would be in the literary vanguard. Richard James Calhoun's study of Southern critics indicates that Southern concern for traditon, Southern reaction to Northern ideas on progress, puffery, positivism, utilitarianism, and utopianism, and Southern desire to educate taste all blended to encourage a dominant judicial view well up to the Civil War. This rational and formal view stressed ideas of unity and close attention to the work itself, although critics never really lost sight of moral and social guidelines. They continued to emphasize common sense, truth, and correct diction. Even Bryant and Wordsworth were tolerated with reservation.[47]

The North too had its share of men who distrusted the agitation for a national literature, chiefly because it appeared so radical and neglectful of tradition or the *consensus gentium*. Their attitude, however, was more conciliatory. So long as the traditional forms and values were not subverted, the fledgling attempts of native writers could be encouraged. Bryant, whose early criticism is in the judicial mode, reproved Solyman Brown's uncritical and chauvinistic nationalism as inappropriate for finding "favor at the bar of criticism." The more moderate view of Washington Irving that we should winnow out the best in foreign literatures to "strengthen and embellish our national character" struck the major note. It was repeated later by Lowell, who argued that a self-imposed historical and geographical isolation would simply "debar us of our rightful share in the past and the ideal." But by then many thought the question tiresome. In 1840 the *Arcturus* confessed to being weary of the whole subject of a national literature; one good writer or genius, it said, would settle the matter in a day *if* he were to appear.

Judicial critics were committed to a cosmopolitan position because they were committed to foreign literary models and critical criteria. William Crafts, a Southerner, violently defended established literary models, attacked literary nationalists, and condemned almost all of the romantic school, including Crabbe and Scott. Crafts's position had its equivalent in the North, where E. S. Gould took Johnson's criticism of Milton as "proof of the perfection to which criticism may attain" in its "impartial analysis" and sharing of valuable insights. There was also the heady influence of the English periodicals. Here Jeffrey, who served as editor of the *Edinburgh Review* from 1802 to 1829, was a major influence on the position taken by American periodical criticism. At the time he was regarded as essentially a conservative judicial critic, and only later were his achievements and innovations noted. Jeffrey, said Francis Bowen, in a belated testament to Jeffrey's liberalism, had been one of the first to describe the genius of Keats and Crabbe; had been instrumental in overthrowing the authority of Queen Anne's age; had popularized the Elizabethans; and had been "a high-priest to the national idolatry of Shakespeare."[48] In addition to the *Edinburgh Review*, there were the American editions of *Blackwood's*, *The Westminster Review* (especially in New York), and Scott's *Quarterly Review*. Together, they confirmed a style of criticism during the early part of the period that complemented our own concern with standards. It was the feeling that these standards were largely foreign and outdated that led to later impatience with their serviceability.

V *The Persistence of Interest in the Epic*

While these standards were in effect they did provide means for gauging the work itself. In their emphasis on cultivation and learning, on the "laws of metrical composition," and on the need to follow "established rules" of creative writing, they tended to look backward rather than forward. The heroes of men like Paulding were the "older" writers like Spenser, Dryden, Swift, and Pope, who intended that "every metaphor and allusion should illustrate its object, that every epithet should produce its effect, and every line be penned for its sense and not for its sound."[49]

The inherent conservatism of the judicial critics prompted them to stick to accepted forms of literature. In the early decades of the period, the epic was still considered the highest form of literary expression. Somewhere near the bottom lay the personal lyric. Hildreth thought Pope our "great moral poet" and said that Homer strengthened in men the "precepts of prudence and morality."[50] As fashions changed in the period, the positions of epic and lyric were almost totally reversed. By 1856 H. B. Wallace lamented that romantic critics were "very limitary and insular" in their sympathies and would "consign Homer himself to neglect" and "push Horace and Virgil quite out of the line of poets."[51]

Part of the reason for this change in fashion, apart from the triumph of romantic literary theory, can be attributed to the utter failure of writers to achieve anything of significance in the epic form. It is doubtful that Emmon's four-volume *Fredoniad,* one of a number of really bad epics, found many readers even at the time of its publication. Yet critics persisted in thinking that America would not come of literary age until an epic was produced. Nationalists revealed an inherent conservatism when they phrased their demand in terms of the epic form. William Tudor, early editor of the *North American Review,* thought there were a large number of subjects (particularly during the Revolution) that could lend themselves to epic treatment, and the same year Walter Channing pointed out that the United States was far behind England in the production of epic poems.[52] As late as 1856 A. P. Peabody (not, however, a judicial critic) felt it a reflection on native efforts that we had not produced a single epic of "even moderate merit."[53]

VI   *Interest in the Novel*

Simply because so many novels were produced, judicial critics had to come to grips with the form. Very early in the period, Samuel Miller listed the demands on the novel: it should possess "utility," should impress the "understanding and the heart," and should provide "pictures of nature." Beyond that, the novel should present "natural and probable exhibitions of *modern* manners and characters" and "descriptions of real life."[54] Later, in a discussion of the novel as genre, its growth and development, and its moral character, W. B. O.

Peabody defended the novel as part of "the department of poetry" whose worth is to be judged by its complete "moral impression." This was quite a departure for Peabody, and represents the influence of Scott. Peabody did not feel that a novel needed a "professed moral" or poetic justice, but he did point out that all novels suffered from a moral taint before Scott and Miss Edgeworth. These two, he felt, made the novel "teach and illustrate the most important practical truth."

Peabody's praise of Maria Edgeworth reflects the period's adulation of women as conservators of social and moral values. The view even entered the list of attributes of the Teutonic race, to be picked up in this century in the *Handbook* of the Daughters of the American Revolution. Critics like F. W. P. Greenwood, J. G. Palfrey, and A. Lamson all praised such women writers as Sedgwick, More, and Barbauld for "rescuing fiction from the service of corruption and profligacy; and converting it into a powerful agent in correcting moral judgments."

On the whole, the novel fared poorly in the first two decades of the century, largely because the novels themselves were poor fare—at least till Scott. But the persistence of the type led critics to wish its improvement. Their suggestions were phrased in terms of the values they entertained in relation to other forms. Novels should present the sober realism and basic good judgment that inheres in organized society. The style should be correct and refined, the characters (and characterizations) balanced, and the dialogue, plot, and description all probable. In the more conservative critics, probability was confused with the eighteenth-century idea of decorum. Finally, action should be appropriate, that is, there should be a strict correspondence between the novel's tone and the reader's impulses to action.

These criteria, in the hands of competent critics, were serviceable for analyzing novels. But the last point—that of appropriate action—was sometimes difficult to apply. A critic, for instance, could react adversely to the titillating sexual suggestiveness occasionally found in Ann Radcliffe's *The Mysteries of Udolpho.* He might even react to Emily as a prying little peeper and eavesdropper. On the other hand, it is obvious that Emily is a woman of great moral sensibility, perhaps overly preoccupied with saving her honor. The tone of the novel is finally within the Christian popular code. On the whole, critics tolerated those "romances" where the action was grounded in sentiment and morality. Here the Scottish principle of sympathy was a factor, although in practice the principle was often translated into sentimentalism.[55]

VII   *Attitudes toward Language*

When dealing with language, judicial critics generally praised economy, plain expression and common sense, smoothness and harmony, as appropriate in a rational universe. These criteria were serviceable in recognizing excesses (particularly extravagances, far-out images or figures, hyperbolic expressions), although the savagery of some of the reviews obscures that value. With the advent of romantic enthusiasm, attempts to preserve the "pure, perspicuous, classical composition" championed early in his career by W. H. Prescott became increasingly difficult. So concerned were some, that in 1820 the American Academy of Language and Belles Lettres was established with John Quincy Adams as president. Its aims were to preserve the purity of the language, and to keep it simple and economical in analogy with the simple order of the universe.[56]

VIII   *The Decline of Judicial Criticism*

Early in the century a critic in the *Monthly Anthology* said that the multiplication of badly written books made it the duty of reviewers to "destroy useless, unnecessary, and pernicious productions."[57] Nearly two decades later Washington Irving was of a like mind in complaining of the "extravagant images and flashing phrases" of E. C. Holland. No reader can reasonably deny the justice of Irving's view, although he might reasonably object to Irving's belief that good writing consists in "conformity to those orders of composition which have had the sanction of time and criticism."[58] Even the gentle Whittier accused critics of becoming effeminate, soft, and particular, and of promoting an imbecile poetry. He acknowledged the relevance of private judgment, but, he said, this should be balanced by time and "the best critical authorities."[59]

Yet romanticism increasingly came to dominate the period, and for the most part Irving and Whittier went along. Irving's shift from judicial criticism to the latitudinarian tone of "Desultory Thoughts on Criticism" (1839) marks almost exactly the path taken by American criticism, although Irving drew up short in a kind of impressionism. One can see the same shift in the *American Quarterly Review*, which has been commonly regarded as a judicial magazine edited by the arch-associationist Robert Walsh. Actually the magazine was fairly eclectic, and under Walsh's editorship published a number of articles written from an historical and liberal point of view. By 1835, C. F. Hoffman growled that "our criticism is comparative, not absolute!"[60] And a year later E. S. Gould observed that criticism had become "superficial" once it had abandoned its duty to analyze "merit and demerit, in detail."[61]

Judicial criticism had its practitioners right up to the Civil War, but by the 1840s it was less a movement than a point of view embraced by various individuals or small isolated clusters of sympathetic souls, although the South continued to present a sturdy front. In the hands of someone like James McHenry, judicial criticism was often absurd in its narrowness and bigotry. But in the hands of a strong conservative classicist, for instance, Hugh Swinton Legaré, judicial criticism could be marked by care, exactness, and firmness without losing its flexibility. Here, criticism was solid and responsible.

CHAPTER 5

Romantic Criticism

ROMANTICISM in America as it relates to literary criticism is a knotty subject, as I have indicated at some length in the first two chapters of this book. Here I wish to isolate a few of the critical attitudes that dramatize the differences between judicial and romantic criticism, and to then examine the importance that the sophisticated critical principles of Coleridge and Carlyle had for American followers.

The judicial point of view, dominant to 1815, slowly declined after that date, although it always enlisted some adherents. As the number of judicial critics diminished, a new group of critics emerged, less committed to the ideal of social solidarity (conservatively defined) and altogether opposed to the working principles of judicial criticism. Stimulated by the spirit of nationalism, the zeal for antiquarian study, liberal associationism, and romantic philosophies imported from England and the Continent, the new group rejected the speculative objectivity that Newtonian cosmology had encouraged and affirmed instead the twin concepts of a dynamic, genetically evolving world and the shaping force of the creative mind. Judgment was deposed and imagination installed. Feelings were extolled as a better index to sincerity than methodical disposition. The lyric was deemed more poetical than the epic. And sympathy became the primary tool for the critic longing to understand rather than to harshly condemn. By 1820 most of these romantic principles had been evolved, and by 1830 they were working principles for a large number of critics.

Criticism in the transition period between judicial and romantic criticism was often tentative and eclectic. Old methods had been rejected, but the new methods were imperfect and not well understood. The immediate effect was to convince critics that they knew what they disliked while uncertain of what they should approve. But they did have some touchstones. Romantically inclined critics insisted that they had "higher objects" than the elaborate detailing of faults. A representative eclectic like William Cox consistently held that true literature should persuade, elevate, and inspire in contrast to the "mere teaching" of the practitioners of the heroic couplet. Literature perfected men to live with themslves and with a divine, higher order. Its final end was thus richer than the simple preparation of man for his role in society.

These are grand aims. Unfortunately, they are not especially helpful for precise criticism, a fact of which some critics were uneasily aware. They wished to avoid rigid value judgments or any theory "which makes the gauge first, and then tries the work by it."[1] But they were unable to work out a flexible critical theory that would get them beyond impressionistic reactions, biographical statements, or general descriptions of the works. Later, under the influence of the soft idealism that followed Emerson and of the sentimentalism of the "feminine fifties"—of which the vogues of Tennyson and Dickens were a part—these critics were encouraged to continue this limp approach to literature.

I *Sympathetic Understanding*

An early attempt had been made by E. T. Channing to evade a mere negative reaction to judicial criticism by stressing catholic appreciation or sympathy. Channing argued in 1816 that men should approve a healthy diversity of taste because it encouraged creative talent while restraining critics from the "bad habit of dictating to great minds."[2] But later Robert Sands noticed that many critics who adopted this view never moved past the first step of appreciation.[3] Such eclecticism clearly shows in Tuckerman, in Whittier's *Literary Recreations and Miscellanies* (1854), and in Henry Giles's *Illustrations of Genius* (1859). After his initial flirtation with judicial views, Washington Irving came to the conclusion that amiability, ease, and cheerfulness were three of the more important virtues of the critic. Part of the critical office, he felt, was simply to "chat sociably with the public as with an old friend, on any chance subject."[4]

A closely reasoned article on Cowper's *Poems* by Willard Phillips stands out among various early attempts to escape such an ennervating impressionism. Phillips was perfectly willing to allow the individual critic his personal reaction to a literary work. But, he said, such reaction should not be extended into "general criticism." A just estimate of a literary work could be made only in terms of the correspondence found to exist between an author's private vision and the particular audience his work addressed. A generation of Americans had accepted Adam Smith's principle, outlined in *The Theory of the Moral Sentiments,* that we come to know ourselves best when we step aside from our persons to view ourselves as "impartial spectators." Phillips proposed to modify the principle to make it useful for romantic criticism. First, the critic must try to understand the "real scene" of a literary work by occupying the same "station at which the artist had sketched the landscape." Following that, the critic should sympathetically "transfuse" himself into the character of the public for whom the work was intended. Then the necessary correspondences could be established.[5]

Phillips's concept of sympathetic understanding was shared by a good many critics, although they did not phrase it quite so well as he. A critic in the *Portfolio,* reviewing Ogilvie's *Philosophical Essays,* wrote that "personal considerations" could never determine the value of a book. A book's "own merit was discovered by acknowledging the author's aim and method".[6] Gulian Verplanck not only recommended consulting the author's purpose, but argued against the current tendency to condemn works of "amusement and escape" or works deficient in their parts.[7] And William Gilmore Simms, in a prefatory apologia for the 1837 edition of *Tales and Sketches,* argued that the "standards of good criticism" required the reader to sympathetically enter the book and realize the same "glow" that had inspired the writer. "The witch-beverage must be quaffed by the reader, or he will never catch a solitary glimmer of the magic show. . . ." Possessed of a feeling heart and a quick mind, the critic, said Simms, should "review the thousand qualities of the writer—his skill as an artist, his moral sense, his taste, his knowledge of a character, of human passion, and foibles, his powers of expression, and the range and the degree of enthusiasm which is possessed by his genius."[8]

Such a shift in critical attitudes led to a reevaluation of authors more conservative critics had previously dismissed. The "personal disgust" felt by early readers of Byron, the uneasiness of critics over Moore's unrestrained and passionate poetry, the angry reaction to Coleridge's poetry and prose, tended to disappear as their work became more familiar and popular. Moreover, familiarity made it easier to develop criteria to deal with such writers. Dennie had been almost alone in his early appreciation of Wordsworth, but by 1817 the *Portfolio* had accepted the entire Lake School plus Scott, Campbell, and Montgomery. By this later date, as Tremaine McDowell has pointed out, Bryant had encountered Wordsworth and under Wordsworth's influence was abandoning Byron as a model.[9] Even the *American Monthly and Critical Review,* long a staunch supporter of neoclassical attitudes, found it could praise the "good taste" shown by Coleridge in *Biographia Literaria* in "depicting the defects and excellencies of his contemporaries."[10] Gulian Verplanck's review in the *Analectic* of the much maligned Leigh Hunt maintained that *The Feast of the Poets* was a delightful and original book that could be thoroughly enjoyed if the reader would drop the outdated "critical fastidiousness which is the bane of all the enjoyments of literature."[11] And in his 1855 Lowell Institute Lectures, Lowell spoke for a breadth of mind capable of appreciating both the natural and the artificial in literature "provided they be only good of their kind."[12]

II *Attitudes Toward the Novel*

Romantic attitudes aided too in alleviating the narrow moral earnestness that characterizes much judicial criticism of the novel. It would be too much to say that moral concerns disappeared with the advent of romantic criticism (witness Emerson and Thoreau), but they become genuinely broadened in conformity with the new stress on imagination. Willard Phillips, a considerably enlightened critic, could still place himself on the side of "virtue and prudence" and condemn the "false views of life" presented by Fielding and Smollett or the "sentimental deliriums of romance" that have their origins in Richardson and Mrs. Radcliffe. But Phillips was far from rejecting the novel as a result, and he rather sided with the view expressed by Jane Austen in *Northanger Abbey* that it is not necessary to eradicate the species in order to control the disease. Even James McHenry, a narrow and often bigoted critic, expressed surprise that the novel was an accepted form in homes that had previously felt they were for only "sickly sentimentalists, or extravagant misspenders of time."[13]

Critics tended to accept the statements of Hawthorne, Cooper, and Simms on the distinctions to be drawn between the novel and the romance. But in practice the two were viewed as having the characteristics of the latter. That is, critics looked for unity, single effect, probability, breadth of view, and verisimilitude rather than adherence to the literal. Not many critics would have insisted so rigorously as Simms that the romance was the modern equivalent of the epic. And even Simms neglected the comparison in his practical criticism.[14]

Some novelists never enjoyed critical regard, but others were rehabilitated for the public. Bulwer, universally read, was almost universally condemned by critics for his "depraved" attempts to "deprecate and undermine virgin and conjugal innocence."[15] But Balzac was made palatable to the American public in John Lothrop Motley's excellent essay in the *North American Review*. Balzac, said Motley, "is neither moral nor immoral, but a calm and profound observer of human society and human passions, and a minute, patient, and powerful delineator of scenes and characters in the world before his eyes. His readers must moralize for themselves."[16] The same point was made in a review of Goethe's *Wilhelm Meister* in the *Southern Review*. Moralists might demand poetic justice, but Goethe's method was to present life as it is, and this, the reviewer argued, presented "the most subtile panacea that could be applied for the cure of [life's] sins and follies."[17]

III   *Attitudes Toward Poetry*

Poetry was also viewed in more liberal fashion. No one seriously questioned the relevance of morality to social conduct. Poets, as Bronson Alcott said in 1834, were still the "most effectual teachers of morality."[18] But critics were no longer drawn to the moral didacticism that characterizes much of the period's poetry. They especially disliked the inclusion of trite and platitudinous themes that relied for their effect on the standard responses of readers. The *Literary and Scientific Repository* wondered if Christian truths were "the better for being put in rhyme." It felt that poets should be less concerned with generally accepted truths and focus instead on the complexities of "poetical invention" and the uses of "imagination."[19] Bryant would not exclude the use of religious themes (he defended Hilhouse's *Hadad* against religious extremists), but he too thought biblical subjects did not reduce the need for probability of character and circumstance. The point made by W. A. Jones, that the really moral writers were precisely those who avoided inculcating morality but simply wrote from experience, was generally accepted at the time he made it. And while the position tends to blur in terms of the accepted poetry, the critical attitude itself helped establish a wider critical receptiveness than had previously obtained.

IV *The Primacy of Genius*

Romantic critics also reacted to the conservative position that writers should discipline themselves to take a subordinate position in a larger, well-defined whole. They argued that genius, not the rules under which genius should labor, was primary. Genius created the taste that subsequently could appreciate its work. It consulted the whole of human potentiality and the bounty of nature. It ranged widely to encounter "new and striking situations" to find worthy subjects, as Irving said, following his new mentor, Campbell.[20] W. E. Channing felt that genius set before us our own natures "in more than human beauty and power."[21] Stressing as they did the imagination, critics endlessly discussed the unifying role of the imagination in genius, the supremacy of genius to mere men of talent and understanding, and the capacity of genius to produce art of passionate intensity and wide moral truth.

Following eighteenth-century attitudes, romantic critics asserted that genius spoke from "the fulness of the heart" spontaneously and lyrically, "without any idea of rules, or pretension to excellence, or fear of criticism."[22] Later romantics, imbued with the notion that nature was vitalized with a spiritual presence, felt that genius "awakened within us a consciousness of our affinities to the great creation and its God."[23] Thus poetry revealed the "divine in man" as "the revelations of God" strike the poet.[24] Such theories, which tend to mysticism and lofty indefiniteness, were apt to disarm criticism before its practitioners could fairly come to grips with the poetry. It was a danger before which lesser critics succumbed into lyrical impressionism. But such theories at least encouraged attempts at understanding poetry that departed from convention and sectarian moralizing.

V *The Place of Originality*

Granting the primacy of genius, critics were less prone to look to literary tradition and convention. Writers were praised for their originality and imagination. Countering Poe's insistence on absolute originality, Philip Pendleton Cooke pointed out that a poem often begins with its author's reading in another, so that even lines and rhythm may be unconsciously indebted to a predecessor.[25] The more common position, however, was that of Irving, who felt as early as

1814 that writers should task their own power and rely solely on their own judgment.[26] Thus, a reviewer in the *Boston Quarterly Review* sought to explain Wordsworth's difficulties as a poet in terms of his reliance on "theory." True genius, said the reviewer, "spurns all fetters, all systems of philosophy, and makes and follows its own rules."[27]

The natural result was to lessen the influence of previously accepted models, especially from classicism and neoclassicism. R. H. Dana, Sr., deplored the influence of ancient authors who were no longer relevant to the modern scene, and E. T. Channing, in his forceful article arguing against models in literature, said that study of the classics resulted in an "acquiescing and unproductive" attitude which substituted rules and models for the "endless change" of natural processes.[28] Other critics, more realistic, simply felt that writers should guard against any straitjacketing influence of models. Bryant recognized the obvious fact that writers are subject to the influence of other writers, but he was opposed to the narrow range the "puerile followers of Pope" imposed on themselves. And reflecting the new interest in seventeenth-century English literature, T. Parsons suggested the American mind would find more "vigor and originality" there than in the "excessive refinement" of the eighteenth century.[29]

In emphasizing self-reliance and originality, these critics also argued that foreign literatures too often served as models rather than as inspiration. American poetry, said E. T. Channing, should avoid being "a bad imitation of popular authors abroad." Even the British *Westminster Review* noticed that Catherine Sedgwick, one of "the most popular writers in the United States," was unduly influenced by British novelists and it recommended to American writers that they cultivate originality by consulting nature and circumstance. Bryant, in his 1825 review of Miss Sedgwick's *Redwood*, strikes a similar note, except that he goes on to say that a writer using native materials has varieties of geography and character at hand which are denied the writer of romance. Bryant's view repeats a position he had taken in his "Essay on American Poetry," published in the *Noth American Review* in 1818, which according to William J. Free was an early attempt to fuse poetry as suggestive art, native materials, and poetic tradition into a comprehensive aesthetic theory.[30] The more knowledgeable American critics took the position that art is creative rather than imitative. Its primary function should be to make nature comprehensible by "completing" its forms. For James Marsh, the Vermont

Transcendentalist, this meant that the writer should consult the dictates of the "inward soul" through introspection in order to find a correspondence between subjective states and the objective forms of nature.[31]

Emphasizing as they did the primacy of the poet, romantic critics viewed their task as a sympathetic exploration of his work and a codification of the results. "From the practice of Genius, we are to learn the laws of Genius. We, critics and system-makers, have no right to frame a code of law for his observance. Our glory is to take our law from him, and interpret it faithfully."[32] Criticism was no precursor of genius, preaching doctrines to the wilderness people about the new joy to come. Genius, allied to imagination, was its own best sermon. Genius was a "law unto itself," and criticism could do little more than discover its causes and appreciate its effects. The resources of man and nature being inexhaustible, each work was a Copernican universe with itself at the center. Criticism explained this universe so that the reader, himself capable as Jones Very said of imaginatively duplicating every personal experience of historical man, could read and understand and profit by the subsequent enlargement of his self.

VI *The Matter of Style*

Romantic critics discarded the mechanics of style as outlined in the various rhetorics as too artificial in their emphasis on elegance and smoothness. They sought instead for a closer vital relation between style and thought which moved beyond regular accents and monotonous cadences. Bryant's essay on "The Use of Trisyllabic Feet in Iambic Verse," published in the *North American* in 1819, was an early venture in this direction. His own use of the trisyllabic foot in his poetry was greeted with mixed reactions, even so good a critic as Willard Phillips finally suspending judgment in the matter. For the most part critics identified the relation between style and thought through what they termed "strong feeling." According to Bryant, style "is a part of the thought, and a bad style is a distortion of the thought."[33] Following Alison, Bryant argued that poetry was primarily suggestive, so that light "touches" work on the imagination as the "best defined objects" do not, provided only that such touches be accompanied by strong emotions. Thought was redeemed when it was associated with emotion. John Neal attacked the "sleepy, milk and water-school of Addison" and advocated a style that would appeal to man's "blood" relationship and the sympathies of the "heart."

Even colloquialisms were tolerated, on the theory that experience was so wide and flexible it could be adequately rendered only with a wide and flexible style.

In time, romantic critics came to see style as organically functional in literature. Horatio Greenough glowingly described the functional beauty of Yankee clippers and New England farmhouses,[34] and Hawthorne, in his *Italian Notebooks,* praised the "moral charm" of Gothic architecture as opposed to classic architecture, which, he said, was "nothing but an outline." Equating style with spirit and form with idea, critics looked to a dynamic blend of form and spirit as constituting an organic whole. John Sullivan Dwight, editing the poems of Goethe and Schiller, said that "The form is not the container of the spirit of a song; the form is thoroughly instinct with the spirit, and, in fact, grew out of it."[35] The same idea was affirmed by a host of critics. In one gesture they swept aside the whole paraphernalia of canons of style, and in their place substituted the principle of organic functionalism.

The principle received many different expressions. Emerson in "The Poet" said that "It is not metres, but a metre-making argument that makes a poem." And Thoreau felt that the writer must rely on that which is "grown from within outward, out of the necessities and the character of the indweller." For Thoreau, style was a "vital function like breathing," and while revision was of course necessary, the poet should never turn to the mechanical execution of form. At its most extreme, the principle took on mysterious dimensions, so that the process of composition, as J. S. Dwight said, was "as much a mystery to the poet as to any one."[36] Generally a more moderate attitude prevailed, holding that while all the constituent parts of a literary composition are genetically modified as the work grows, it is finally the "shaping spirit" of the imagination that gives the work unity and a harmonious tone. The higher form of imagination, said Lowell, "masters us at last with a sense of indefinable completeness."[37]

VII   *Coleridge and the Imagination*

In many respects, romantic criticism comes of age when it discards the neoclassical ideal of judgment and accepts Coleridge's definition of the imagination as an ordering power. Coleridge's distinction between reason and understanding allowed Americans to keep the best parts of critical judgment and historical pluralism. Reason established the primacy of art once and for all. It intuited the great moral truths applicable to the human condition and testified to the unity of mankind. These truths, embodied in art, endowed art with transcendental importance. Understanding, on the other hand, by acknowledging the role of necessity on the mundane level, allowed the critic to trace conditioning factors on the work of art and on the artist, to admit the effect of change (and continuity) on man's eternal quest for universal expression, and to stress in general the rhetorical elements of art.

These twin elements of art—truth through reason and history through the understanding—were blended by the imagination into organic forms which critics could both understand and evaluate. The theory of organic form, by focusing attention on ontological considerations, effectively put to rout exponents of literary genres or types. The work stood by itself as a unique comprehensible form, independent of rules, literary kinds, moral judgment, historical considerations. On the other hand, the doctrine of organic relations promoted a semimonistic view of the interrelatedness of mind and matter which could be analyzed in terms of historical antecedents. This dual capacity of the doctrine appealed immensely to such critics as Frederic H. Hedge, J. F. Clarke, G. H. Calvert, and G. B. Cheever. It led to the elaboration of what some called "reproductive criticism," a species of criticism which had as its purpose, as George Allen said, the reproduction of the specific creative process of the artist. In its main outlines it does not differ appreciably from Croce's theory of expressionism.

Coleridge held to the primacy of genius and its freedom from constraint, as did many Americans, but more generally he saw that "times and manners lend their form and pressure to genius." This blend of freedom and necessity allowed Coleridge to be cognizant of two critical points: the end the writer had in view, and the "local accidents" that modified the work of art. Both points assumed a critic of "philosophical" vision, one who understood the need for apprehending relations. The first point required the critic to place himself in sympathetic proximity to the writer, without confusing the personal life of the artist with his work. The critic had to take the writer's point of view, and adopt, for the moment, his habits of thinking and feeling. The second point recognized what was inescapably true, that genius in adapting to its age, place, and manners, voices through them the universal spirit of man. Both points introduced the note of critical toleration. The true critic, said Coleridge, was incapable of despotism. The method is well illustrated in the essay on Milton, where Coleridge assumes the original genius of Milton as "the immediate agent and efficient cause," and then explores the "conditions" imposed by the "character of the times" and Milton's own personality.

As Norman Fruman has demonstrated in *Coleridge, The Damaged Archangel* (1971), one can very nearly assume that when Coleridge develops an idea at length he has plagiarized the performance from another. This sorry fact was unknown to most Americans who paid him tribute as a genuine philosopher. F. H. Hedge, J. F. Clarke, Frothingham, and others were all impressed with Coleridge's doctrine of the interior consciousness, his antipathy to the sensationist philosophy, and his distinction between understanding and reason. They had little to say about Coleridge's critical theory. But his critical breadth drew respectful attention from such men as James Marsh, George Allen, G. H. Calvert, and E. P. Whipple. These men regarded him as "the first critic of the century." They were less confident of his rank when he left the realm of theory to engage in practical criticism.

Both James Marsh and George Allen were instrumental in disseminating Coleridge's critical theory. Prior to 1821, Marsh was an enthusiastic reader and student of the Cambridge Platonists, de Staël, Schiller, Schelling, Schlegel, and Coleridge. He was the first American translator of Herder, Bellerman, and Hedgewisch. Coleridge recognized him as his official disciple in America. Marsh's importance lies mainly in his translations, teaching, and editorial work. As a teacher at the University of Vermot and a recognized authority on religious matters, second perhaps only to Moses Stuart, Marsh was in a position to strongly influence many men.[38]

VIII   *The "Reproductive Criticism" of Allen and Whipple*

It was Marsh who indtroduced George Allen to Coleridge and Wordsworth, as well as to the Germans, and who encouraged Allen's religious inquiries, which went slightly sour when Allen converted to Roman Catholicism in 1847. Allen's two critical essays in the *New-York Review* were concerned with working out the implications of romantic doctrines as they were received from Coleridge and such Germans as A. W. Schlegel and Heine. They feature the relation of Christianity and art, the role of fancy and imagination, and the idea of organic unity and form. Allen hoped to fully comprehend all the implications of a work of art by a close, sympathetic study of the work itself. The method, he thought, was unique, and he gave Coleridge full credit as the "one unparalleled mind" who in a series of fragmentary directions had pointed the way. The "reproductive" critic (a term borrowed from Heine but considerably modified) came "alongside" the work of genius "with the specific purpose of reproducing, step by step, the creative process of the artist." This entailed a close approximation of the writer's point of view, thought, and feeling. Reacting to contemporary critics who confused the personal lives of authors with their works, Allen insisted that reproductive criticism must "separate the work-master from the work, and [must] follow him in his productive process."[39]

Edwin Whipple's essay on Coleridge's principles of literary criticism develops many of the same points. Appalled by the party and personal criticism that distorted so much of contemporary second-rate criticism, Whipple offered Coleridge as the emancipating alternative to the dry pedanticism of Francis Jeffrey, whom he accused of lacking principles or a philosophy of criticism. Whipple's portrait of Jeffrey as a narrow, dogmatic, faultfinding, reactionary critic is itself narrow, but fortunately he soon lost himself in an examination of Coleridge's theory and regained the urbane tone which is his trademark in the period. Whipple deduced five principles from Coleridge that would reconcile historical pluralism and the need to evaluate a literary work. First, unity and organic life must be intuited in the work. Then historical investigation discriminates between the organic and external accretions. Following this, the critic assumes "the writer's own point of view" and enters into the inner life of the work of art. Here the critic determines the ends that the writer had in mind and adjusts his critical capacities to fit the case. The result, Whipple felt, contributed to "catholicity and comprehension," and prevented the kind of critical errors made by the neoclassicists and party hacks.[40]

The essays of Allen and Whipple are first-rate statements of what later in the century became known as critical expressionism. Whatever we might think of the theory now, it had a considerable number of exponents and an even more considerable number who borrowed many of the principles as working tools of the craft. The theory gave the artist complete freedom in determining literary form and structure. The artist himself was conditioned by nature and yet rose superior to its modifying influence. Historical considerations accompanied the nature-genius-art relationships. Here sympathetic understanding and historical method were desirable. But in addition, and really more importantly, a poem, play, or other art form was unique in itself. Insofar as genius was transcendentally creative, free of trammeling circumstances, the work of art assumed ontological significance. It possessed its own necessity, therefore its own value. Completeness and perfection characterize the art work. No critical study can legitimately break up its organic unity, for, as Wordsworth said, we must murder to dissect. In the order of creation, the imagination assumed priority, coming even before thought. Working freely, imagination creates its own forms. Each work of art is therefore completely unique, whole, organic, and vital, and it becomes the business of the critic to sympathetically enter the work, imaginatively duplicate the artist's original experience, and come to a revelation of what the artist has done for man.

IX   Thomas Carlyle and American Criticism

Carlyle's work was also influential in the American quest for a practical but liberal critical theory. In Carlyle could be found one of the favorite doctrines of Americans, the idea that universal history assures historical continuity and progress through its cumulative effect on natural processes. Reason and justice were constantly at work subverting the forces of destruction, and man achieved his highest happiness in conforming to the design of Providence, for humanity was the great end. The genetic view is thus a large aspect of Carlyle's overall theory. It is typical of the century in its emphasis on the transcendental meaning of aggregate human conduct. Only within the limits of history could man freely exercise his will; in a broader view his fate lay in the hands of God, in the genius of the nation, in his physical environment. These views form the philosophical underpinning for Carlyle's essays in practical criticism. Genius transcends the limitations of its age in intuiting great universal truths, but it speaks through the age to acquaint men with their destiny—the need to subscribe to the great ends Divinity has shaped for man.[41]

Carlyle enjoyed a high personal reputation with Americans, but he was also known as a popularizer of German philosophy and literature. His essays on aspects of German literary theory began in the *Edinburgh Review* with the article on Jean Paul Richter in 1827, and ended with his article on Goethe's works in the *Foreign Quarterly* in 1832. Hedge credited these essays with prompting German study in

America, as did J. F. Clarke, who said that Carlyle's "wild bugle-call" influenced him and Margaret Fuller to begin the study of German in 1832. There was, of course, considerable interest in matters German at this time, as evidenced by American study in Germany and George Bancroft's influential series of essays on German literature in the *American Quarterly Review*. Emerson's publication in four volumes in 1838–1839 of Carlyle's *Critical and Miscellaneous Essays* did much to advance Carlyle's reputation beyond the small circle of Concord avant-gardists. W. B. O. Peabody doubted whether any of Carlyle's "subsequent work" was so much read in America. These essays are primary examples of Carlyle's analytical and biographical methods, and Americans were quick to note the manner in which they could be used for analytical and evaluative purposes.

What Americans especially remarked in Carlyle's criticism, in addition to the manner in which he placed his subject in historical context, were his great tolerance and sympathy and stress on biographical data. They liked the way in which Carlyle tried to explain a man's moral character, in the process offering instruction and wisdom and pointing up the universality of law. Carlyle traced the "history of a mind" from its inception to its full maturity. The way he placed the literary work within the context of the man's social and philosophical development struck many as creating an "epoch in biography and criticism," as James Freeman Clarke said in his essay, "Nineteenth Century Questions." Carlyle determined the boundaries of his problem, and all his facts fell neatly into place within them. The study became one whole. The individual items related to one another so perfectly that Carlyle's criticism itself established the same organic form he sought in the creativity of others. He seemed to see, said the *American Quarterly Review*, that all events "form one great chain of causes and effects, and a whole history of the world is necessary to enable us to understand a single moment."[42]

Hedge's review of Follen's edition of Carlyle's *Life of Schiller* is typical of American attitudes in the way it catches up many of these ideas and works them into a theory of biography.[43] Hedge, who did not know that Carlyle was the author, praised the book's "clear and happy method." The biography was what it should be, a history of a mind rather than a history of a person. Hedge was not too clear on Carlyle's attitude toward genius and necessity, and at several points he sharply debated Carlyle's tendency to explain poetic talents by natural events. Hedge admitted that the "mortal part" of genius is subject to "necessary and everlasting laws," but he felt that its free

spirit transcends them. The mortal and spiritual are so often intri-
cately involved, however, that the writing of biography is difficult.
"The biographer must not only exhibit each part of his subject in its
individual distinctness and fulness, but he must also explain the
relation between them; he must show how the intellectual life has
sprung from the earthly condition, and how the earthly condition has
in turn been modified by the intellectual life" (377). Like Carlyle,
Hedge appealed to universal progress to reconcile history and
poetical truth. But he acknowledged that "finite understanding" can
not always see the compatibility of the real and ideal or "detect the
harmony which exists between the movements of destiny and the
rules of art" which the great artist automatically intuits.

Carlyle's American admirers continually stress their belief that
criticism can be conducted "scientifically" if the roles of genius and
sympathy are properly understood. Speaking of Carlyle's unique
ability to show how innate power and circumstances blend in the
artist, Emerson wisely pointed out that Carlyle countenances neither
an "unconscious law of Fate" nor a "wild chance," but locates
aesthetic qualities in the artist's appreciation of the laws promulgated
by "divine love."[44] As a result, said C. S. Henry in a carefully
analytical appraisal of Carlyle's work, Carlyle never engages in
"unsatisfactory comparison" or "unsympathizing rebuke." Carlyle
assesses the work of art in terms of the author's "spirit" and aims. He
sees the "infinite connexions of every event." In reconceiving and
reproducing the work, he establishes a pattern of intricate relationships that is far removed from the kind of narrative "line" that had
previously been popular. Henry's interpretation brings Carlyle's
theory into close harmony with Coleridge's. Both historical analysis
and evaluation through sympathetic recreation are the respon-
sibilities of the critic.[45]

While most reviewers of Carlyle duly pointed out his doctrine of
sympathetic understanding, it was mainly members of the Transcendentalist group that took the trouble to abstract Carlyle's principles in
order to arrive at a clear knowledge of his critical method. Men like
Hedge, G. H. Calvert, and C. S. Henry, all of them in reaction to
criticism based on party or individual dislikes and to elaborately
formulated standards for literary works, readily embraced Carlyle's
invitation to ascertain the purpose of the author, to adopt the author's
point of view, and to shed one's own prejudices. And they were at one
with Emerson in maintaining that there was a law for man as well as a
law for thing. Thus one did not look for causality on the material level

alone. One found it in the realm of spirit too, in the direct play of mind between divinity and genius, or the almost unconscious manner in which genius perceived the laws of universal history and adapted to them. This explains the tendency, evident in most of these critics, to critically assess not only literary movements of the past but even the lives of individuals; the tendency is especially noticeable in discussions of the eighteenth century, to them a century of lamentable indifference to the wide-ranging potential of the human mind.

The influence of Coleridge and Carlyle led to a much more sophisticated critical theory than has usually been recognized. The impressionistic jumble of reactions that scholars have professed to find in the criticism of Whipple or G. B. Cheever is not the whole matter. Whipple's historical-social attitudes, which he shared with other admirers of Coleridge and Carlyle, did make him into a sort of American Macaulay, as Denham Sutcliffe suggested some years ago. But the romantic stress on expression, creative in the artist, recreative in the critic, promoted concern for the work itself. Emotional response was thus an important element, and expressionism is just cloudy enough in its method to encourage a relaxation into impressionism. But some important steps had been taken. Insofar as Coleridge and Carlyle spoke of the importance of organic unity and transcendent ideas, a consistency and consequence was assigned the individual work that set it apart from all others, even those of its kind. The work had its own "spirit," its own form, its own unique being, all of which could be known, not in terms of any rich explication of the parts (Americans do not seem to have sensed the possibilities here of Coleridge's writing on the imagination), but in a sympathetic awareness of the author's aims and an intuition—by virtue of the transcendental reason—of his success.

CHAPTER 6

Historical Criticism

BY about 1830 critics brought together a strain of nationalism and a strain of philosophical romanticism, and inspired a type of historical criticism whose frame was shaped by new theories of national and racial psychology. These theories in turn rested on the idea that social forces were really the unfolding of God's plan for history. While romantic antiquarianism of the type associated with Sir Walter Scott was invaluable in the early development of the historical attitude, historical criticism as a method did not really emerge until Americans adopted romantic statements on the nature of ultimate reality.[1] The result was a theory of criticism which sought to understand literary origins in terms of cause and effect by attention to temporal sequence. Subjectivity and judicial appraisal of a moralistic sort were minimized.

Three main facts stand out in a study of the rise of historical criticism in the period. First, a substratum of religious belief helped to encourage rather than to hinder a type of historical relativism. It provided cosmic security. Scholars were quick to react to any suggestion that natural law obviated the need to refer phenomena to a spiritual agency. As Theodore Parker said, God spoke through nature to man. Nature testified to providential direction. Following as it does the eighteenth-century Deist interpretation of nature, which isolated God from the creation, this view placed Him back in nature. God as both Person and Force could be a sustaining energy guaranteeing the universality of intellectual progress and the common brotherhood of man.

Second, since God's immanence in nature suggested that he was personally involved in processes of change, men were able to elaborate a more complex theory of causation. Newtonian mechanics continued to confirm the universality of law relative to cause-and-effect relationships in nature and the universe. But as God came to be viewed as a force residing in nature, and nature itself seen as evolving along fairly progressive lines, another dimension to thinking on the question of cause and effect was introduced: the old doctrine that natural phenomena is explicable by mechanical principles was supplemented by the idea that matter, individuals, groups, and classes all contained some internal principle that like a seed controlled and directed change along the lines of growth. Nature and society, said George Bancroft, "resembled living plants" suffused with "inward energies." These energies served to divide both nature and societies into various classes or orders, each possessed of distinctive characteristics. As the new attitude toward causation was applied to American society, questions were inevitably raised about how a multiracial democracy might coalesce into one whole. These quesions were never satisfactorily resolved, but the general tendency was to develop a theory of national character in which diverse social and racial groups shared in an underlying group mind. This mind was not subject to direct empirical observation, but it could be inferred from its effects on social processes and behavior.

Finally, this theory of genetic causation prompted men to modify their view, also romantic, that literature was self-expressive or that it stated truths incommunicable by other means. Men now came to see literature as expressive of society at large. Literature was an integral part of the greater life of the community. "Good poetry, like other possessions of knowledge," said Samuel Knapp in *Lectures on American Literature* (1829), "more often belongs to the age in which it was written than to the genius of the individual poet" (193). Again, genetic causation moved critics to regard the individual work of art as a growth or development out of its own internal principles rather than as a mechanical composition. The doctrine of kinds and the theory of imitation were played down, and creativity raised to a new level. Even comparative criticism was disallowed. "The rules of criticism, founded upon the example of a successful author in one country," Samuel Worcester concluded, "may be inapplicable to the work of an author in another country, though the work of the last may belong to the same species of composition as the work of the first."[2] Thus historical criticism could either explain the individual work of art through studying the conditions that governed its development, or it could use the work to illustrate the spirit and manners of the community.

I *Ethnology and Historical Criticism*

The relatively new field of ethnology played an important role in broadening the scope of historical inquiry in the nineteenth century. As ethnology developed from the relatively simple views of men like Benjamin Rush and Jefferson, it spread from a study of the filiation of the earth's races to the study of geographical and climatic conditions, the physical characteristics of the people, religion and mythology, polity, customs and manners. The *Transactions* of the American Ethnological Society, a group founded in 1842 by Albert Gallatin (it included such well-known critics as Edward Robinson, Evert Duyckinck, and E. G. Squier), show that by that date a strictly scientific temperament was taking hold in ethnological study. The political economist, the statesman, the man of letters, as well as the scientist, were expected to familiarize themselves with this new "science of the age." One had to understand the origins of races, the influence of climate and other physical elements, the relations in roots and structures of languages, and the modifying and controlling forces of great natural boundaries.

One of the great controversies in the period, until Darwin's book in 1859 changed the tack of ethnological inquiry, was the debate between the polygenists and the monogenists.[3] The polygenists, of whom Louis Agassiz was the greatest American exponent, asserted that the unity of mankind did not require a unity of origin. Nor did they believe that a diversity of origin involved a plurality of species. The origins of the various races followed a pattern set by God. Americans had already encountered these views in Lord Kames's *Sketches of the History of Man* (1774), which they read in both English and American editions. By mid-century, polygenist views were held by such men as James Cowles Prichard, Samuel George Morton, Josiah Clarke Nott, George R. Gliddon, James De Bow, Edwin Whipple, and Theodore Parker. Pushed to its ultimate conclusion, the polygenist theory that the races were adapted to their particular regions made large-scale migration of race impossible. Such a doctrine, of course, would be unpopular in America, which was composed of various foreign racial elements. This was why Americans so largely opposed Robert Knox, although he counted men like Emerson among his sympathetic readers.[4]

Polygenists had difficulty in reconciling their view that mankind had multiple origins with the biblical account in Genesis. To counter accusations of infidelity, they sometimes argued that their theory

made it unncessary to ascribe human origins to "the crime of incest."
Some others disclaimed all theological and political intent, and said
that such questions were simply outside the realm of inquiry of the
scientist. Others relied on the obscurantist argument. The ways of God
are inscrutable to man. For the most part, they were religiously
conservative. Agassiz was strongly pro-Paley and antidevelopment.
Whipple felt that Agassiz had authoritatively answered believers in
the developmental theory (the monogenists) who argued God out of
creation in favor of a life produced by natural causes.[5]

In the social sphere, polygenists were more argumentative. Agassiz's statement that it was "mock-philanthropy and mock-philosophy"
to assume that races had the same abilities and powers was especially
galling to abolitionists. Theodore Parker had reservations about both
the Irish and the Negro.[6] In the South, where polygeny butted
head-on into religious fundamentalism, Josiah Nott, a well-known
popularizer of the Southern position on racial inequality, edited
Gobineau's *Essay on the Inequality of the Races,* which denied
progress and the efficacy of Christianity on civilization. And James
De Bow praised Calhoun for using ethnological findings to answer
Jefferson's "strained dogma" that all men are born free and equal.[7]

Most monogenists adhered to some form of religious orthodoxy,
while their political thought ran the gamut from conservatism to
radicalism. They stressed similarities of form, structure, and faculties
in man as evidence of his common origin. Man formed one species,
and from this the races were variations, caused either by external
circumstances or inherent tendencies within the group, or by a
combination of these.

A strong argument for the monogenist view was the presumed
similarity of languages. While languages were studied as examples of
inherent national characteristics, in the larger view similarities
observed in roots and syntax grouped the nations in a fraternal bond.
In this period the concept that Western languages referred back to an
Indo-European background was becoming popular. The *New-York
Review* felt that the study of languages was "one of the most powerful
means" at hand for ethnological research and pointed out that such
study tended to sustain the theory of the single origin of the human
race. The article did not dwell on the mental characteristics of the
various races, but it did note that "Deity always operates by
secondary causes," so that differences in race could be ascribed to
"physical causes."[8]

The Nordic myth, and especially its offshoot, Anglo-Saxonism, was an important aspect of historical theory. It formed the focal point for ethnological inquiry and seems to have been a ground on which most racial theorists could meet. A few men, notably Irishmen like Henry Giles and Henry Cruse Murphy, argued that Anglo-Saxon superiority was only brute superiority. According to this view, the Celt was the civilizing force, and the greater poet, orator, or philosopher. Others, like Emerson, were doubtful that any race existed in pristine purity, but even Emerson observed that "race avails much" in contributing to a hereditary "symmetry" that reached even to the mind.[9] The great majority were all for the Anglo-Saxon and especially for its three major "instincts": an aggressive and frank spirit of inquiry; civil and religious freedom; and the elevation of woman as the conservator of racial values.[10] F. H. Hedge spoke for this majority when he said that the Anglo-Saxon race held the "torch" of progress. Only the Russian could be considered a potential rival, Hedge said, and at the present time the Russian had neither the means nor the literature to exert world-wide influence.[11]

Ethnological scholarship broadened the scope of historical inquiry to include belletristic literature as a repository of racial psychology. Barnas Sears thought that historical studies should give an impetus to literary study on the grounds that "all literary productions" alluded to the religion, laws, and customs of a race.[12] This procedure was actually followed in a number of histories published in the period. W. H. Prescott's *Conquest of Mexico* had a two-hundred page foreword which included a summary of characteristic art forms of the Aztec race. Henry Wheaton's *History of the Northmen* (1831) carefully analyzed the sagas as the best source of information on contemporary manners and beliefs. The monogenist George Ticknor wrote his three-volume *History of Spanish Literature* (1849) entirely in terms of race, language, national character, soil, and climate.[13] The work of Thomas Dew, president of William and Mary, was also organized around the biological uniqueness of races of men. Dew, who was influenced by German ethnological theory, included in *A Digest of the Laws, Customs, Manners, and Institutions of the Ancient and Modern Nations* (1856) a number of long chapters which trace how each nation subtly modified the heritage of the past to blend with its own spirit.

The work of Henry Wheaton provides a good illustration of how exponents of north European racial superiority used the various literatures to implement their historical point of view, especially since Wheaton can by no means be called a Germanophile. As charge d'affaires to the court of Denmark (1827–1833), he was in a postion to study Scandinavian literature at firsthand, and became such an enthusiast that he was elected an honorary member of the Scandinavian and Icelandic Literary Societies at Copenhagen. Relying mainly on Erasmus Rask's researches into Anglo-Saxon antiquities and origins, Wheaton devoted himself to refuting the idea that Icelandic poetry was derived from the Anglo-Saxon. He cited differences in grammatical structure and sought to disprove the contentions of German scholars that Icelandic form, metrics, and language were indebted to the Anglo-Saxon. Wheaton's reliance on Rask serves to point up the fact that he was an amateur in a complex and exacting game. But his theory is consistent and is applied in a surprisingly sophisticated way.[14]

As the idea gained currency that the Anglo-Saxon race was favored by God to lead the world to health and happiness, its literature was correspondingly elevated in the eyes of scholars. All the world could take pride in Shakespeare, but nevertheless he was peculiarly Anglo-Saxon. The racial character, as Andrew Lipscomb put it, was free from morbid and ultra speculations and distrustful of system-making; its genius was rooted in common sense that saw immediately the absurdity of Deism, pantheism, or transcendentalism; and the race as a whole was marked by intellectual catholicity.[15] Most of these points are conservative when cast against the background of the period. But it should be remembered that the great majority of scholars were against all ultraisms, were quite conservative in their views, and hoped for the melioration of society by slow easy stages.

Anglo-Saxonism was at least influential in encouraging research into early English literature. Loammi Ware and others became interested in "ethnic myths" like the legends of King Arthur as illustrative of the national character. The "Old English" literature of the seventeenth century was explored, and attention was given to Chaucer and his contemporaries. Lowell found *Piers Plowman* "characteristically Saxon." Longfellow wrote romantically of the "dark chambers and mouldering walls of an old national literature." But others, studying early English "folk" literature, pictured the Anglo-Saxon muse as bucolic and sly, satirical of the Norman masters, and wont to create fairies like Titania, Mab, and Puck. Such "rude and antique composition" was invaluable to scholarship, said the *New-York Review*: "We are bound by the canons of good scholarship, to receive and accredit them in the guise in which they come to us, as the envoy and representative of a people who have produced, and by their traditon authenticated them."[16]

The salient point in a study of racial thought in historical criticism is that, whatever the absurdities, race reinforced and helped to systematize the historical study of literature. Ideas on race were not complex; neither the polygenists nor monogenists seem to have anticipated the modern concept of "genetic drift" to explain racial composition. As the United States moved toward civil war, efforts were made, particularly in the South, to deny to "inferior" races any artistic ability. But this attitude was maintained even in New England. The South, thinking itself the preserver of the genteel heritage, was not especially inclined to give up the authority vested in the classics that a historical view of literature seemed to require. Consequently, the greatest application of racial thought to national literatures was made in New England. By the 1850s New England literary historians were regularly using race psychology to lend continuity to their historical studies of diverse literatures.

II *Associationism and Historical Criticism*

As one of the most influential philosophical movements of the period, associationism, which basically tried to establish a physiological explanation for the process of learning, was also a primary element in the rise of historical criticism.[17] Two key points were largely responsible. Associationism embraced the principle of change (usually associated with universal history), and it emphasized the psychological nature of conduct. As associationism engaged in a tentative and to some extent critical empirical study of psychological phenomena, it increasingly modified its views on the unity of human nature and consequently put greater stress on the study of historical antecedents. This shift from authority to psychology was immensely important for historical criticism. The strange compound of moral freedom and mechanistic necessity in associationism that resulted from the postulation of an innate moral sense and the empirical study of the physiological nature of association actually helped to promote historical study. For the critic could at once insist upon an orthodox morality and at the same time undertake the "scientific" study of literary works according to the "great law of human nature, the principle of associaton."[18]

The associationist stress on the descriptive method and the analytic examination of mental laws can best be seen by reference to discussions of taste, beauty, sympathy, and the "laws" of association. Its early belief in the "universal principles" of human nature had sanctioned an absolute standard of taste. But a relative view was explicitly set forth by the Scots Thomas Brown and Archibald Alison, both of whom related taste to secondary laws of association, that is, to laws governing those conditions (environmental or familial) that affect the existence and development of general laws of primary association common to all mankind.

Alison's views were widely disseminated by Francis Jeffrey, whose editorship of the *Edinburgh Review* (which had a large American edition) and successful visit to America earned him a wide audience. By relating taste to secondary laws of association, its diversity due to differences in mental attitudes, habits, and institutions was admitted. This allowed for considerable flexibility in critical approach and prompted such men as Willard Phillips, E. T. Channing, and A. P. Peabody, and magazines like the *American Quarterly Review* and *North American Review*, to more charitably assess the literature under review as relative to the historical time in which the literature had been produced.

Associationism was again psychological in its inquiries into the sense of beauty. There was an increasing tendency to make beauty a part of man's emotional experience and to seek its sources in his behavior. Thomas Reid and other early associationists had held to the objective and inherent beauty of particular objects. Later Scots, like Dugald Stewart and Alison, were partly subjectivists or primarily so. Hawthorne's Bowdoin teacher, Thomas Cogswell Upham, in his *Elements of Mental Philosophy* (1845) clearly illustrates the impact of later associationist thought. Upham followed Stewart in attributing *some* objective qualities to objects which could stir the emotion of the beautiful. But most of Upham's energy was spent on illustrating the emotional origins of the apperception of beauty, which again led to extending the boundaries of critical investigation to encompass the historical study of literary backgrounds.

Sympathy had been one method to enforce the bonds of a common brotherhood in the thought of Reid and Adam Smith. Known popularly as "the doctrine of felt relations," it was possible for association to either destroy or create sympathy. Reid and Smith thus ranked sympathy below universal association and intrinsic beauty. It was described as "a feeling of interest which frequently attaches itself to objects of little or no original beauty, or even agreeableness." It was, in fact, a sort of "relative beauty."[19]

Liberal critics were prepared to grant sympathy a greater role in literary criticism. It became the basis for imaginatively realizing the original circumstances and emotions that entered into the work of art. There was still a close connection between association and sympathy. But in the new scheme, sympathy as "moral sensibility" sought to discover and to duplicate original associations in order to form a "right estimate of the abilities of the author, or of the tendency and importance of his work."[20] Criticism had to assume the same station as the writer. It had to "take into consideration the relations of the writer, and the character of the readers for whom his production is intended."[21]

The seminal element in developing an associationist historical view was the emphasis put on "laws" of association. Later important in Taine's methodology, the cataloging and descriptions of these laws introduced method into the examination of a writer's background. The laws could be scientifically described, in other words, which assured critics of some objective criteria. Thomas Brown was quoted to the effect that "the Physics of mind are like those of matter, only an analysis and arrangement of its phenomena." This position was echoed by the influential A. P. Peabody in a more explicit statement: "Phenomena and results in the intellectual world, are governed by laws no less determinate and unbending than those which regulate and modify the annual products of agricultural skill and labor; and, in the finely reticulated system of correspondences between the outward and the spiritual universe, we may trace the application of the same principles to the harvest of wheat and barley, and to that of enduring and effective thought and sentiment."[22]

Like the sense of beauty, the associative principle was imbedded in man's emotional nature, which in turn affected his thought processes. Associations took place below the threshold of consciousness. Hence it was necessary to make full inquiry into all the circumstances that had affected a work of art if one were to become wholly familiar with it. But these very circumstances often constituted the book's attractiveness. Upham praised secondary association for illustrating "endless diversities" in human nature. And, like other associationists (such as Samuel Gilman), he felt that a "slight acquaintance with literary history" showed the great need for understanding "peculiarities of the associating principle."[23] Views like Upham's were greatly responsible for breaking down established canons of criticism and in substituting a critical method cognizant of differences.

Associationist critics paid some attention to biography as an element in historical criticism. But it was not greatly emphasized. Willard Phillips, A. P. Peabody, and E. T. Channing particularly emphasized the idea that the history of opinions is the history of individual men. Channing asked that "literary biography" show how a writer's experiences affected his judgment, purposes, and feelings: in short, "the history of his mind." The prime example of biographical writing, according to Channing, was Southey's *Life of Cowper*. Even the so-called digressions, in which Southey sketched in background literary history, were "important in connexion with the growth of Cowper's mind and the formation of his taste."[24]

Of far more importance to associationist critics was the relation between literature and racial and national backgrounds. Theoretically such critics allowed the individual writer his material and his method of handling it. Yet as a member of a social group, and presumably sharing in its characteristics, the writer was expected to show "some peculiar operation of familiar principles" existing in society. Such an expectation could, of course, be turned to a barefaced defense of the political or religious status quo—and sometimes was. Or it could be used to argue for the kind of genteel realism later derided by Frank Norris. But critics were genuinely concerned in asking for a literature that mirrored the religion, laws, imagination, moral outlook, and cast of thought of a particular society, all that would make the study of literature something more than an amusement.

In one's own country the various social "pockets" were closely knit, and there was little trouble in apprehending the national relevance of a literary work. But foreign literatures confronted readers with sequences of association that were unfamiliar. This fact had two consequences for associationist critical theory. First, critics were asked to extend their mental horizons as broadly as possible, to familiarize themselves with climatic and other natural conditions and with social institutions, and to study the moral, religious, and political bent of individual men in order to come to some conclusions about the society. Second, critics were warned against engaging in comparative criticism of national literatures—which supplied an indirect aid to literary nationalists. For if comparative criticism could be discouraged on the grounds that feelings and associations differed according to culture, then American authors would not have to hazard a comparative appraisal with the past or with their European contemporaries, an appraisal which might deflate American books.

Associationist critics were understandably pleased in having worked out a method for analyzing literary works in terms of time and place. R. Wheaton said in 1847 that forty or fifty years before, inquiries into sources or relations would have met with "general disapprobation." It was possible, he felt, to recognize the indebtedness of men like Shakespeare and Dante to the past without denigrating their greatness.[25] But knowledge of time and place could work the reverse, too, by raising previously unacknowledged writers to higher station. Thus E. T. Channing's defense of Lord Chesterfield sketched in eighteenth-century literature and manners, commented on Chesterfield's merits, and stated the belief that once literary history had reached maturity critics would appreciate the eighteenth century as a connected part of the past.[26]

III   History and Historical Criticism

The cross-fertilization of historiography and literary study was also instrumental in turning critics from standards of evaluation, based on supposedly immutable principles, to historical investigation. Historians of the period firmly believed that historical examination of the complex of causal sequences would reveal pattern and progressive order, although Prescott observed in 1843 that relativism was so strong that "unity of interest" was the only principle held of "much importance by modern critics." For the most part, the ideals of historians followed those set down by Prescott in his review of Irving's *Conquest of Granada.* The philosophical historian must be an impartial and sympathetic recorder of forms of government and social relations, be conscious of geographical and chronological details, and possess something of the powers of the novelist and dramatist.[27]

While the practice was not always equal to the theory, historians like Prescott, Bancroft, Motley, Simms, and to a lesser extent George Tucker, Jared Sparks, and John Palfrey, professed to write history which included pictures of "the intellectual culture and manners of the people" of whom they were writing, rather than a straight chronological narrative of political events.[28] Francis Parkman's *The Old Regime in Canada* was almost solely an essay in social history. Prescott, in his preface to *History of the Reign of Ferdinand and Isabella,* wrote that he had devoted "a liberal portion of the work to the literary progress of the nation, conceiving this quite as essential a part of its history as civil and military details."

These views, when carried over into literary criticism, immediately undercut critical infallibility. Prescott early observed that the claims to infallibility of the *Edinburgh Review* and *Quarterly Review* were ludicrous, and "fell to the ground when thus stoutly asserted by conflicting parties."[29] Jared Sparks felt that literary history should encompass the origins of language and balladry and should explore their relevance to social history. He recognized that literary history did not give complete "truth of narrative," but, he said, a delineation of "local associations," manners, customs, religions, and morals, acted as a "source of history" and led to an appreciation of the "varied forms" of different ages and nations.[30] As one of the first strictly academic figures in America to seriously turn to such concerns, Sparks occupies a distinctive place in early American criticism. Ordained a Unitarian minister in 1819, he was editor of the *North American Review* for six years (buying it for ten thousand dollars and later selling it for twice that amount). He was thus in a position to slant the magazine toward his major interests. He was also an instructor in ancient and modern history at Harvard, and for five years (1849–1853) president of that institution.

Like their contemporaries in related disciplines, historians demanded that literature promote some ideal social order. They believed in social hegemony because they believed that people in the aggregate form one moral being. However striking individual features might be, they are lost in the general outline of national physiognomy and national spirit. Conservative historians like George Washington Greene used this theory to promote a species of political quietism by making the group mind dependent on natural forces and the divine plan. Liberals like Bancroft, on the other hand, attributed original dynamic qualities to the group mind in order to underscore the impermanence of existing institutions. As the destiny of the people evolved, their institutions likewise evolved. These differences in emphasis and point of view can readily be detected in the criticism. But at the very center of the historians' work is the Lockean concept of the aggregate democratic man. And closely associated with this is the historical view of literature as the distinct embodiment, as Simms said (he wrote in addition to novels some eleven histories dealing directly with the South), of the nation's attitudes, polity, taste, amusements, and social conditions.[31]

Thus every change in the structure of a dynamic culture-complex was "an unfolding of its own internal nature." An "indwelling necessity" (the special psychic forces characterizing a people) advanced the "unconstrained development" of a community of thought completely typical and yet unique. Consequently, as Merrill Lewis has pointed out, God, nature, and man shared in a common purpose. "Neither philosophy, nor government, nor political institutions, nor religious knowledge, can remain behind, or go much in advance, of the totality of contemporary intelligence," said Bancroft.[32] The artist could no more avoid reflecting his time and place than the common hod carrier; indeed, to these critics the prime merit of the artist was that he was so accurately the spokesman of the particular spirit of his time. "A great poet is the mirror of his time," Bancroft wrote, "just as a great philosopher is the exponent of its general culture". Consequently Bancroft believed that a nation's literature "commends itself to the attention of enlightened curiosity, even independently of its intrinsic merits, from the knowledge it sheds on the nature of man."[33]

These views are admirably illustrated in the critical work of Mrs. Therese Robinson, a German emigrant to America who became a warm friend of such intellectuals as William Cullen Bryant, George Bancroft, and Bayard Taylor. In Germany she had interested herself in Serbian popular poetry through the influence of Jacob Grimm. Goethe and Herder were also influences on her work. In 1834 she published her first literary work in English, *Historical View of the Slavic Language*. Later, under Bancroft's influence, she wrote her cultural study, *Geschicte der Colonisation von Neu-England* (1847), which was based on the idea that democracy and colonization in America were coincident. (Motley in his review questioned this thesis of the "Bancroft school.") Throughout these works Mrs. Robinson reveals the belief that deep in the collective heart of a nation are the mysterious, dynamic forces that mold its peculiar patterns of action. When these subliminal forces are found in all their vigor, as they are in the literature, one is insensibly close to the very roots of the social organism.

It is W. H. Prescott, as might be expected, who best exemplifies how the principles of historiography came slowly to bear on literary history. He was never narrowly judicial or partisan. His criticisms, however, contained at first the familiar touchstones of morality and fidelity to "nature." He held the two in some sort of orthodox relationship. Associationism led him to transitional ground. He still believed that poets could be ranked. But at the same time he was akin to the new romantic attitude in stressing feeling (although he deprecated the Lake and Cockney schools), and in calling for the natural over the artistic in order to stir corresponding associations in the reader.

The next few years moved Prescott further away from fixed principles. A fine article on "Essay Writing" (1822) was not only evaluatory but also an inquiry into origins. The following year he borrowed Schlegel's definition of the romantic, and while he could not quiet his prejudice, he sought to explain literatures on the basis of national types. Some ten years later his criticism reached its final stage. He thought considerations of climate, race, and national character, in combination with secondary causes, sufficient to explain the genesis and character of any writing. In a long article entitled "English Literature of the Nineteenth Century" (1832), Prescott used these criteria to trace out a "literary history of our time" which ascertained the state of literature of his day and the channels from which it sprang.[34]

IV *Biblical Criticism and Historical Criticism*

Biblical criticism was another discipline that helped turn literary criticism toward history. A majority of the schools and colleges were denominational, concerned with educating young men for the ministry. At a time when writing for periodicals was very much an avocation, the educated clergy constituted a large percentage on periodical staffs. The magazines themselves were often sponsored by religious sects. Others, like the nonsectarian *North American Review*, published articles by many of the leading theologians of the country.

The orthodox and conservative Congregational and Presbyterian *Quarterly Christian Spectator* (1819–1838), the Baptist *Christian Review* (1836–1863), and the Calvinst *Literary and Theological Review* (1834–1839) published remarkably good articles on literary and biblical subjects. But the liberal *Christian Examiner* (1824–1869) and the Calvinst *Bibliotheca Sacra* (1843–) hold the first rank. The *Christian Examiner*, which grew out of the *Christian Disciple* (1813–1823), was a Unitarian magazine that had a succession of capable editors like John Palfrey, William Ware, Alvan Lamson, and G. E. Ellis. It specialized in theological discussions, but by the 1830s devoted considerable attention to literature. The *Bibliotheca Sacra*, founded by Edward Robinson and representative of orthodox Calvinism, was edited by such scholars as Bela Edwards, E. A. Park, and S. H. Taylor. It was notably historical in its approach, although conservative in its conclusions. In 1857 the magazine declared its independence from sectarian religious policy.

Biblical criticism was a concomitant part of the radical change in point of view which resulted from the decline of old ideas of order and stability, changed views of human nature, and the criticism of ideas begun by the eighteenth century. These factors, plus the rise of the natural sciences and the general acceptance of the inductive method, tended to fix attention on historical continuity. As the emphasis came to be placed on the affective faculties of man, Christianity came to be viewed as a life, not a system. It was to be experienced, as Coleridge said. Thus a sense of moral absolutism could be retained, even though its authority, the Bible, was studied in terms of its human genesis and development.

The aims and methods of biblical criticism can be reduced to two general considerations, since most scholars followed the categories established early in the century by Eichhorn. First, it was necessary to have as perfect a reconstruction of the biblical text as possible. Once the text was established, then a close study of the various books and Gospels could be undertaken in terms of their relation, the order in which they were written, their philological peculiarities, and their characteristic and unusual modes of presentation. All this was the task of the "lower criticism," which involved a large number of American scholars. Second, there was the external evidence to be considered, which moved beyond the study of any one text. Critics concentrated on relating whatever was known in the Bible to information derived from outside it, such as accounts of ancient writers like Pliny and Josephus, geological findings, or antiquarian research. This was the task of the "higher criticism."[35]

Both approaches were based on a philosophical view of historical causation in which the principle of genetically continuous causation (the principle of organicism) was central. The concept of historical criticism led men to think that God communicated with man in a "regular way." "I look at such things historically," Theodore Parker wrote the Reverend M. A. Miles in 1845, "and cannot settle matters of fact *a priori;* and looking in this way, I don't find evidence which makes it probable to me that God, even in his communication with men, departed from this normal method."[36]

No one school or sect had a monopoly on biblical criticism.

Catholics and Methodists did little. But Congregationalists, Baptists, Unitarians, and Episcopalians interested themselves in the new method and sought to appropriate findings to validate their positions. One encounters men as different as Andrews Norton, Moses Stuart, Gulian Verplanck, and Theodore Parker. Norton's *General Repository and Review* (1812–1813), primarily instructive and judicial, was nevertheless a pioneer in the new discipline. According to Jerry Brown in *The Rise of Biblical Criticism in America, 1800–1870* (1969), Harvard made a faculty appointment in biblical studies as early as 1811. Moses Stuart, a professor of theology in Congregationalist Andover Academy and an ardent student of German philosophical and theological writings, was immensely influential in encouraging the textual and literary criticism of the Bible. Verplanck, an Episcopalian, was professor of revealed religion at the General Theological Seminary for four years, a position that interested him in biblical study and largely prompted his study of the genuineness of the Scriptures. Later he used historical principles in his edition of Shakespeare. Parker was not the most influential of biblical scholars, but his belligerent and learned discussions attracted wide attention. Influenced by Convers Francis and George Ripley (Ripley was well-known for his pamphlet war with Andrews Norton over Transcendentalism and for his critical writings in the *Harbinger* and the New York *Tribune*), Parker mediated between the schools of Norton and Emerson, particularly in his belief that even *a priori* judgments and intuitive conclusions had to be justified historically. Experience was his criterion. But it was experience as modified by Parker's philosophical view of history.[37]

Many biblical critics approached the Bible from the point of view of scholar-historians. They were interested in internal matters of theme, style, and language, and external facts of its historical genesis and development. Germany was an inspiration, the theories of Schwegler, Baur, Zeller, Planck, Schwitzer, Griesbach, De Wette, Herder, Neander, and many others being excitedly discussed. While many distrusted German liberalism, they felt that their doctrinal views of Christianity provided sufficient protection against potentially heretical views. This positon was defined by W. G. T. Shedd, the editor and disciple of Coleridge and professor of English literature at the University of Vermont, who said that history was important because it promoted "Scripturality," induced a correct estimate of creeds and systematic theology, protected theologians from false views respecting the external church, and promoted "profound and genial agreement on essential points."[38]

Thus assured, scholars began an intensive study of all aspects of Scripture. Here they enlisted the natural sciences in the search for the "local and peculiar" conditions affecting biblical literature. E. A. Park cited anthropology, psychology, and rhetoric as sciences auxiliary to practical theology. He then went on to divide biblical exegesis into biblical hermeneutics, linguistics, history, antiquities, and criticism.[39] Park's friend, B. B. Edwards, also stressed the fundamental importance of historical interpretation according to "certain fixed principles." Such a program, he felt, would harmonize the Scriptures with the new discoveries in the natural sciences, would provide a means for interpreting the Bible in perfect consistency with the laws of the human constitution, and would encourage a "real sympathy" with biblical truths.[40]

Since a great part of biblical criticism was concerned with problems of language, much of the credit for the intensive study of languages in the United States can be attributed to the clergy. Shedd looked at language as a part of "the sphere of life and living organization," as opposed to "mechanical principles."[41] This position was seconded by Henry M. Goodwin, whose writings in *Bibliotheca Sacra* sound eminently Emersonian, especially in their concern with the doctrine of the correspondence of the physical and the metaphysical.

Scholars, regarding the Bible as the only sufficient rule of faith and conduct, undertook its extensive study by cultivating the languages in which it was originally written. The novelty of Christianity in its early years was embedded in the freshness and urgency of the New Testament language. But because of long familiarity with the New Testament, scholars of the nineteenth century could not easily apprehend these characteristics. It took a deliberate effort to place oneself in the spirit of early times. Only the severest labor could recapture the primitive qualities of the Bible. G. B. Cheever explained how the "peculiar construction" of the Hebrew language rendered it highly poetical, and he quoted Herder on its sonorousness. And D. Fosdick said that the figurative phraseology of the Bible was drawn from surrounding objects, Jewish art and society. Fosdick's view emphasized the great differences between Jewish and neighboring cultures. But Samuel Turner, professor of biblical learning and interpreter of Scripture in the Episcopal Theological Seminary and professor of Hebrew language and literature at Columbia College, said it was absurd to deny the influence of foreign customs, laws, and usages in biblical literature. Originality consisted in a judicious borrowing of foreign ideas in order to enrich the native.[42]

Concern with language led to a close and intensive reading of the text. The Reverend George Hastings believed that a close analysis of the Old Testament revealed the presence of the thoughts, imagery, passions, and even the style of Moses in the whole line of Hebrew prophets and poets. The essentials of Moses' great ode at the Red Sea could be found everywhere, including Deborah's song and Psalm 68. Samuel Turner took the songs of Moses and Deborah as the embodiment of the "religious and martial heroism of the nation" and studied them for clues to important patterns of Jewish character and history. Analyzing the Book of Job in terms of authorship, time, and place, George Rapall Noyes defended it as a dramatic poem having a consciously ambiguous ending. The strongest point against the antiquity of the book, Noyes thought, was Satan, whose character had been given the Jews at a date later than the conjectured date for the book.[43]

The modern practice of making artificial divisions in the Bible, of cutting it up into "verses," was deplored by scholars as a loss of poetic sensibility. The *Old Testament* had been alive to Jesus. But it was dead to moderns. Consequently theologians attempted to recreate the original purpose of biblical poetry and to realize its influence on the character and fortunes of the Jews. Biblical poetry was not judged by "our own associations." Such thinking was an important contribution (as in Timothy Dwight) to revolt from neoclassical rules and genres, since classification was virtually impossible. Following in the path of Herder, American scholars shed the doctrine of kinds, saying it was "unimportant" whether Hebrew poetry belonged to any particular class of composition. The Bible was of other ages, and could not be studied according to classical values. It was absurd to call this part epic, that lyric, another elegaic.[44]

In working with secular writing, the clergy continued to view literature in terms of national phenomena. Here their philosophical attitudes do not differ appreciably from those of lay exponents of philosophical history. But their work with the Bible made clerical critics especially aware of textual variations, language problems, the usefulness of the new sciences, and the desirability of good documentary evidence. The lower and higher criticisms, with their elaborate schemes for understanding the Bible in all its rich variety, provided both a philosophical underpinning and a significant method for the historical study of literature.

This background was least useful in discussing an American national literature. Here clerical critics engaged in the same platitudes, used the same clichés, and flattered the national vanity quite as much as their lay contemporaries.[45] The American "blood-relationship" with the English led to considerable interest in English national legends and ethnic myths. The sources of the English spirit were explored in long recondite articles on the King Arthur stories, the cast of Chaucer's mind and poetry, Anglo-Saxon language and history.[46] Most of these articles were dependent on previous scholarship. But they all show unquestioning acceptance of literary history as a "scientific method" of scholarly investigation.

While clerical scholars were interested in American and English literature as repositories of the racial mind, their interests really leaned more toward surveying the cultures of southeastern Europe and Asia Minor. Implicitly, at least, these critics viewed the Bible as an essential part of the Western tradition. The other essential part, the Greek, received less attention, but the articles were usually good. A number were concerned with Wolf's denial of the authorship of Homer because of the feeling that "irreligious" scholars would apply Wolf's method to the Pentateuch. The elaborately documented essay of R. D. C. Robbins on Greek drama is a fine example of historical criticism. Robbins, a professor of languages at Middlebury College, was well acquainted with Warton, Schlegel, and Taylor, and much of his essay is indebted to Donaldson's *Greek Theatre*. He minutely traces the rise of the chorus and of dialogue to show the religious origins of Greek drama, studies its early choruses, the Dorian source of choral poetry and the Doric dithyramb, discusses the influence of the Peisistratids (560–510 B.C.), and ends by analyzing the union of the chorus and dialogue.[47]

The long, detailed article on Slavic language and literature by Edward Robinson is one of the best produced by a biblical scholar. Robinson had a vigorously critical mind and was a respected figure in intellectual circles. His book on the geography of the Holy Land was a pioneering venture in the field. Throughout his article on the Slavs, he dealt with the various divisions of the Slav race in terms of their overall comparative traits and diverse national characters. He found these especially illustrated in the languages, which he discussed at considerable length. He noted, for instance, the copiousness of the

Russian language, its ability to assimilate foreign words, the freedom of construction allowed, the nature of the alphabet, and how all this made for an indigenous literature. Robinson also translated a lecture of Eugen Burnouf, a professor of Sanskirt, which he described as opening up unexpected possibilities "in the field of ethnographic and historical speculation."[48]

The most rewarding instances of the cross-fertilization of biblical and literary criticism seem to have occurred in the periodicals of the Congregationalists, Presbyterians, and Unitarians.[49] These periodicals, which ran the gamut from Orthodox Calvinism to Transcendentalism, employed learned and highly skilled scholars capable of writing in a number of fields. The wish of American critics to see with biblical eyes and to hear with biblical ears prompted them to develop a remarkably precise historical method. One critic, in relating the Apocalypse to its age and race, observed that "No enlightened critic now thinks of adopting anything like the old ways of exposition."

V *Shakespeare and Historical Criticism*

Historical criticism of Shakespeare is instructive because it shows how the theory could apply even to a writer who above all others was universally appealing. In the eighteenth century, Shakespeare criticism had helped to modify neoclassical theory. Samuel Johnson, for example, repudiated the unities, and Pope related Shakespeare to his age to explain away his faults. To nineteenth-century critics, Shakespeare was the great exemplar. His individual men and women always showed their common basis in humanity. His breadth of imagination was unsurpassed. He grew with one's growth in knowledge. "No English writer is so generally and constantly kept in the public mind," E. A. Abbott wrote in 1859 in the *North American*. "Where one person reads Milton, five read Shakespeare."

There was a small but persistent segment of American criticism that continued to judge Shakespeare in the light of neoclassical criticism. Reporting to the *North American* on a visit to Scotland in 1815, T. Lyman found in Edinburgh a "most important literary faction" composed of men like Alison and Brown which denigrated Shakespeare for "want of taste, of classical purity and precision, and those other faults which have always been perceived in Shakespeare."[50] Men of these views especially disliked unquestioning adulation of any writer, and they found faults enough in Shakespeare.

They disapproved of his lack of formal unity, and his taste for buffoonery, vulgarity, and rant. As late as 1847 Leonard Withington wrote a scathing attack on Shakespeare's "imperfections," praised the vernacular language of Milton, Dryden, Pope, Johnson, and Hume, and attacked the current veneration of the "new" criticism of Coleridge and the Germans.[51]

But most Americans seem to have preferred the work of Warton, Whately, Morgann, Richardson, and Kames to that of Rymer and Hume.[52] Part of this was due to American dislike for the "rules." Shakespeare was great because he surpassed the writers of antiquity who were the models for the rules. W. H. Prescott praised him for his "calculated" neglect of rules and for his presumed indebtedness to the "national ballads" of Elizabethan times. Shakespeare's historical and romantic drama everywhere afforded glimpses of the "feudal spirit" of olden days.[53] The *Southern Literary Messenger* defended Shakespeare's learning against Ben Jonson's famed remark and said that he forsook the rules for much the same reason that the Greeks observed them: "He had as much right as they to establish a school of his own, for he had as much genius as they, and he had the same guide which had led them forward. The taste of the audience was, in both cases, the governing motive."[54]

Biographical criticism of Shakespeare variously viewed him as one of the first moderns, as a spokesman for the Protestant Germanic element of Europe, as a man exclusively concerned with the exigencies of contemporary theater, as a man responding to the artistic ferment of the time, as one who could not transcend the moral tone of the period. But the paucity of biographical information either discouraged such criticism or drove critics to such large generalizations that they could be made to apply to anyone. Some critics rejected the "prattle" about poaching and horse-holding. Others, like H. W. Barrett, regarded the sonnets as autobiographical "self-revelations" addressed to a man and woman, which must be read in relation to Elizabethan style. Others recommended the construction of an "inner history" based on the plays and poems which would show the man "more truly than any mere external record." And still others viewed him as the prodigy of the Anglo-Saxon race. Lowell, at the time in the very midst of his nationalistic period, felt that Shakespeare was "doubly fortunate" in having a Saxon father and a Norman mother; the lobes of his brain, Lowell said, were "Normanly refined" and "Saxonly sagacious."[55]

Francis Bacon's famous phrase that poetry is like "history made visible" accounts in great part for the strong historical cast to nineteenth-century Shakespearian criticism.[56] Delia Bacon felt that her own period was one of "historical inquiry and criticism" and professed not to understand why the "commonest rules of historical investigation" had not been applied to the study of Shakespeare's authorship."[57] While her views were generally regarded as recondite and theoretical, critics felt that she had made a genuine contribution to an understanding of the compass of Shakespeare's thought.[58] According to Emerson, genius had to live the same life as other men, come under the influence of the same events, and feel the same necessities and the same emotions. Shakespeare proved that even "the greatest genius is the most indebted man." "Thus", said Emerson, "all originality is relative. Every thinker is retrospective."[59]

In general, critics viewed Shakespeare as Protestant, humanist, and philosopher, a participant in the great surge of human progress that accompanied the Reformation. By seeing him in the light of these relations, criticism added another dimension to scholarship. It allowed a great deal of critical leeway. In the hands of such men as the German Ulrici, who believed that each play centered on a single philosophical theme, studies bogged down in verbal gymnastics. But the practice of relating Shakespeare to the larger intellectual trends of his time assumed that Shakespeare had the talents to make these trends answer to his own dramatic ends. Thus a broader sweep was given to criticism, and the study of Shakespeare became in part the study of intellectual history.

As the attitude toward Shakespeare's work became increasingly historical, and as material concerning his work and that of his contemporaries was uncovered, a more constructive critical attitude toward the text was adopted. Dyce's edition was favorably reviewed. Many critics strenuously objected to the critical overloading of the Johnson-Steevens text, the most popular of English editions, even while they agreed with the basic historical motivation of Steevens. With Collier's edition, critical interest increased. It soon became something of a test of a critic whether he agreed with or opposed Collier. Francis Bowen defended Collier and attacked the "false principles of criticism" of Dyce and the Germans, who went afield in the "antiquarian and bibliomaniac mode." But N. L. Frothingham looked upon Collier's discoveries as "the greatest piece of literary audacity that has moved the laughter or the wrath of men since Dr. Bentley published his edition of the 'Paradise Lost.' "[60] As time went on, opposition to Collier increased until Richard Grant White published *Shakespeare's Scholar* (1854) as an outspoken refutation of most of Collier's contentions without actually accusing Collier of a lack of literary conscience.

American editions of the plays, from Dennie's to O. W. B. Peabody's, were all copies of English editions. Peabody's edition (seven volumes, 1836) was the first to explicitly attempt a reconstruction of Shakespeare's text by a collation of the 1623 folio and the quartos, although actually he based most of his text on Singer's English edition.[61] The editions of Verplanck and Hudson pushed Shakespeare scholarship further into "philosophical" historical criticism. Verplanck's notes, which included material on contemporary customs, clothes, and architecture, were designed to provide the reader with whatever data were necessary for a clear understanding of the plays. The order of the plays themselves was slanted toward depicting Shakespeare's artistic and intellectual growth. Verplanck felt that the order of the plays could be given with "reasonable confidence" through a careful analysis of internal evidence, and the external evidence of earlier editions, the Stationer's Register, Shakespeare's contemporaries, and the style and versification.[62] Hudson's edition betrays indebtedness to Coleridge and Schlegel. In addition, his strong religious and political bias (that of a High Church Anglican and aristocratic Whig) and his tendency to forget to acknowledge indebtedness to other scholars mar his work. But his edition gives evidence of historical interest. With the 1872 revision of *Lectures on Shakespeare* (1848), Hudson placed even more emphasis on the history of Elizabethan drama and the influence of Shakespeare's predecessors on his thought and art.[63]

Insofar as historical method descended from theory to practice, Shakespearian scholarship came of age with Richard Grant White. Romantics in the trains of Schlegel and Coleridge had placed their major emphasis on large perspectives which were in essence abstractions of the real situations existing in Shakespeare's time. Despite the considerable amount of research and scholarship that went into the study of sources, this rule of theory over an inductive critical approach caused the scholarship to suffer. White's work was undertaken in reaction to the followers of Coleridge and Schlegel. But in his zeal to deflate the "inflated nonsense" of the philosophical critics, White wound up at the other extreme of emphasizing Shakespeare's monetary interests.

Prior to his interpretative study, *Memoirs of the Life of William*

Shakespeare (1865), White's work was mainly textual. His twelve-volume edition of the *Works* was published in the period 1857–1865. *Shakespeare's Scholar*, directed mainly against Collier's folio of 1632, attacked previous scholars as "critical Dogberries" who failed to study the text of the plays in relation to "the theatrical customs of Shakespeare's day and the probable exigencies of his early career." White explicitly followed this line of inquiry in determining the authorship of *King Henry the Sixth*. He concluded that about 1587 or 1588 Shakespeare assisted Marlowe, Greene, and perhaps Peele to write the *True Tragedy* and the *First Part of the Contention*. He then revised the plays into the folio form as we know it, leading to Greene's charge of plagiarism. White's work represents a turn from excessive generalization to a concrete, inductive historical approach. Explicitly basing his work on the 1623 folio, and not following the editorial work of any others, although remaining aware of their contributions, White sought to present to the reader Shakespeare's words exactly as they had been written.[64]

VI The Practice of Historical Criticism

Historical criticism was indigenous in its origins. By the 1830s, a combination of native and foreign elements had molded it into a confident, consistent body of principles characterized by seven main points: (1) it was cognizant of a continuous but changing cultural tradition as the focal point in literary history; (2) it was oriented to a religious and moral view of literature on racial grounds; (3) it saw the work of art as sociologically important; (4) it interpreted the work of art along the lines of national and racial psychology; (5) it was mainly anti-Lockean (antipositivist), although a few Lockeans like A. H. Everett and Francis Bowen occasionally adopted historical principles; (6) it took for granted an intimate knowledge of the text (Shakespeare, for example), but it generally focused on the larger implications of literary expression; (7) it stressed the organic structure of the individual work of art and the interrelatedness of literature and society.

Americans in the period 1800–1860 guarded against the monism implicit in the theory of historical criticism by emphasizing Providential guidance. This allowed them to give more recognition, by implication at least, to free will and individuality than in the following period, dominated by Taine. In tone and philosophy the period 1800–1860 is romantic and intuitive. It insisted on the group unconscious mind as a sort of mystical, irrational force, which it then elaborated into a nationalistic *Volksgeist*. At the same time, the period held tenaciously to the idea that a general human nature having intellectual content could be abstracted from the social community. However much this abstraction was modified by doctrines of national and individual uniqueness, it lurks in the background and provides a solid basis of argument for proponents of cosmopolitanism through a frank acceptance of diversity.

New England was in the vanguard in accepting historical principles. Generally speaking, the other sections of the country lagged behind. The West, of course, was still in the process of establishing itself, and, while its magazines actively promoted regional and national literature, it lacked a varied group of writers who were abreast of new developments. The South, owing to its greater emphasis on tradition and gentility, was slower in abandoning adherence to models and absolute critical principles, although in time men like Simms and A. B. Meek represented a position considerably more popular than that of Legaré. Criticism in Philadelphia and New York shows an unevenness that finally subtracts from its importance. Walsh's *American Quarterly Review* was among the first to print historical criticism of a remarkably fine kind. And the *New York Review* (1837–1842) printed some admirable articles of a historical nature during its brief career. Historical criticism was also printed sporadically in the *Portfolio*, the *American (Whig) Review*, and the *Democratic Review*.

Advocates of historical criticism were of every class and religious persuasion. Liberals like the early Brownson and Theodore Parker were perhaps more strident in pushing historical criticism. But in the final analysis their critical position was little different from that of Edward Everett, George Ticknor, Edward Robinson, and C. C. Shackford. Indeed, the fact that historical criticism was accepted by men of conservative standing and was printed in the respected pages of such periodicals as the *North American Review* and *Bibliotheca Sacra* probably did more for its acceptance than all the writings of the Transcendentalist circle.

CHAPTER 7

Theories in Practice: Poe and Emerson

IN reputation and influence Poe and Emerson are two of the leading figures in American criticism. Both were very much men of their time, affected by and responsive to most of the issues with which their contemporaries were also grappling. Both were idealists, yet differed so fundamentally on the limits and purpose of literature as to present two radically distinct aesthetic theories. They jolted and jogged their readers in order to promote clearheadedness where parochialism prevailed, and for this reason were considered important but controversial. In the period 1860–1905 the critical idealists especially would try to mitigate some of the controversy through a synthesis of their respective positions.

I *Views of Contemporary America*

Poe and Emerson bleakly viewed their period as one of dissociation and decomposition. Its philosophy was critical, utilitarian, and cheap. Universal principles were no longer natural or binding. America exhibited a "certain maniacal activity," said Emerson, which in its vast churning spewed out "some Nuremberg toys."[1] Expectations had not been fulfilled. Material prosperity yielded only a derivative philosophy, a spiritually impoverished society, and a graceless art.

Poe's mind was essentially conservative, Emerson's liberal, but both abhorred the the Benthamite ideal of social democracy, which seemed to them to exalt mediocrity and the commonness of everyday activity. Inclined naturally to Whiggery, Poe's aristocratic intellect, devoted to social as well as natural "laws of gradation," led him to be violently abusive toward democracy, which he thought "could *never* be anything but a rascally one."[2] Emerson also endorsed an aristocracy of intellect: "Certainly I go for culture, and not for multitudes."[3] But Emerson had faith in man if not men, because man possessed "the Divine Reason" which justified an equalitarian social organiza-

137

tion based on love. He could therefore reject social stratification. "People who wash much have a high mind about it, and talk down to those who wash little."

The gimcrack condition of American society was reflected in its literature. As a cultured people, Poe charged, Americans were "one vast perambulating humbug." Poe's vision of readers surfeited on lady's tales, melodramas, and miniatures of low life was shared by Emerson. The times were sterile in invention. The romance left no lingering trace once the book was closed. Readers fled the "evils of life" to seek "asylum" in art. Art had become solace and compensation, divorced from intimate relation with the life from which it flowed.

II   Views of Current Criticism

Neither man had much patience with the prevailing criticism of his day. To Emerson, current criticism was "infested with a cant of materialism." Critics were preoccupied with "manual skill and activity." They confused form with convention, and they continually misjudged the grace and power of the "natural sayers," the true poets.[4]

Poe condemned American criticism as "corrupt." Works were judged by "literary Titmice" who valued them by the sole criterion of whether they sold or were popular. Where formerly Americans had "enacted a perfect farce of subversience to the *dicta* of Great Britain," they were now too arrogant in their pride, puffing books and involving themselves in "the gross paradox of liking a stupid book the better, because, sure enough, its stupidity is American." American criticism was generally of two kinds, both shoddy. On the one hand, there was an unhealthy intercourse between critic and publisher, especially in the New York coteries, where Fay, for instance, was admired though he lacked merit. On the other hand, criticism fell into the "cant of generality," especially in the quarterlies. Here the aim was no longer to analyze a book's contents and to pass judgment on its merits, but simply to conceal the poverty of critical perception through anonymity and "systematized rigmarole."[5]

III   Approaches to Criticism

Both Emerson and Poe had their formulas for correcting this spiritless situation. Criticism had to become aware of the inspirational power of books, Emerson thought, in order to heal the split between the beautiful and the useful, a split that did not exist in nature. He anticipated the day when criticism would examine books in terms of their ability to describe the immortal, to stimulate moral power in the reader, and to address the reader's imagination. His preface to the first issue of the *Massachusetts Quarterly Review* explicitly stated that the magazine was established to translate this anticipation into practice. Interested in such matters as the English literary mind, the scholar, the nature of art and of beauty, literary ethics, poetry and the imagination, these interests often became the titles for general essays. He had a theory that time winnowed the truth in books, so that he wrote few sustained essays on living authors. "In contemporaries, it is not so easy to distinguish betwixt notoriety and fame."[6]

Poe called for dignity and dependence on one's native resources as essential principles of criticism. The magazines for which he wrote required the journalistic article rather than the discursive essay favored by Emerson. While Poe's work on various magazines was markedly successful, at least at each beginning, he seems to have been congenitally incapable of compromising principle in a workaday world. The result was one restless move after another, always with the purpose of finding a position in which he might entrench himself to attack the trivial and the ordinary. Thus his prospectuses in the early 1840s for the *Penn Magazine* and the *Stylus,* projects designed to give him sole authority to advance the cause of letters and thought.[7] Poe necessarily had to review much drivel, never a challenge to the competent critic, and it is possible that his frequent loss of exactness can be attributed to the sheer volume of his reading in meaningless stuff. His judgment was certainly awry in regard to Chivers and Willis, as well as a whole bevy of female writers. The vituperative attacks on the New York literati, answered in kind, were unbecoming, and his demolition of Fay's *Norman Leslie* was equivalent to squashing a cream puff. Nor can one explain away his appalling lack of taste in mounting his attacks on Longfellow and Lowell.[8]

Yet Poe had a perspicuous judgment which he often used effectively. He failed to see the value of Emerson, but he correctly assessed the strengths and weaknesses of Bryant (1837) and Hawthorne (1842). The 1836 essay on Drake and Halleck is on the whole a fair review. It is particularly strong in pointing out in Drake such problems as bathos, inversions of language, artificial versification, and badly conceived conceits. Poe was probably correct in saying that

Bulwer's tendency to philosophize resulted from a nagging suspicion of shallowness. He was excellent in his assessment of Dickens— except for his habitual phobia on plagiarism—and while he over-praised Thomas Moore's poetry as "inspired," he hit on Moore's strength in versification, vigorous style, and robust fancy.

A. *Idealism*

Idealism was the controlling impulse in the thought of both men. Having abandoned the traditional view of God, their cosmic vision pictured the creation as a unified "plot of God" pulsating with creative power. "To look upward from any existence, material or immaterial, to its *design*," said Poe, moved us toward "Nature's God." And Emerson remarked that Nature "is ever as is our sensibility; it is hostile to ignorance,—plastic, transparent, delightful, to knowledge. Mind carries the law; history is the slow and atomic unfolding." Such exalted cosmic views, they thought, were lost on the majority of their contemporaries. Their contemporaries had yielded to a machine world of bolts and nuts through the adoption of a too narrow empiricism. This false precision in viewing the fact led to a loss of perspective, and vision became fragmented. As a conse-quence, human beings had become estranged from the very world in which they lived, and compensated by pursuing an arrogant form of freedom that merely intensified the estrangement. In reality, Poe said, man's freedom lay in acknowledging "principles which have taught our race to submit to the guidance of the natural laws, rather than attempt their control."[9] And Emerson argued that self-surrender to "a necessitated freedom" constituted man's happiness.

B. *Imagination*

A man of extraordinary vision was needed, namely the poet, to regain, or to recreate, the primal unity. A writer could live in his time and translate it into literature of some power, but it was better to succumb to inspiration and to aim "higher" at the "idea of absolute, eternal truth." For Poe, the desire to apprehend the "beauty above" was an *"immortal* essence of man's nature." The poet, more sensitive than most men, was impelled to poetry in a feverish desire to render supernal beauty. If the poet lacked imagination, the attempt became meaningless. In "Letter to B . . ." imagination seems little more than passionate intensity of spirit. By 1836, under the influence of phrenology, Poe viewed imagination as "a lesser degree of the creative power in God." It was the "soul" of Ideality or the Poetic Sentiment, terms Poe used interchangeably to describe "the sense of the beautiful, of the sublime, and of the mystical." The imagination vanquished the shallowness of the factual, and made art seem a "happy modification of Nature." Emerson was of like mind. "Whoever discredits analogy and requires heaps of facts before any theories can be attempted, has no poetic power, and nothing original or beautiful will be produced by him."[10]

Yet there is a fundamental difference between Emerson's and Poe's kinds of artistic commitments. Poe thought the imagination functioned to stimulate the poetic sentiment to a flight toward supernal beauty. In this view the true poet is essentially a person of exquisite suggestiveness, whose power lies in the ability to *nearly* reach a world beyond our own. In his later career, as Robert Jacobs has demonstrated in *Poe: Journalist and Critic* (1969), Poe tried to reconcile this view of the imagination with an increasing sense of the public role of the writer, but was largely unsuccessful. For Emerson, the imagination achieved its "highest unity" in the moral sentiment. Emerson's true poet was essentially a man of ideas. "He is a beholder of ideas and an utterer of the necessary and causal." The poet's imagination was receptive to the continuous revelations of the "Divine Mind," humbly reporting them to the masses of men, and it methodically ordered the matter of nature and history to reveal the ideal as it interpenetrated matter.

Both men accepted Coleridge's distinction between imagination and fancy, and both often dissolved, as did Coleridge, into high-flown but vague phrasing when talking of the imagination. Emerson came across the concept at least by 1829, when he read James Marsh's editon of Coleridge's *Aids to Reflection*. By the mid 1830s he was praising the poet's imaginative insight as a "very high sort of seeing" not gotten from study or emulation. A special kind of intellect, the imagination encouraged the poet to abandon himself to nature and to be receptive to a "new energy." Emerson admitted that we do not know the "laws" by which the imagination operates. But we are familiar with the fact of its operation, and some conclusions can be drawn. It has literally nothing to do with amusement, accidental resemblances, or colorful presentations of material forms, since these are all properly the office of fancy. Imagination is intensely spiritual.

It detects the correspondence between the mental image and the physical fact, and passionately reveals the correspondence. "Passion adds eyes; is a magnifying glass." The imagination thus invests the physical fact with a "certain cosmical quality" which lifts it "out of a pitiful individuality." But more than that, the imagination is a metamorphosing faculty. It transmutes objects into "new forms" of symbolic intensity. "The feat of the imagination is in showing the convertibility of every thing into every other thing."[11]

Poe's radical disjunctions of intellect, imagination, and passion, which he maintained throughout his career (with some modifications in the latter period), result from his persistent tendency to intellectually discriminate and categorize ideas. He restricted imagination to the poetical and exempted it from intellectual and moral considerations. Imagination, to Poe, is creative, although it does not create from nothing, and it transcends our world of phenomenal relations. It necessarily heightens poetic insights. Examining Bryant's "The Ages," Poe observed that it possessed "higher beauties" of tonal unity and completeness, but the poem was deficient in imagination and originality of thought, a view pretty much the same as now. And in a passage peculiarly close to the textual criticism of our time, Poe analyzes how the imagination creates the "purely ideal" through an intensification of meaning in various phrases. If the passage does not reach Emerson's theory of symbolic expression, it parallels Emerson's theories of metonymy, inspiration, and organic original form.[12]

C. *Art as an Ordering Power*

Poe and Emerson viewed art in the abstract from a Platonic elevation. Art reflected high seriousness, elevated composition, earnestness. Poe would exclude all reason and humor from poetry, and therefore he discounted Pope's *Essay on Man* or Butler's *Hudibras*, although he admitted they possessed "peculiar merits." The artist had to maintain a severe relation with beauty, and, Poe thought, only Keats might lay claim to having upheld that relation. Similarly, Emerson thought art could contain "nothing frivolous." The poet sought veracity. "God and Nature are altogether sincere, and Art should be as sincere."[13] In the universal sense, art was "the spirit creative." It was the "decalogue," not the consoler, of mankind.

The artist expanded on nature by isolating natural forms, imposing unity on these obstinate materials, and to that extent molding our perceptions and extending our vision. Here art triumphed over the diversity and seeming randomness of nature. "Were we to copy nature with accuracy," Poe wrote, "the object copied would seem unnatural." Unity, he felt, was a "vital requisite in all works of Art." The ideal forms of art corresponded vaguely to a world beyond our own. Emerson, more cheerfully disposed toward our world, denied that art had a "separate and contrasted existence" to nature, and asserted that "true" art and the "kingdom of nature" shared a common character. But both men agreed that art was creative and not imitative. Art aimed at the *sense* or the *idea* rather than at faithful reproduction. The artist, said Emerson, values "the expression of nature and not nature itself."[14]

The primary difference between the two men lies in their conceptions of the uses of art. Poe consistently maintained that art sought a "very lofty region of the ideal." The ideal was approached, if not reached, through the creation of beauty. And beauty itself was a separable source of pleasure from truth or passion. In *Eureka,* Poe pictured our entire universe as fragmented pieces of the original unity of God, so that the ideal, in the sense of primal unity, existed nowhere but in the mind of man. Art was the means for capturing that ideal unity and giving it expression.

Emerson synthesized the real and the ideal, and made truth, beauty, and goodness all parts of one original and continuing unity. He could thus reason that "the great works are always attuned to moral nature," a position with which Poe might have agreed in the abstract but which forms no essential part of his aesthetic theory. The element of the real leads to artistic convention, itself superior to "individual talent," as if "a gigantic hand" had inscribed "a line in the history of the human race." The element of the ideal leads to originality and ultimately to spiritual truth. This truth is the precipitant gotten by the artist when he filters his experience of the world through his own intelligence. "Thus is Art a nature passed through the alembic of man," said Emerson, while Poe stated that "We do not paint an object to be true, but to appear true to the beholder."[15]

D. *Beauty*

Poe and Emerson accepted beauty as an essential principle in art, and viewed it as a psychological effect rather than a quality. Beauty, said Emerson, is "not in the form, but in the mind." And Poe maintained that beauty is known as an "intense and pure elevation of soul."[16] Neither man attempted a definition of beauty, but both did remark on some of its qualities. For Emerson, beauty must be simple, must have no superfluous parts, must exactly answer to its ends, must be enduring, and must have an "ascending quality." Poe felt that beauty is indirectly related to form, color, sound, and sentiment or tone. The measure of beauty was whether the work possessed originality, invention, or imagination—terms which he thought in 1842, at any rate, were synonymous. Beauty also included felicity of design which in its origins was vaguely sexual. Emerson thought that design reached "perfection" in mankind and especially in feminine forms. When a woman reveals her beauty she "confers a favor on the world," especially if she inspires deep passion. "Beauty without grace is the hook without the bait."[17] Emerson reacted frankly and openly to the beauty of women. But Poe, who thought that our pursuit of beauty was in the final sense abortive, made their deaths one of the highest, most melancholy, subjects of poetry.

Poe was in many respects a better Platonist than Emerson, and therefore had a healthier respect for the limitations under which human beings acted. Deprived of the experience of ideal unity in a world that consisted of only discriminate forms, poetry provided man "brief and indeterminate glimpses" of another world of perfect beauty the contemplation of which was the "most intense, the most elevating, and the most pure" form of pleasure. Yet that contemplation ultimately resulted in "a certain petulant, impatient sorrow" because it could not be sustained or completely captured. Consequently the highest tonal quality of beauty is sadness or melancholy.[18]

Unlike Poe, Emerson was buoyantly confident that beauty could be caught and contained in the consciousness of man. Beauty was firmly established in the material and spiritual necessity of nature, in which man also participated. Logically speaking the infinitude of Emerson's nature should thwart any attempt to classify the forms of beauty. But Emerson commonly viewed beauty in terms of several gradations: as physical delight, as virtue, and at its highest as consciousness of spiritual form. Since man is the measure of beauty, and since man is a composite of sense, moral virtue, and intellect, the most beautiful poetry will be found to have relations with all three. Emerson was thus at odds with Poe, who argued that beauty had only "collateral" relations with virtue and truth.

E. *Art and the Moral*

Given this fundamental disagreement on beauty, it is natural to expect them to disagree on the moral relevance of art. Poe could be as morally prudish as the next critic. He attacked Wilmer's *The Quacks of Helicon* for its "filth" and "gross obscenity," and remarked parenthetically at one point that "nothing vulgar [should] be *ever* said or conceived." But the logical cast of his mind, which reveled in distinctions, worked at cross purposes to his idealism. Noting that this world is one of particulars, of values separate from one another, he divided mind into pure intellect, taste, and the moral sense. The moral sense (conscience) appertained to duty, and intellect to truth, while taste was related to beauty. Coleridge, from whom Poe had gotten these divisions, had used them flexibly. But Poe cast them in concrete. In the 1840s Poe partially granted the right of poetry to "depict" moral concerns, provided they were made "the *undercurrent* of a poetical thesis." But the whole tide of his aesthetics runs counter to a reconciliation of intellect, beauty, and the moral sense. In discounting intellect and the moral sense in poetry, Poe stands as progenitor for the aesthetic movement in the last decades of the century.

Raised in an area in which the Puritan tradition still exerted influence, and himself trained for the ministry, Emerson habitually viewed man as subject to worship and moral integrity. "The foundation of culture, as of character," he said, "is at last the moral sentiment." When this statement is coupled with his view that man is uniquely an expressive creature, and that man is incomplete until expression is at one with moral truth, it is possible to understand what he meant when he said that poetry is "the piety of the intellect." At its most profound, art is ideal, addressed to a should or would rather than the mundanely existent. Poe assumed that virtue in poetry reasoned or preached, Emerson that it illuminated the mind.[19]

F. *Originality*

Despite their sometimes high-flown statements about idealism in art, both Poe and Emerson had a sturdy appreciation of the role of sound ordinary sense. "The restraining grace of common-sense is the mark of all the valid minds," said Emerson; and Poe argued that feeling and taste should be regulated by the "*dicta* of common sense" which are of "universal application."[20]

Emerson was opposed to the American tendency to promote "culture" through excessive adherence to outmoded models, but he was nevertheless suspicious of "our petulant demand for originality." Great writers do not spin their work out of their bowels. They are indebted to time and place, so that their "materials" are ready at hand. "Thus all originality is relative. Every thinker is retrospective." Early in an artist's career, borrowing would show. With increase in skill borrowings would be adapted to the writer's temperament until they became his own. More important than originality, for Emerson, were "range and extent" of spiritual vision, sympathy for one's native people, and "love for the material with which one works."[21]

Poe based his argument for originality on the practical ground of common sense. Like Emerson, he thought it necessary to "burn and bury" past efforts and to have writers consider what they were *capable* of doing rather than rely on what had conventionally been done. But where Emerson stressed intellectual breadth and sensibility in art, Poe was disposed to value originality most, simply because it was an obvious and easily attainable "source of interest." In "The American Drama" Poe identified four possible kinds of originality: originality of the "general thesis"; originality in developing the thesis through incidents; originality in giving a new tone to even well-known theses; and originality of effect. Of these four, the last, "to produce a fully original effect," was the end the writer should keep "truly in view."[22] By 1842, when Poe reviewed Hawthorne's *Tales,* he had reached the position that originality was the equivalent of invention, creation, and imagination. The expanded version of this review, published five years later in *Godey's,* listed originality as the first criterion for judging a writer's genius.

G. *Language*

Both men had an almost absolute faith in the efficacy of the word. "A man of no conversation," said Emerson, "should smoke." Nothing was beyond the power of the writer, or at least he so supposed. "He believes that all that can be thought can be written, first or last," Emerson observed, "and he would report the Holy Ghost, or attempt it." To the more practical Poe, the resources of languages were sufficient to document all experience, including even dreams, visions, and ecstasies.

Some of Poe's best practical criticism is devoted to how language functions in poetry. He was averse to what Emerson called "correspondences." A poet departed from his "true province" when he strained his resources to discover in the moral world a parallel to some natural phenomenon. But he was also averse to similes as too artificial and ordinary, since such comparisons stop short of the full exploration of what is contained in the language. An artist, Poe said, should "always contrive to weave his illustrations into the metaphorical form."[23]

Yet when a poem moved beyond metaphor to some spiritual insight or symbolic statement through its own logical development, Poe was perfectly willing to follow in its train. In this respect, he was especially effective in dealing with Bryant's poetry. He acknowledged the beauty of "To a Waterfowl," the force of its central image, and its elements of melody and versifications, all of which he thought fine even though they did not push through to first-class poetry. And he goes unerringly to the finer lines of the poem: the "abyss of heaven" image and the parenthetical "The desert, and illimitable air." Poe also acknowledged the "rich simplicity" and congruity of design and expression of "Oh, Fairest of the Rural Maids," even to saying that linking the maid's physical and moral character to qualities of the forest scenery constituted "a far higher and more strictly *ideal* beauty."

Emerson's reflections on language are lively and provocative, and closely parallel much that I. A. Richards was to say later. The singular expression of the fact, Emerson thought, was nearly impossible, for inevitably the fact is incorporated into some figure of speech. The resources of language are multiple, and men speak in metaphor. "Conversation," he said, "is not permitted without tropes." All language is enlivened by this most natural tendency to figurative expression. Hence there is nothing mysterious or uniquely special about tropes or figures. Language abounds in their use. We cannot, he said, "utter a sentence in sprightly conversation without a similitude."[24]

Emerson maintained that there was a "climbing scale of culture" which moves from the direct object through its definition to an understanding of its form, thence to "signs and tokens" created by human intelligence, and finally to "ineffable mysteries of the intellect." Each object in nature literally contains a sense of the whole. Man has lost sight of this fact, and so the poet's function is at least partly restorative. The poet's deeper insight, symbolically expressed, reestablishes the original unity of nature. "The very design of imagination is to domesticate us in another, in a celestial nature."[25]

Thus language at its highest creates symbols that point beyond themselves to dimensions of reality that can be apprehended in no other fashion. They cannot be created at will, but must evolve as all things natural evolve, through the dynamic and "fluxional" interaction of language and artistic insight.

H. *Form*

Along with language, both men were intensely interested in how works of art were shaped into newly existent independent entities. In Emerson's words, they were "students of the mystery of Form." If a literary work lacked form, it consisted of little more than a random pattern of fragments strung together, and in a fundamental sense the work was not art at all. But if the parts of a literary work could be subordinated to and made a functional constitutent of form, then the work gained a constitutional symmetry that made it intelligible and a delight to behold.

When Emerson and Poe talked of organic form, they had in mind a standard of excellence far superior to the nice adjustment of parts in individual poems. Organic form was a model of the highest perfection, the ideal statement that made our crabbed lives more bearable by showing us the illusion of circumstance, a beauty that transcends the world, and sublime visions of universal order. To Poe, the best poets (the Shelleys, Coleridges, Wordsworths, Keatses) gave testimony to a broad poetical vision that encompassed all "objects in the moral or physical universe." The breadth of this vision measured the poet's worth. Similarly, Emerson held that "each work is the tyrant of the hour and concentrates attention on itself." Art in this sense teaches us "the immensity of the world" and the "opulence of human nature."[26]

Rhythm and tone testified most directly to perfect form. Poe's statements about the relation of music to beauty are well-known. As poetry moves toward its "highest possible development," it tends naturally to become more rhythmical in nature. Emerson was of like opinion. As intensity of thought increases, so does its rhythms, for order and harmony in the ideal are one. "Substance is much, but so are mode and form much," he said, and the nature of a poet's rhythm was a "pretty good measure" of his genius.[27] Tone—that is, the general quality or "pitch" of a literary work—was valued for different reasons by the two men. For Poe, tone was objective, and provided a work "its indispensable air of consequence." Hawthorne's sustained purity of tone, especially as it complemented his themes, stamped him as an "indisputable genius"; on the other hand, tonal incongruities such as one found in Halleck's "Alnwick Castle" disrupted the poem, robbed it of all unity of effect, and bore witness to the poet's inferior ability. Emerson, too, thought that the chief value of tone lay in its effect. However, he valued poems for the "record of intuitions" that they contained, and paid relatively little attention to the objective properties of tone. For him, tone chiefly served to stimulate internal responses in the reader in the most profound and concentrated way possible. Poems and their properties may be objective, but they are revealed subjectively. It was this strict interdependence of objective tone and subjective echo that most interested him, for it suggested that the best poetry was revelatory, and that the revelation could not take place until the responding chord had been struck.[28]

Poe also speculated on structural unity as a lesser mode of ideal organic form. His basic position was that "every work of art should contain within itself all that is requisite for its own comprehension." Hence the understanding must be able to contemplate the poem "as a whole, that is, upon the nice adaptation of its constituent parts," a position he correctly referred to Schlegel's "unity or totality of interest" one year after he had mistakenly said that Schlegel viewed plot as mere complexity of incident.[29] Too narrow a focus on plot, however, worked against the higher interests of art, as illustrated by the interest of the *hoi polloi* in the narrative continuity of popular fiction. And some of our finest tales—*Pilgrim's Progress,* for instance—have no significant plot. Poe concluded that unity of plot is at best "a secondary and rigidly artistical merit," and should not be pursued at the cost of higher merits "founded in nature."

IV   *The Specific Arts*

Both Poe and Emerson carefully drew the line between ideal art and the specific arts. The former was an abstract model existent only in men's minds, whereas the specific arts were the imperfect objects left over when men pursue their instinctive impulse to create something. Man aims for the ideal, but in the nature of the case he falls short. Consequently, said Emerson, a poem can only suggest the "immeasurable and divine." Throughout his career Poe held the same view. In "Letter to B . . ." Poe cribbed his definition of a poem from Coleridge, but the point of divergence reveals a significant difference between the two men. Poe misses Coleridge's important dictum that a poem proposes a delight in the whole compatible with liking the parts. Instead, Poe talks of "indefinite" pleasure and "indefinite" sensations as essential qualities of good poems. Later, in *Marginalia* and "The Philosophy of Composition," Poe continued to stress "indefinitiveness" as a desirable element in poems, even though it should function as a undercurrent rather than as a dominant motif.[30]

The problem with the specific arts is that they have a "material basis" through which the spiritual must be filtered. Because the specific arts must employ such tools of general usage as language and literary types, they are lodged in matter, decline to the specific, and finally inhibit and modify the energy of genius. Consequently the specific arts are imperfect transcriptions of man's attempt to capture infinity. They are, as Emerson said, "abortive births of an imperfect or vitiated instinct."[31]

The two men sought to skirt this problem in different ways. Emerson stressed the antecedence of thought to form; if the thought was sufficiently "passionate and alive" the poem acquired an "architecture of its own." While vaguely stated, the position has the virtue of completely removing the arbitrary from composition, even the rational element. Great poets find their verse; they do not make it. Poe's poet could be quite as fervent as Emerson's in his giddy flight after the ideal. But Poe would have none of Emerson's poet ravished by the revelations of the oversoul and serving almost as its amanuensis. Poe's poet was a craftsman, lucid, deliberate, fully possessed of his reasoning faculties. Such a poet excelled in invention; he knew how to combine the "parts" of a poem and what to exclude; and he was constantly guided by his "one pre-established design."[32] After discounting some of its extravagances, "The Philosophy of Composition" does convince us that Poe wrote "The Raven" in the fashion he describes. The essay helps to explain how Poe could have become the virtual creator of the detective story, why he could have promulgated "five laws" for the short story (totality, compression, immediacy, verisimilitude, and finality), and why he could have assigned five qualities to a "proper" poem (strength, unity, compression, point, and completeness).[33]

V   *Ultimate Variety of Vision*

What now is to be made of the two? They share a common enthusiasm and to a considerable extent a common vocabulary, but they face one another over an intellectual fence. To Emerson, Poe was only "the jingle man," while Poe in his turn spoke contemptuously of Emerson as prince of the "Frogpondian Euphuists." Both are in their ways Platonists, but Emerson stresses organic wholeness and the eventual absorption of everything into the universal body, whereas Poe sought to discriminate prototypical ideas which stand massive and complete in themselves. At the very heart of Emerson's organicism is his theory of correspondence, which holds to the perfect parallelism between the laws of nature and the laws of thought. He does not deny the baneful influence of matter on man, but he has a Pelagian confidence that the entire universe is shot through with divine purpose. Poe's universe is fractured, its original unity now separated into various components. Parts and pieces are scattered everywhere, as in Milton's little story on truth.

The two follow out everywhere the implications of their respective doctrines, and especially, since both are writers, in the attitudes they strike toward genius. Emerson comes legitimately to his optimism on the future of literature because he sees that above man is the "infinite Reason" in infinite variety. Genius intuits this Reason, and is thereby granted "a power to carry on and complete the metamorphosis of natural into spiritual facts." Genius gains its insights by remaining "passive to the superincumbent spirit," removes the blinders fashioned by malnurture and maleducation, and turns the eyes of humanity toward the spiritual reality embedded in experience.

To Poe, genius is active rather than passive. It self-consciously puts its imagination in the service of the Form under which it chooses to work: science, philosophy, literature and the like. In each case, the job is to define the craft intellectually in order to make it a discipline in its own right. If a person serves Beauty, he owes allegiance to no other idea, and part of his task is to make sure that he does not wander from his particular province. If a writer, the person uses those elements that subserve the cause of Beauty: narration, unity, language, tone. In a perfectly professional manner he ritualistically fashions these elements through his imagination into a poem. The poem stands as a symbolic representation of Beauty, and at the same time it encourages the reader to an imaginative flight toward Beauty itself.

Both men had spiritual needs that the current, washed-out, nerveless condition of society could not nourish. Society had grown so used to the implacable weight of custom as to become well-nigh crippled in spirit. A regenerative force was needed. Poe and Emerson found it in the imagination. Through the imagination they could explore the far boundaries of human experience in order to extend the possible range of thought and action, and to finally make sense of the actual world in which we have our existence.

Poe's imagination pursued his ideal order beyond the edge of the actual. The gothic tales seem to suggest that infinity inheres in the physical world by virtue of the subconscious, and that it is characterized by fathomless terror and appalling perversity. In most respects, however, Poe's physical world was a grim counterfeit. The ideal world, on the other hand, was an absolute point of unity, order, and harmony. It may not have had objective existence, but it at least had poetic existence in man's imagination. Through suggestion, indefiniteness, and a kind of verbal sorcery, the poet acquainted the reader with this ideal world, and encouraged the same kind of melancholy desire that the poet himself had experienced. What is so fascinating in Poe is the technical precision with which he shaped an aesthetic the final end of which is indefiniteness. Technical precision created an artistic perfection otherwise absent in this world. At the same time Poe was able to undercut the idea that artistic perfection is sufficient to man's needs by using idefiniteness to suggest spiritual dimensions which we in this world cannot comprehend.

Emerson's vision of an ideal reality corresponding point for point with the actual prompted him to discount the blemishes that inhere in the actual. Blemishes were a small matter when time testified to the presence of timeless things. Too intense a preoccupation with the defects of this world can make us passive observers of change, whereas if we focus our attention on the timeless we can become active participants in the universal creation. There is a certain mystery to all this, of which Emerson was aware, and even more a moral grandeur. What we can most admire and least appreciate is the confidence that gave these views birth.

Notes and References

Chapter One

1. "The Periodical Press," *Southern Quarterly Review* 1 (January, 1842), 42.

2. "Irving's Sketch Book," *Analectic* 14 (July, 1819), 78–79.

3. See the relevant sections in Benjamin Spencer, *The Quest for Nationality* (Syracuse, 1957).

4. Gulian Verplanck, *Discourses and Addresses* (New York, 1833), p. 78.

5. Margaret Fuller, *Life Without and Life Within,* ed. Arthur Fuller (Boston, 1895), pp. 108–9.

6. Daniel Webster, "The State of Our Literature," in *Writings and Speeches of Daniel Webster* (Boston, 1903), p. 575.

7. James Russell Lowell, "Nationality in Literature," *North American Review* 69 (July, 1849), 198, 209.

8. James Mulqueen, "Conservatism and Criticism: The Literary Standards of American Whigs, 1845–1852," *American Literature* 44 (1969), 355–72.

9. James Russell Lowell, *Works* (Boston, 1892), II, 131.

10. Ralph Waldo Emerson, "Thoughts on Modern Literature," *Dial* 1 (October, 1840), 137.

11. Joseph Buckminster, *Boston Literary Miscellany* 1 (1804), 82, 92.

12. "Early American Poetry" 2 (December, 1827), 492.

13. George Tucker, "Discourse on American Literature," *Southern Literary Messenger* 4 (1838), 81–88.

14. Samuel Osgood, "The Real and the Ideal in New England," *North American Review* 84 (April, 1857), 542.

15. Dexter Clapp, "The Fine Arts in America," *Christian Examiner* 39 (November, 1845), 314–30.

16. William Tudor, Review of Pickering's *English Language, North American Review* 1 (September, 1815), 386.

17. Joseph Dennie, "Philology," *Portfolio* 1 (February 7, 1801), 42–43; "Americanisms," *Portfolio* 4 (February 18, 1804), 53.

18. Quoted by Allen W. Read, "Edward Everett's Attitude Towards American English," *New England Quarterly* 12 (1939), 115.

19. Quoted by David Shulman, "N. P. Willis and the American Language," *American Speech* 23 (February, 1938), 39.

20. Samuel Knapp, *Lectures on American Literature* (New York, 1829), p.

10; Jared Sparks, "Professor Everett's Orations," *North American Review* 20 (April, 1825), 437; Alexander Kinmont, *Twelve Lectures on the Natural History of Man* (Cincinnati, 1839), p. 278.

21. See Michael Crowell, "John Russell Bartlett's *Dictionary of Americanisms*," *American Quarterly* 24 (May, 1972), 228–42.

22. Joseph Worcester, *A Comprehensive . . . Dictionary of the English Language* (Boston, 1848), p. lvii.

23. Cf. Eleanor Bryce Scott, "Early Literary Clubs in New York City," *American Literature* 5 (March, 1933), 31–46; and Ervin Shoemaker, *Noah Webster, Pioneer of Learning* (New York, 1936), especially the chapter on "Language Reform." Webster's arguments regarding the grammar of the Bible, irregularities in English authors, orthography and etymology can be found in his essay "State of English Philology," in *A Collection of Papers on Political, Literary and Moral Subjects* (New York, 1843).

24. Noah Porter, "A Universal and Critical Dictionary of the English Language," *American (Whig) Review* 5 (May, 1847), 509.

25. "Etymology," *Southern Review* 5 (May, 1830), 338–39.

26. "Language as a Means of Classifying Man," *Christian Review* 24 (1859), 355. See also "Historical and Critical View of Cases in the Indo-European Languages," *Quarterly Christian Spectator* 9 (March, September, 1837), 109–34, 415–33.

27. B. W. Dwight, "An Historical Sketch of the Indo-European Languages," *Bibliotheca Sacra* 14 (1857), 753–69; 15 (1858), 97–127.

28. Henry Wadsworth Longfellow, *Origin and Growth of the Languages of Southern Europe and of their Literatures* (Brunswick, Maine, 1907), pp. 6–7.

29. "National Minstrelsy," *Southern Literary Journal* 4 (December, 1838), 424. The article ends by admonishing American writers to emulate ballad literature in order to "preserve the national character" and elevate the national spirit.

30. G. Harrison Orians is the acknowledged authority on Scott in America. See especially his chapter in *Transitions in American Literary History*, ed. Harry Hayden Clark (Durham, 1953). For other discussions of Scott's influence, see Grace W. Landrum, "Sir Walter Scott and His Literary Rivals in the Old South," *American Literature* 2 (November, 1930), 256–76; J. B. Hubbell, "Literary Nationalism in the Old South," in *American Studies in Honor of W. K. Boyd* (Durham, 1940), pp. 175–220; and G. H. Maynaider, "*Ivanhoe* and its Literary Consequences," in *Essays in Honor of Barrett Wendell* (Cambridge, 1926).

31. Jared Sparks, "Recent American Novels," *North American Review* 21 (July, 1825), 80.

32. "Bulwer's Last of the Barons," *Southern Quarterly Review* 4 (July, 1843), 217.

33. "The Fair Maid of Perth," *Southern Review* 2 (August, 1828), 231.

34. A. P. Peabody, "Philosophy of Fiction," *Christian Examiner* 32 (March, 1842), 10–11.

35. W. B. O. Peabody, "Waverley Novels," *North American Review* 32 (April, 1831), 393.

36. G. Harrison Orians, in *A Short History of American Literature* (New York, 1940), p. 131, gives a partial list of American anthologies in the 1840s, citing the period as "The Triumph of the Anthology." See also the long list in *Minor Knickerbockers*, ed. Kandall Taft (New York, 1947), pp. cxii–cxvi.

37. Henry Tuckerman, "American Literature," *North American Review* 82 (April, 1856), 319.

38. With the decline of romanticism in Germany, Longfellow's interest correspondingly declined. See Frederick Burwick, "Longfellow and German Romanticism," *Comparative Literature Studies* 7 (March, 1970), 12–42.

39. See Margaret Denny, "Cheever's Anthology and American Romanticism," *American Literature* 15 (March, 1943), 1–9, who suggests Cheever's romantic anthology promoted acceptance of romanticism in America.

40. See the reviews of Griswold's work in *Democratic Review* 20 (1847), 384–86, and *Literary World* 1 (1847), 61.

41. For good appraisals of Griswold as man and critic, see Jacob L. Neu, *Rufus Wilmot Griswold*, University of Texas Studies in English no. 5 (Austin, 1925); and Joy Bayless, *Rufus Wilmot Griswold* (Nashville, Tennessee, 1943).

42. William Gilmore Simms, "Modern Prose Fiction," *Southern Quarterly Review* 15 (April, 1849), 64–65.

43. For general orientation see Donald Davidson, "Regionalism and Nationalism in American Literature," *American Review* 5 (April, 1935), 48–61; and Benjamin Spencer, "Regionalism in American Literature," *Regionalism in America*, ed. Merrill Jensen (Madison, 1951), 219–60.

44. Margaret Fuller in New York *Daily Tribune*, December 7, 1844, p. 1.

45. Samuel Osgood, "The Real and the Ideal in New England," *North American Review* 84 (April, 1857), 554.

46. Ralph Rusk, *The Literature of the Middle Western Frontier* (New York, 1926), I, 273. See also David Donald and Frederick Palmer, "Toward a Western Literature, 1820–1860," *Mississippi Valley Historical Review* 35 (1948–1949), 413–28.

47. The best general histories are Kendall Taft, *Minor Knickerbockers* (New York, 1947); J. P. Pritchard, *Literary Wise Men of Gotham* (Baton Rouge, 1963); and Perry Miller, *The Raven and the Whale* (New York, 1956).

48. John Stafford, *The Literary Criticism of "Young America"* (Berkeley, 1952).

49. Quoted by Jay Hubbell in "Literary Nationalism in the Old South," *American Studies in Honor of William Kenneth Boyd* (Durham, 1940), p. 219, n. Discussions of Southern sectionalism can be found in Charles Sydnor, *The Development of Southern Sectionalism, 1819–1848* (Baton Rouge, 1948); Eugene Current-Garcia, "Southern Literary Criticism and the Southern

Dilemma," *Journal of Southern History* 15 (August, 1949), 325–41; and Benjamin Spencer, *The Quest for Nationality* (Syracuse, 1957).

50. See especially Edd Winfield Parks, *Ante-Bellum Southern Literary Critics* (Athens, Georgia, 1962), and Richard J. Calhoun, "Literary Criticism in Southern Periodicals During the American Renaissance," *Emerson Society Quarterly* 55 (Spring, 1969), 76–82. I have generally relied on the work of these two men in the next few pages.

51. Quoted by Parks, *Ante-Bellum Southern Literary Critics*, p. 134.

52. Gregory Paine, *Southern Prose Writers* (New York, 1947), p. lxxix.

53. Spencer, *The Quest for Nationality*, p. 274. Two good articles that illustrate the quandry of southern sectionalism are Robert Jacobs, "Campaign for a Southern Literature: *The Southern Literary Messenger*," *Southern Literary Journal* 2 (1969), 66–98; and Richard J. Calhoun, "The Ante-Bellum Literary Twilight: *Russell's Magazine*," *Southern Literary Journal* 3 (1970), 89–110.

Chapter Two

1. As quoted by Philip Rahv, *Discovery of Europe* (Boston, 1947), p. 141.

2. Angelina La Piana, *Dante's American Pilgrimmage* (New Haven, 1948), pp. 12–13.

3. Ibid., p. 12.

4. One of the better studies of Dusseldorf influence in the United States is James Thomas Flexner, *That Wilder Image* (Boston, 1962), passim.

5. M. L. Green, "Stendhal in America," *Revue de Littérature Comparée* 10 (April–June, 1930), 304–12.

6. Robert Mahieu, *Saine-Beuve aux États-Unis* (Princeton, 1945), pp. 1–2, cites religious differences and the German vogue as reasons for the lack of enthusiasm for French literature.

7. See Harry Hayden Clark, "The Influence of Science on American Literary Criticism, 1860–1910, including the Vogue of Taine," *Transactions of the Wisconsin Academy of Sciences, Arts and Letters* 44 (1955), 138–64.

8. Francis Bowen, "Works of George Sand," *North American Review* 53 (July, 1841), 103–39.

9. A. R. Spofford, "Genius and Writings of Victor Hugo," *North American Review* 81 (October, 1855), 329–46; F. W. Palfrey, "Early French Poetry," *North American Review* 78 (January, 1854), 214–37; de Bury, "Contemporary French Literature," *North American Review* 84 (January, 1857), 203–26; and de Bury, "Literature in France under the Empire," *North American Review*, 84 (October, 1857), 476–503.

10. Howard Mumford Jones, *America and French Culture* (Chapel Hill, 1927), p. 467.

11. Orestes Brownson, "Benjamin Constant," *Christian Examiner* 21 (September, 1836), 63–77; Brownson, "Cousin's Philosophy," *Christian Examiner* 21 (September, 1836), 33–64; and Brownson, "Recent Contribu-

tions to Philosophy," *Christian Examiner* 22 (May, 1837), 181–217. See also Edward Powers, "Orestes Brownson," *Records of the American Catholic Historical Society* 62 (1951), 82–161. George Joyaux, "Victor Cousin and American Transcendentalism," *French Review* 29 (December, 1955), 117–30, sets 1842 as the peak for the popularity of eclecticism.

12. "Specimens of Foreign Literature," *Boston Quarterly Review* 1 (October, 1838), 433.

13. Scholarship on German culture in America is extensive. See especially Henry Pochmann, *German Culture in America* (Madison, 1956); Harold Jantz, "German Thought and Literature in New England," *Journal of English and German Philology* 41 (1942), 1–46; and Stanley Vogel, *German Literary Influences on the American Transcendentalists* (New Haven, 1955). René Wellek has written extensively on the relations between German philosophy and American writing. English influence on German thought was powerful; see John Louis Kind, *Edward Young in Germany* (London, 1906), and Henry Pochmann's *German Culture in America*, which notes three "waves" of English influence in Germany.

14. Henry E. Dwight, "Education in Germany," *Southern Review* 4 (1829), 109; W. H. Prescott, *Biographical and Critical Miscellanies* (Philadelphia, 1857), p. 254; John Weiss, *Life and Correspondence of Theodore Parker* (New York, 1864), I, 271; Emerson, "Thoughts on Modern Literature," *Dial* 1 (October, 1840), 146. Modern scholarship has increasingly supported Brownson's contention that Transcendentalism was essentially an indigenous development. For a balanced view, see Alexander Kern, "The Rise of Transcendentalism," in *Transitions in American Literary History*, ed. Clark, pp. 245–314.

15. Edward Everett, "Orphic Poetry," *North American Review* 21 (October, 1825), 390; George Bancroft, two articles in the *North American Review:* "Herder's Writings" 20 (January, 1825), 138–47, and "Von Dohm's Memoirs" 26 (April, 1828), 285–316; and among the more important of George Bancroft's articles in *American Quarterly Review:* "German Literature" 2 (1827), 171–86; 3 (1828), 150–73; 4 (1828), 157–90. See also Russell Nye, *George Bancroft, Brahmin Rebel* (New York, 1944), and John W. Rathbun, "George Bancroft on Man and History," *Transactions of the Wisconsin Academy of Sciences, Arts and Letters* 43 (1954), 51–73.

16. W. H. Hurlbut, "Religious Poetry of Modern Germany," *Christian Examiner* 46 (March, 1849), 268.

17. C. de la Barca, "The Italian Drama," *North American Review* 39 (October, 1834), 329–70; J. B. Angell, "Influence of English Literature on the German," *North American Review* 84 (April, 1857), 311–45; and J. B. Angell, "Influence of English Literature on the French," *North American Review* 86 (April, 1858), 412–34.

18. Cf. John W. Rathbun, "The Philosophical Setting of George Ticknor's 'History of Spanish Literature,' " *Hispania* 43 (March, 1960), 37–42, on which this paragraph is based.

19. See especially Gertrude Jaeck, *Madame de Staël and the Spread of German Literature* (New York, 1915); and R. G. Whitford, "Madame de Staël's Literary Reputation in America," *Modern Language Notes* 33 (1918), 476–80. These should be supplemented by the interpretation of Howard Mumford Jones, *The Theory of American Literature* (Ithaca, 1948), passim.

20. C. de la Barca, "Madame de Staël," *North American Review* 37 (July, 1833), 1–20.

21. Cf. William Charvat, *The Origins of American Critical Thought, 1810–1835* (Philadelphia, 1936), for an extended discussion of the influence of the Schlegel brothers.

22. "Philosophy of Criticism," *Portfolio* 18 (1817), 505–7, 477–80; "Schlegel's Lectures," *American Monthly Magazine* 2 (September, 1833), 115–22; and "Present State of German Literature," *American Monthly Magazine* 8 (1836), 1–13.

23. Hannah-Beate Schilling, "The Role of the Brothers Schlegel in American Literary Criticism as Found in Selected Periodicals, 1812–1833," *American Literature* 43 (January, 1972), 563–79.

24. For general orientation, see especially Edith Amalia Runge, *Primitivism and Related Ideas in Sturm und Drang Literature* (Baltimore, 1946), and F. McEachran, *The Life and Philosophy of Johann Gottfried Herder* (Oxford, 1939). There is no study of Herder's vogue in America other than that of M. D. Learned, "Herder and America," *German American Annals* 6 (September, 1904), 531–70. In Richard Arthur Firda, "German Philosophy of History and Literature in *The North American Review:* 1815–1860," *Journal of the History of Ideas* 32 (1971), 133–42, Herder is pictured as the most influential German in encouraging a romantic tone in American criticism.

25. John W. Griffith, "Longfellow and Herder and the Sense of History," *Texas Studies in Literature and Language* 13 (1971), 249–62; George Bancroft, "John G. Herder's Complete Works," *North American Review* 20 (1825), 138–47; A. Everett, *An Address to the Literary Societies of Dartmouth College on the Character and Influence of German Literature* (Boston, 1839).

26. Review of Herder's *Remains*, Littell's *Living Age* 54 (1857), 119.

27. The literature on Goethe's critical theory is extensive. See especially Julien I. Rouge, "Goethe critique: l'acheminement à la methode 'genetique,'" *Revue de littérature comparée* 12 (1932), 99–121, John Blankenagel, "Goethe, Madame de Staël, and *Weltliteratur*," *Modern Language Notes* 40 (March, 1925), 143–8.

28. Edward Everett, "Goethe's Life—By Himself," *North American Review* 4 (January, 1817), 217–62; Leonard Woods, Jr., "Goethe's Works," *Literary and Theological Review* 2 (1835), 282–307.

29. "Hermann and Dorothea," *Democratic Review* 23 (1948), 259; "Hermann and Dorothea," *Literary World* 2 (September 18, 1847), 149.

30. Those who followed Bancroft were disposed to use the same method without the moral criticism in which he engaged. Longfellow, who in 1829

continued the New England tradition of study at the University of Göttingen, eventually came to consider Goethe Germany's finest writer, although in *Hyperion* he wrote that he could not tolerate bad morals in such as Goethe. See W. A. Chamberlin, "Longfellow's Attitude toward Goethe," *Modern Philology* 16 (1919), 57–76, and Orie Long, "Goethe and Longfellow," *Germanic Review* 8 (1932), 145–75, reprinted in Long's *Literary Pioneers*.

31. J. L. Motley, "Goethe," *New-York Review* 3 (October, 1838), 397–44; Motley, "Goethe," *New York Review* 5 (July, 1839), 1–48.

32. See Lowell's *Works* (Boston, 1892), II, 85; XI, 217, and George Wurfl, "Lowell's Debt to Goethe, a Study of Literary Influence," *Pennsylvania State College Bulletin* 1 (1936), 1–89. Parke Godwin, "Lewes's Life and Works of Goethe," *Putnam's Magazine* 7 (February, 1856), 192–203; "The Autobiography of Goethe," *Democratic Review* 19 (1846), 439–47 and 20 (1847), 14–22; and "Goethe's Auto-Biography," *Southern Quarterly Review* 11 (1847), 441–67.

33. O. Frothingham, *Transcendentalism in New England* (New York, 1876), p. 287; Mason Wade, ed., *Selected Writings of Margaret Fuller* (New York, 1941), pp. 221, vii. Frederick Braun, *Margaret Fuller and Goethe* (New York, 1910), is still the best study of the subject.

34. See the relevant essays in *Selected Writings of Margaret Fuller, Life Without and Life Within*, ed. Arthur Fuller (Boston, 1895), and *Art, Literature, and the Drama*, ed. Arthur Fuller (Boston, 1889).

Chapter Three

1. Channing, *Lectures Read to the Seniors of Harvard College* (Boston, 1856), p. 180. For the Lyceum see Waldo Braden, "The Beginnings of the Lyceum, 1826–1840," *Southern Speech Journal* 20 (Winter, 1954), 125–35; also Herbert Wichelns, "The Literary Criticism of Oratory," in *Studies in Rhetoric and Public Speaking*, ed. by A. M. Drummond (New York, 1962), pp. 181–216, which poses a distinction (probably too sharply) between rhetorical and literary criticism.

2. For a different view see Stephen Chambers and G. P. Mohrmann, "Rhetoric in Some American Periodicals, 1815–1850," *Speech Monographs* 27 (1970), 111–20, who say that religion was linked to freedom and eloquence to "form a triumvirate" of rhetorical concerns in the period.

3. John Hoshor, "American Contributions to Rhetorical Theory and Homiletics," in *History of Speech Education in America*, ed. Karl Wallace (New York, 1954), 131, 133, passim.

4. For an excellent presentation of this point, see Craig La Driere, "Rhetoric and 'Merely Verbal' Art," in *English Institute Essays* (1948), 123–52. Also Marvin Herrick, *The Fusion of Horatian and Aristotelian Literary Criticism, 1531–1555*)Urbana, 1946).

5. Henry Day, *Elements of the Art of Rhetoric* (Hudson, Ohio, 1850), p. 4.

6. William Charvat, *Origins of American Critical Thought, 1815–1835* (Philadelphia, 1936), provides a useful listing of critical principles. "Scraps from a Correspondent," *Monthly Anthology* 1 (December, 1803), 62; "Literary Indolence," *Portfolio,* 5th ser. 17 (January, 1824), 499–500.

7. J. Q. Adams, *Lectures on Rhetoric and Oratory* (Cambridge, 1810), I, 40–41; Channing, quoted by Maria Hochmuth and Richard Murphy, "Rhetorical and Elocutionary Training in Nineteenth-Century Colleges," in Wallace, *History of Speech Education in America,* p. 160. Especially useful as background to rhetorical theory at Harvard is Eugene Ried, "The Philosophy of American Rhetoric as it Developed in the Boylston Chair of Rhetoric and Oratory at Harvard University" (Ph.D. diss. Ohio State University, 1959). J. Q. Adams, Joseph McKean, E. T. Channing, and F. J. Child were the first four occupants of the chair.

8. Channing, *Lectures Read to the Seniors of Harvard College,* p. 176.

9. Emerson, *Works* (Boston, 1903), I, 354–55. See also Barnet Baskerville, "Emerson as a Critic of Oratory," *Southern Speech Journal* 18 (March, 1953), 150–62.

10. This point was used in Emerson's defense by the *Democratic Review* 1 (February, 1838), 319, when it said that Emerson like all great men of a particular kind showed a "natural tendency to withdraw from the conventions" of his own day in order to avoid the effects of "temporary institutions and local peculiarities."

11. Review of Longfellow's *Ballads and Poems, Democratic Review* 10 (February, 1842), 191; Day, *Elements of the Art of Rhetoric,* p. 241.

12. James R. Boyd, *Elements of Rhetoric and Literary Criticism* (New York, 1847), 44–45, passim. The book was used in many colleges but was intended for the academies and secondary schools, and was a loose compilation of material drawn from Connel's *Catechism of Composition,* Reid, Blair, Beattie, Cheever, and others, and magazines like *North American Review* and *Democratic Review.* Review of Alexis Eustaphieve's *Demetrius, Portfolio* 6 (July, 1818), 90; Matthew Boyd Hope *The Princeton Text Book of Rhetoric* (Princeton, 1859), pp. 155–60. Even though Hope is primarily indebted to Whately and Theremin, his phrasing is often close to Blair, whom Hope cites on occasion. According to Charvat, Blair "dominated criticism of style" in these early years. See Douglas Ehninger and James Golden, "The Intrinsic Sources of Blair's Popularity," *Southern Speech Journal* 21 (Fall, 1955), 12–30.

13. See Samuel Newman, *A Practical System of Rhetoric* (Boston, 1832, pp. 206–7.

14. Review of *The Last of the Mohicans, United States Literary Gazette* 4 (May 1, 1826), 89; the remark on probabilities is in a review of Samuel Beach's *Escalala, United States Literary Gazette* 1 (January 1, 1825), 280; Gardiner and Phillips are quoted by Charvat, *Origins of American Critical Thought, 1815–1835*, p. 145.

15. The remark on taste is from "Romances of the Baron de la Motte Fouque," *Southern Review* 3 (February, 1829), 37.

16. "Mrs. Hemans's Poems," *American Quarterly Review* 1 (March, 1827), 155.

17. J. Q. Adams, "Othello," *New England Magazine*, n.s. 1 (1836), 209–17; "Fugitive Thoughts and Random Criticism," *Democratic Review* 30 (1854), 42–48.

18. E. T. Channing, "The Life of Charles Brockden Brown," *North American Review* 9 (June, 1819), 65.

19. Russell, *A Grammar of Composition* (New Haven, 1823), p. 146; Hope, *The Princeton Text Book in Rhetoric*, p. 109.

20. For the specifics of analysis see Samuel Newman, *A Practical System of Rhetoric*, p. ix; the Bulwer review is in *Southern Review* 3 (May, 1829), 467–95. Composition in Latin was also a means for learning one's lessons in criticism. See "On Composition in Prose and Verse," *Portfolio*, 5th ser. 17 (January, 1824), 102–8.

21. Russell, *A Grammar of Composition*, pp. 64–65.

22. Percival review, *United States Literary Gazette* 1 (June 15, 1824), 66–67; *Hobomok* review by W. H. Gardiner, *North American Review* 19 (1824), 262.

23. Quoted by Kendall B. Taft, *Minor Knickerbockers* (New York, 1947), p. lxv.

24. This was especially true of American advocates of Campbell's *Philosophy of Rhetoric*.

25. Adams, *Lectures on Rhetoric and Oratory*, III, 330.

26. Review of Eustaphieve's *Demetrius*, *Portfolio* 6 (July, 1818), 89.

27. Russell, *A Grammar of Composition*, p. 56.

28. *American Quarterly Review* 2 (December, 1827), 484–85.

29. Newman, *A Practical System of Rhetoric*, p. 207.

30. Ibid., p. 151.

31. See Hochmuth and Murphy, "Rhetorical and Elocutionary Training in Nineteenth-Century Colleges," p. 164.

32. As Day said, *Elements of the Art of Rhetoric*, p. 22, in literature "the subject is at the choice of the writer; and in his selection he has the opportunity of displaying the elevation and correctness of his taste."

Chapter Four

1. Arthur Edward Jones, "Early American Criticism: A Study of American Literary Opinions and Attitudes, 1741–1820" (Ph.D. diss., Syracuse University, 1950), p. 221.

2. Robert Spiller, "Critical Standards in the American Romantic Movement," *College English* 8 (April, 1947), 344–52; Howard Mumford Jones,

"The Drift to Liberalism in the American Eighteenth Century," in *Ideas in America* (Cambridge, 1945). For the other side of the argument, see Merrill Heiser's "The Decline of Neoclassicism, 1801–1848," in *Transitions in American Literary History*, ed. Clark.

3. Quoted by Parks, *Ante-Bellum Southern Literary Critics*, p. 315.

4. W. B. O. Peabody, "Aiken's Life of Addison," *North American Review* 44 (April, 1847), 314–72.

5. Of. Leon Howard, "The American Revolt Against Pope," *Studies in Philology* 49 (January, 1952), 48–65, and Agnes M. Sibley, *Alexander Pope's Prestige in America, 1725–1835* (New York, 1949).

6. J. S. Gardiner, "Pope: Poet of the Human Species," in *The Federalist Literary Mind* (Baton Rouge, 1962), p. 191.

7. Ibid., p. 25.

8. Willard Phillips, "Cowper's Poems," *North American Review* 2 (January, 1816), 234.

9. "Of Criticism, Rhetorick, and the Belles Lettres," *Portico* 1 (1816), 202–4.

10. Robert Walsh, *Didactics: Social, Literary, and Political* (Philadelphia, 1836), I, viii.

11. "Imitation," *Portfolio* 21 (1819), 333.

12. *Sermons of Samuel Stanhope Smith* (New York, 1821), I, 53–5.

13. Review of *Memoirs and Poetical Remains of the Late Jane Taylor*, *Christian Examiner* 3 (1826), 481.

14. Review of Sedgwick's *The Poor Rich Man*, *American Quarterly Review* 21 (March, 1836), 20.

15. Fisher Amers, *Works* (Philadelphia, 1854), II, 430–31.

16. *Monthly Anthology* 4 (May, 1807), 252.

17. "Criticism and Authors," *American Monthly Magazine* 3 (1834), 313–18.

18. Charles Card Smith, "Whipple's Essays and Reviews," *Christian Examiner* 46 (March, 1849), 191.

19. Quoted by Parks, *Ante-Bellum Southern Literary Critics*, p. 315.

20. "Paul Clifford," *Christian Examiner* 9 (September, 1830), 50–51.

21. Quoted from Gulian Verplanck by Taft, *Minor Knickerbockers*, p. xlvi.

22. "Coleridge's *Christabel*," *American Monthly Magazine* 1 (May, 1817), 12.

23. "Sir James Mackintosh," *Christian Disciple* n.s. 3 (1821), 267.

24. Samuel Gilman, "Cause and Effect," *North American Review* 12 (April, 1821), 396. Cf. Merle Curti, "The Great Mr. Locke: America's Philosopher, 1783–1861," in *Probing Our Past* (New York, 1955).

25. Samuel Miller, *A Brief Retrospect of the Eighteenth Century* (New York, 1803), p. 14.

26. Cf. Martin Kallich, "The Associationist Criticism of Francis Hutcheson and David Hume," *Studies in Philology* 43 (October, 1946), 644–67.

27. A. P. Peabody, "Sir James Mackintosh," *North American Review* 66 (April, 1848), 261.

28. John Kirkland in *The Federalist Literary Mind*, p. 142.

29. Cf. Edward Niles Hooker, "The Reviewers and the New Criticism, 1754–1770," *Philological Quarterly* 13 (April, 1934), 189–202.

30. Abraham Mills, *Literature and Literary Men of Great Britain* (New York, 1856), II, 503.

31. Theodore Dehon, "Criticism," *Monthly Anthology* 4 (1807), 472.

32. Andrews Norton, "Poetry of Mrs. Hemens," *Christian Examiner* 3 (1826), 404.

33. Francis Jeffrey, *Essay on Taste* (London, 1871), p. 60.

34. F. W. Winthrop, "Beauty," *North American Review* 7 (May, 1818), 23.

35. Ibid., pp. 22–23.

36. "Alison on Taste," *General Repository and Review* 3 (1813), 193.

37. "French Drama," *American Quarterly Review* 7 (1830), 280–305. For background, see Martin Kallich, "The Meaning of Archibald Alison's *Essays on Taste,*" *Philological Quarterly* 27 (October, 1948), 314–25.

38. Thomas Cogswell Upham, *Elements of Mental Philosophy* (New York, 1845), p. 274.

39. Winthrop, "Beauty," p. 5.

40. "Brown's Philosophy," *American Quarterly Review* 4 (1828), 21.

41. "Theory of Association in Matters of Taste," *Southern Review* 7 (August, 1831), 376–77.

42. Winthrop, "Beauty," p. 18.

43. Hugh Swinton Legaré, *Writings* (Charleston, 1867), II, 5–51.

44. Cf. Walter Channing, "Literary Delinquency of America," *North American Review* 2 (1815), 33–43, and *Portico* 2 (1817), 161–26.

45. "American Literature," *Southern Review* 7 (1831), 436–59.

46. "Mutual Influence of National Literatures," *Southern Quarterly Review* 12 (1847), 306–29.

47. Richard James Calhoun, "Literary Criticism in Southern Periodicals: 1828–1860" (Ph.D. diss., University of North Carolina, 1959).

48. Francis Bowen, "Jeffrey's Life and Letters," *North American Review* 75 (October, 1852), 296–331.

49. J. K. Paulding in *Portfolio*, 4th ser. 2 (November, 1816), 386–87.

50. Richard Hildreth, "Homer," *American Monthly Magazine* 1 (1829), 172–73.

51. H. B. Wallace, *Literary Criticism and Other Papers* (Philadelphia, 1856), p. 434.

52. William Tudor, Phi Beta Kappa Address, *North American Review* 1 (1815), 13–32; Walter Channing, "Reflections on the Literary Delinquency of America," pp. 33–43.

53. A. P. Peabody, "American Poetry," *North American Review* 82

(January, 1856), 236–47. For a survey of the attitudes toward the epic in America, see Donald Foerster, *The Fortunes of Epic Poetry* (Washington, 1962), chap. 4.

54. Samuel Miller, *A Brief Retrospect of the Eighteenth Century*, II, 172–79.

55. For background on this whole business of morality and literature, see the section on "The Moral Yardstick" in chapter 4 of John Paul Pritchard, *Literary Wise Men of Gotham* (Baton Rouge, 1963).

56. See Allen Walker Read, "American Projects for an Academy to Regulate Speech," *Publications of the Modern Language Association of America* 51 (December, 1936), 1141–49.

57. *The Federalist Literary Mind*, p. 177.

58. Quoted by Harry Hayden Clark, in *The Development of American Literary Criticism*, ed. Floyd Stovall (Chapel Hill, 1955), p. 44.

59. J. G. Whittier, *The American Manufacturer*, July 16, 1829, p. 1.

60. C. F. Hoffman, "Criticism," *American Monthly Magazine* 5 (March, 1835), 11.

61. R. S. Gould in the New York *Mirror* 13 (April 9, 1836), 322.

Chapter Five

1. *Portfolio* 17 (May, 1817), 417. According to J. P. Pritchard, *Criticism in America* (Norman, 1956), p. 20, the romantics preserved concepts of taste, genius, and originality in slightly modified form; considerably changed theories of artistic imitation and of nature; and carried over almost intact artistic finish and sound scholarship.

2. E. T. Channing, "On Models in Literature," *North American Review* 3 (July, 1816), 203.

3. Robert Sands, "Wordsworth's Poems," *Atlantic Magazine* 2 (March, 1825), 335.

4. Washington Irving, "Letter from Geoffrey Crayon," *Knickerbocker* 13 (March, 1839), 206.

5. Willard Phillips, "Cowper's Poems," *North American Review* 2 (January, 1816), 234–35.

6. "Ogilvie's Essays," *Portfolio* 16 (December, 1816), 497.

7. Gulian Verplanck, Review of Leigh Hunt's *The Feast of the Poets*, *Analectic Magazine*, n.s. 4 (September, 1814), 243–49.

8. Quoted by Edd Parks, *William Gilmore Simms as a Literary Critic* (Athens, Georgia, 1961), pp. 110–11. Pritchard, *Literary Wise Men of Gotham*, pp. 109–11, discusses the point as it appears in New York criticism.

9. Joseph Dennie, Review of *Child Harold's Pilgrimage*, *Portfolio* 17 (June, 1817), 498; Tremaine McDowell, *William Cullen Bryant* (New York, 1935), pp. xlii–xliii.

10. "Coleridge's Biographia Literaria," *American Monthly and Critical Review* 2 (December, 1817), 24.

11. Gulian Verplanck, Review of Leigh Hunt's *The Feast of the Poets,* p. 245.

12. James Russell Lowell, *Lectures on the English Poets* (Cleveland, 1897), p. 98.

13. James McHenry in *American Monthly Magazine* 2 (July, 1824), 1; quoted by G. H. Orians, "Censure of Fiction in American Romances and Magazines, 1789–1810," *Publications of the Modern Language Association of America* 52 (March, 1937), 197.

14. Cf. Edd Parks, *William Gilmore Simms as a Literary Critic,* pp. 11–13.

15. "Bulwer's Novels," *Literary and Theological Review* 1 (1834), 425.

16. J. L. Motley, "The Novels of Balzac," *North American Review* 65 (July, 1847), 87.

17. "Goethe's *Wilhelm Meister,*" *Southern Review* 3 (May, 1829), 379.

18. *The Journals of Bronson Alcott,* ed. Odell Shepard (Port Washington, New York, 1966), I, 44.

19. *Literary and Scientific Repository* 3 (1821), 478–80.

20. Washington Irving, "A Biographical Sketch of Thomas Campbell," *Analectic* 5 (March, 1815), 234–50.

21. Quoted by Perry Miller, *The Transcendentalists* (Cambridge, 1950), p. 24.

22. "Early Spanish Ballads," *Southern Review* 5 (February, 1830), 86.

23. "Dana's Poems and Prose Writings," *Literary and Theological Review* 1 (June, 1834), 219.

24. "Wordsworth's Poems," *Boston Quarterly Review* 2 (April, 1839), 149.

25. Cited by Parks, *Ante-Bellum Southern Literary Critics,* p. 149.

26. Washington Irving, Review of E. C. Holland's *Odes, Naval Songs, Analectic* 3 (March, 1814), 242–52.

27. "Wordsworth's Poems," *Boston Quarterly Review,* 159.

28. E. T. Channing, "On Models in Literature," p. 205.

29. T. Parsons, "Comparative Merits of the Earlier and Later English Writers," *North American Review* 10 (January, 1820), 21.

30. William J. Free, "William Cullen Bryant on Nationalism, Imitation, and Originality in Poetry," *Studies in Philology* 56 (1969), 672–87.

31. James Marsh, "Present Literature of Italy," *North American Review* 15 (July, 1822), 103–4.

32. "Wordsworth's Poems," *Boston Quarterly Review,* p. 159.

33. *Bryant's Works,* ed. Parke Godwin (New York, 1884), VI, 340.

34. Richard McLanathan, *The American Tradition in the Arts* (New York, 1968), p. 193.

35. J. S. Dwight, *Select Minor Poems Translated from the German of Goethe and Schiller* (Boston, 1839), p. 362.

36. Ibid.

37. James Russell Lowell, "Shakespeare Once More," *Complete Writings* (New York, 1904), III, 249.

38. Cf. Marjorie Nicolson, "James Marsh and the Vermont Transcenden-

talists," *Philosophical Review* 34 (January, 1925), 28–30; and John Dewey, "James Marsh and American Philosophy," in *Problems of Men* (New York, 1946).

39. George Allen, "Reproductive Criticism," *New-York Review* 2 (January, 1838), 58–89.

40. Edwin Whipple, "Coleridge as a Philosophical Critic," in *Essays and Reviews* (Boston, 1878), I, 405–21; it was reprinted from the *American Review* for June, 1846.

41. For studies of Carlyle's criticism see Alfredo Obertell, *Carlyle's Critical Theories* (Genoa, Italy, 1948); Frederick William Roe, *Thomas Carlyle as a Critic of Literature* (New York, 1910); and Elizabeth Nichols, *The Consistency of Carlyle's Literary Criticism* (Cambridge, England, 1931). These should be supplemented by Louise Merwin Young's excellent *Thomas Carlyle and the Art of History* (Philadelphia, 1939).

42. William S. Vance, "Carlyle in America Before *Sartor Resartus*," *American Literature* 7 (1936), 363–75, shows that Carlyle's essays were widely read and appreciated, although Vance's main conclusion has been controverted by George Kummer, "Anonymity and Carlyle's Early Reputation in America," *American Literature* 8 (November, 1936), 297–99. Kummer concludes that Carlyle's fame dates from Emerson's pilgrimage to Craigenputtock. However, in the age of the anonymous article, most readers were shrewd at noting identifications and similarities of style.

43. W. H. Hedge, "Life of Schiller," *Christian Examiner* 16 (July, 1834), 365–92.

44. Emerson, "Carlyle's French Revolution," *Boston Quarterly Review* 1 (October, 1838), 412.

45. C. S. Henry, "Writings of Thomas Carlyle," *New-York Review* 4 (January, 1839), 179–208.

Chapter Six

1. See especially Arthur Lovejoy, *Essays in the History of Ideas* (Baltimore, 1948). Important studies of this phase of American criticism are Charvat, *The Origins of American Critical Thought, 1810–1835*, passim; Ernest Hassold, *American Literary Criticism Before the Civil War* (Chicago, 1935); Harry Hayden Clark, "Changing Trends and Criteria in American Literary Criticism, ed. Stovall, pp. 55–65; and Clarence Brown, *The Achievement of American Criticism* (New York, 1954), pp. 28, 153–81. Rene Wellek's *The Rise of English Literary History* (Chapel Hill, 1941), is informative for its parallel study of English criticism.

2. Samuel Knapp, *Lectures on American Literature* (New York, 1829), p. 1932; Samuel Worcester, "The Qualifications of a Critic," *American Quarterly Observer* 1 (1833), 287.

3. Details of the controversy need greater study, but see two articles by John Greene, "The American Debate on the Negro's Place in History,

1780–1815," *Journal of the History of Ideas* 15 (June, 1954), 384–96, and "Some Early Speculations on the Origin of Human Races," *American Anthropologist* 56 (February, 1954), 31–41.

4. A race, said Knox, "may be destroyed but not sensibly modified by climate" (*The Races of Men* [London, 1850], p. 572).

5. E. P. Whipple, *Character and Characteristic Men* (Boston, 1899), p. 270.

6. Theodore Parker, Review of Lieutenant Colonel Charles Hamilton Smith's *The Natural History of the Human Species, Massachusetts Quarterly Review* 1 (March, 1849), 255–60.

7. James De Bow, "The Earth and Man," *De Bow's Review* 10 (March, 1851), 287. For background, see John Greene, "The American Debate on the Negro's Place in History, 1780–1815"; William Sumner Jenkins, *Pro-Slavery Thought in the Old South* (Chapel Hill, 1935); and Arthur Lloyd, *The Slavery Controversy, 1831–1860* (Chapel Hill, 1939).

8. Review of the Baron de Merian's *Principes de l'étude comparative des Langues, New-York Review* 1 (March, 1837), 110.

9. R. W. Emerson, *English Traits* (Boston, 1903), p. 47. Emerson's letters are full of references to race, and he even prepared lectures on the subject. See *The Letters of Ralph Waldo Emerson,* ed. Ralph L. Rusk (New York, 1939), III, 452; IV, 9, 13, 62, 76, 93, 328, 346, 391; V, 40; IX, 265. Max Cosman, "Emerson's English Traits and the English," *Mark Twain Quarterly* 8 (1948), 7–9, and Samuel Kliger, "Emerson and the Usable Anglo-Saxon Past," *Journal of the History of Ideas* 16 (October, 1955), 476–93, give fruitful comments on Emerson's racial theory.

10. Not so surprisingly, the first paragraph of the *Handbook* of the Daughters of the American Revolution repeats these three characteristics.

11. Quoted by Ronald Vale Wells, *Three Christian Transcendentalists* (New York, 1943), p. 112, n.

12. Barnas Sears, "Historical Studies," *Bibliotheca Sacra* 3 (August, 1846), 584.

13. See John Rathbun, "The Philosophical Setting of George Ticknor's 'History of Spanish Literature,' " *Hispania* 43 (March, 1960), 37–42.

14. See Henry Wheaton's various articles "Scandinavian Literature," *American Quarterly Review* 3 (June, 1828), 481–90; "Scandinavian Mythology, Poetry, and History," *North American Review* 28 (January, 1829), 18–37; "Anglo-Saxon Language and Literature," *North American Review* 33 (October, 1831), 325–50; and his *History of the Northmen* (Philadelphia, 1831). See also A. B. Benson, "Henry Wheaton's Writings on Scandinavia," *Journal of English and Germanic Philology* 19 (1930), 546–61.

15. Andrew Lipscomb, "Editor's Table," *Harper's* 21 (September, 1860), 552.

16. "Early English Poetry," *New-York Review* 7 (October, 1840), 375. Longfellow's early historicism results from associationist views, which were then reinforced by his study in German scholarship. See John W. Griffith,

"Longfellow and Herder and the Sense of History," *Texas Studies in Literature and Language* 13 (1971), 249–65.

17. The following paragraphs are based on John Rathbun, "The Historical Sense in American Associationist Literary Criticism," *Philological Quarterly* 40 (October, 1961), 468–84.

18. Gulian Verplanck, *Discourses and Addresses* (New York, 1833), p. 180. Important studies of this aspect of associationism are Lois Whitney, *Primitivism and the Idea of Progress* (Baltimore, 1934); Gladys Bryson, *Man and Society* (Princeton, 1945); Gordon McKenzie, *Critical Responsiveness* (Berkeley, 1949); and Francis Gallaway, *Reason, Rule, and Revolt in English Classicism* (New York, 1940).

19. "Theory of Association in Matters of Taste," *Southern Review* 7 (August, 1831), 376.

20. James R. Boyd, *Elements of Rhetoric and Literary Criticism* (New York, 1847), pp. 44–55.

21. Willard Phillips, "Cowper's Poems," *North American Review* 2 (January, 1816), 235.

22. A. P. Peabody, "Sir James Mackintosh," *North American Review* 66 (April, 1848), 261.

23. T. C. Upham, *Elements of Mental Philosophy* (New York, 1845), p. 160.

24. E. T. Channing, "Southey's *Life of Cowper*," *North American Review* 44 (January, 1837), 36.

25. R. Wheaton, "The Sources of the Divina Commedia," *North American Review* 44 (January, 1847), 97.

26. E. T. Channing, "Lord Chesterfield," *North American Review* 50 (April, 1840), 404–32.

27. W. H. Prescott, *Biographical and Critical Miscellanies* (Philadelphia, 1856), pp. 88–89.

28. According to Richard Arthur Firda, for instance, Palfrey as editor of the *North American Review* was with his successor, Francis Bowen, "among the last of the *NAR* editors who placed special emphasis upon the form and content of written history" ("German Philosophy of History in the *North American Review*: 1815–1860," *Journal of the History of Ideas* 32 [1971], 136). The standard book on Palfrey is Frank Gatell, *John Gorham Palfrey and the New England Conscience* (Cambridge, 1963).

29. W. H. Prescott, *Biographical and Critical Miscellanies*, p. 194.

30. Jared Sparks, "Servian Popular Poetry," *North American Review* 25 (October, 1827), 352–67.

31. *Letters of William Gilmore Simms* (Columbia, 1952), I, 264, 207.

32. Merrill Lewis, "Organic Metaphor and Edenic Myth in George Bancroft's *History of the United States*," *Journal of the History of Ideas* 26 (1965), 592; Bancroft, *Literary and Historical Miscellanies* (New York, 1857), p. 485; John Rathbun, "George Bancroft on Man and History," *Transactions of the Wisconsin Academy of Sciences, Arts and Letters* 43 (1954), 53.

33. G. Bancroft, *Literary and Historical Miscellanies,* pp. 198, 104.

34. This view of Prescott's changing critical theory is based on William Charvat and Michael Kraus, *William Hickling Prescott* (New York, 1943).

35. Basic studies of biblical criticism are R. H. Lightfoot, "The Critical Approach to the Bible in the Nineteenth Century," in *The Interpretation of the Bible,* ed. C. W. Dugmore (London, 1944); and J. Estlin Carpenter, *The Bible in the Nineteenth Century* (New York, 1903).

36. John Weiss, *Life and Correspondence of Theodore Parker* (New York, 1864), I, 473.

37. John Dirks, *The Critical Theology of Theodore Parker* (New York, 1948), p. 63, says that Parker was "the prophet of historical criticism in the New World."

38. W. G. T. Shedd, "The Nature and Influence of the Historic Spirit," *Bibliotheca Sacra* 11 (1854), 345–94.

39. E. A. Park, "Theological Encyclopedia and Methodology," *Bibliotheca Sacra* 1 (1844), 332, 367.

40. B. B. Edwards, "Present State of Biblical Science," *Bibliotheca Sacra* 7 (1850), 1–13.

41. W. G. T. Shedd, "The Relation of Language to Thought," *Bibliotheca Sacra* 5 (1848), 651.

42. G. B. Cheever, "Lowth's Hebrew Poetry," *North American Review* 31 (October, 1830), 337–79; D. Fosdick, "Noyes's Translation of the Psalms," *Christian Examiner* 43 (September, 1842), 207; Samuel Turner, "Claims of the Hebrew Language and Literature," *Biblical Repository* 1 (1831), 496–97.

43. George Hastings, "Lyrical Poetry of the Bible," *American Biblical Repository,* 3d ser. 3 (1847), 330–31; Samuel Turner, "Claims of the Hebrew Language and Literature," pp. 505–6;; George Rapall Noyes, "The Book of Job," *Christian Examiner* 23 (September, 1837), 29–53.

44. Samuel Turner, "Claims of the Hebrew Language and Literature," p. 495; Sidney Willard, "Noyes's Translation of Job," *North American Review* 26 (January, 1828), 43; "Herder's *Letters Relating to the Study of Divinity,*" *Christian Disciple and Theological Review,* n.s. 2 (1820), 418–19. Timothy Dwight had made a point of the Bible's embodying a revolt from Aristotle's rules and genres.

45. Leonard Bacon, "The Proper Character and Functions of American Literature," *American Biblical Repository* 3 (1840), 2–3; Noah Porter, "Prognostics of American Literature," *American Biblical Repository,* 3d ser. 3 (1847), 507.

46. Samuel Smith, "Anglo-Saxon History of Literature," *Christian Review* 8 (1843), 96–114; Loammi Ware, "Literature of the Legends of King Arthur," *Christian Examiner* 67 (November, 1859), 391–408; M. P. Case, "Chaucer and His Times," *Bibliotheca Sacra* 11 (1854), 394–416.

47. R. D. C. Robbins, "The Greek Drama," *Bibliotheca Sacra* 6 (1849), 84–114. See also A. P. Peabody, "The Classic Mythology and Christianity," *North American Review* 86 (April, 1858), 515–29, and the remarks of

Theodore Parker on Homer in *Life and Correspondence of Theodore Parker*, II, 15.

48. Edward Robinson, "Historical View of the Slavic Language in its Various Dialects; with Special Reference to Theological Literature," *Biblical Repository* 4 (1834), 328–431, 517–32; and Robinson, "Discourse on the Sanskrit Language and Literature," *Biblical Repository* 3 (1833), 707–21.

49. I did not have access to the Lutheran *Evangelical Review*, founded in 1849. But see Edward Gimmestad, "A History of the *Evangelical Review*" (Ph.D diss., University of Wisconsin, 1950). For a discussion of religious periodicals see the first two volumes of Frank Luther Mott, *A History of American Magazines* (Cambridge, 1938).

50. T. Lyman, "Letters from Edinburgh," *North American Review* 1 (September, 1815), 345–46.

51. Leonard Withington, "Shakespeare—The Old and the New Criticism of Him," *Bibliotheca Sacra* 4 (1847), 522–40.

52. The popular Kames was one of the first to develop the idea that the classical unities evolved from the religious nature of drama and the use of the chorus, and his *The Present State of the Theatre* is full of historical argument on Shakespeare.

53. W. H. Prescott, "French and English Tragedy," *North American Review* 16 (January, 1823), 124–56.

54. "Shakespeare," *Southern Literary Messenger* 16 (March, 1850), 137.

55. H. W. Barrett, "Shakespeare's Sonnets," *American (Whig) Review* 6 (September, 1847), 305–07; C. C. Shackford, "Shakespeare in Modern Thought," *North American Review* 85 (October, 1857), 505; J. R. Lowell, "White's Shakespeare," *Atlantic Monthly* 3 (January, 1859), 112, 114.

56. There was a general tendency at this time to view Bacon as a historical critic. For evidence that people gave Bacon more credit than he deserved see Edward Flugel, "Bacon's Historia Literaria," *Anglia* 21 (1899), 259ff.

57. Delia Bacon, "William Shakespeare and his Plays, an Inquiry Concerning Them," *Putnam's Monthly* 7 (1856), 2, 19; and her *The Philosophy of the Plays of Shakespeare Unfolded* (Boston, 1857), p. xxxix.

58. See C. C. Shackford, "Shakespeare in Modern Thought," pp. 495–96.

59. R. W. Emerson, "Shakespeare, or, The Poet," in *Writings* (Boston, 1885), IV, 181, 189. See Robert Falk, "Emerson and Shakespeare," *Publications of the Modern Language Association of America* 56 (June, 1941), 532–43, which strikes the balance of Emerson's appreciation of Shakespeare, and Thomas A. Perry, "Emerson, the Historical Frame, and Shakespeare," *Modern Language Quarterly* 9 (December, 1948), 440–47. Emerson was well acquainted with Shakespearian scholarship. See his letter to Gore Ripley, in *Letters*, ed. Rusk, II, 424–26.

60. Francis Bowen, "Restoration of the Text of Shakespeare," *North American Review* 78 (1854), 423; N. L. Frothingham, Review of Collier's *Works of Shakespeare, Christian Examiner* 55 (November, 1853), 454. For background, see Jane Sherzer, "American Editions of Shakespeare," *Publi-*

cations of the Modern Language Association 22 (1907), 633–96; and Robert Falk, "Representative American Criticism of Shakespeare, 1830–1885" (Ph.D. diss., University of Wisconsin, 1940).

61. Sherzer, "American Editions of Shakespeare," p. 659, calls Peabody "the father of textual criticism in America."

62. Whipple said that Verplanck's edition was the "first connected attempt to trace out Shakespeare's intellectual history and character," a verdict confirmed by Augustus Ralli, *A History of Shakespearian Criticism* (London, 1932), I, 277, and Robert July, *The Essential New Yorker, Gulian Crommelin Verplanck* (Durham, 1951). Alfred Westfall, *American Shakespearian Criticism, 1607–1865* (New York, 1939), p. 132, is inclined to see the influence of men like Knight and Collier.

63. This was first noticed by E. P. Whipple, "Shakespeare's Plays," *North American Review* 67 (July, 1848), 96. See also John Stafford, "Henry Norman Hudson and the Whig Use of Shakespeare," *Publications of the Modern Language Association* 66 (1951), 649–61.

64. See Robert Falk, "Critical Tendencies in Richard Grant White's Shakespeare Commentary," *American Literature* 20 (May, 1948), 144–54. The article deals with changes in White's point of view toward Shakespeare's artistry after 1860.

Chapter Seven

1. Emerson, *Works* (Riverside Edition, Boston, 1884), XI, 326. All subsequent references are to this edition.

2. Poe, *Works,* Virginia Edition (New York, 1902), VI, 207–9. All subsequence references are to this edition. For convincing evidence that Poe maintained a citizen's interest in the world about him, see Killis Campbell, *The Mind of Poe and Other Studies* (Cambridge, 1933), especially the first chapter.

3. Emerson, *Journals* (Cambridge, 1912), VIII, 365.

4. Emerson, *Works,* III, 13.

5. Poe, *Works,* XI, 39; XI, 2; X, 185–86, 188.

6. Emerson, *Works,* VII, 187.

7. See, for instance, Lewis Simpson, " 'Touching "The Stylus" '; Notes on Poe's Vision of Literary Order," in *Studies in American Literature,* edited by Waldo McNeir and Leo Levy (Baton Rouge, 1960).

8. Poe's literary controversies are well documented. See especially Sarah Whitman, *Edgar Poe and His Critics* (New Brunswick, 1949); Sidney Moss, *Poe's Literary Battles* (Durham, 1963); and Vincent Buranelli, *Edgar Allan Poe* (New York, 1961).

9. Poe, *Works,* VIII, 281; Emerson, *Works,* VIII, 212; Poe, *Works,* IV, 202. For the role of unity in Poe, see Margaret Alterton, *Origins of Poe's Critical Theory* (Iowa City, 1925), especially chap. 5.

10. Emerson, *Works,* IV, 274; V, 227.

11. Emerson, *Works*, VIII, 15, 32–33; VI, 288; V, 242.

12. Poe, *Works*, IX, 279; VIII, 302.

13. Poe, *Works*, XI, 76; Emerson, *Works*, X, 244.

14. Poe, *Works*, X, 152–53; Emerson, *Works*, II, 328.

15. Emerson, *Works*, I, 29; Poe, *Works*, X, 152. For Emerson's effort to link art, truth, and ethics, see Wendell Glick, "The Moral and Ethical Dimensions of Emerson's Aesthetics," *Emerson Society Quarterly*, 55 (Spring, 1969), 11–18.

16. Emerson, *Works*, VI, 287; Poe, *Works*, XIV, 197.

17. Emerson, *Works*, I, 28; Poe, *Works*, XIV, 275; Emerson, *Works*, VI, 274; Poe, *Works*, XI, 76; XI, 73; Emerson, *Works*, VI, 284.

18. Cf. George Kelly, "Poe's Theory of Beauty," *American Literature*, 37 (January, 1956), 522: "he posits a realm of pure beauty wherein beauty is a transcendental reality whose essence is beyond the empirical world of humanity."

19. Emerson, *Works*, VIII, 216, 65, 34; VI, 284.

20. Emerson, *Works*, VIII, 9. Poe, *Works*, XIII, 37, 43. On occasion the view led Poe to be unnecessarily anticonvention. He thought, for instance, that the use of asides in drama affects verisimilitude, for it is unreasonable to think that an audience at fifty feet can hear things another actor cannot hear at three.

21. Emerson, *Works*, IV, 189, 179. For the relation of this attitude to American democracy, see Perry Miller, "Emersonian Genius and the American Democracy," in *Emerson: A Collection of Critical Essays*, edited by Milton Konvitz and Stephen Whicher (Englewood Cliffs, N.J., 1962), pp. 72–84.

22. Poe, *Works*, XIV, 194; XIII, 59. On at least one occasion, Poe admitted that what a poet "intensely admires" in another comes to have a "secondary origination within his own soul," so that "no one in the world is more entirely astounded than himself" when charged with plagiarism. Quoted by Thomas P. Haviland, "How Well Did Poe Know Milton?" *Publications of the Modern Language Association*, 69 (September, 1954), 857.

23. Poe, *Works*, XVI, 27.

24. Emerson, *Works*, VIII, 17.

25. Emerson, *Works*, VI, 290; I, 32; *Journals*, IV, 146; *Works*, VIII, 25.

26. Poe, *Works*, IX, 304; Emerson, *Works*, III, 21–22. Here and later in the chapter I am indebted to Richard P. Adams, "Emerson and the Organic Metaphor," *Publications of the Modern Language Association*, 69 (March, 1954), 117–30. Despite Poe's statement about the relation between organic form and ideality, it would make some sense to adopt the terminology of Adams and to distinguish between "formism" and "organicism." The former, into which Poe would conveniently fit, is, according to Adams, descended from Platonic idealism and post-Cartesian humanism, and involves heavy stress on the importance of distinctions and categories due to the fact that

each idea, being eternal, differs fundamentally from every other idea. The organicist, on the other hand, stresses wholeness and is reluctant to analyze.

27. Emerson, *Works*, VIII, 54.

28. Poe, *Works*, XIV, 268; VIII, 309; XI, 104; Emerson, *Works*, III, 35; VIII, 278.

29. Poe, *Works*, XI, 78. In reviewing Kennedy's *Horse-Shoe Robinson*, Poe described structure as "that connecting chain which unites into one whole the varied events of the Novel" (*Works*, VIII, 7). George Kelly, "Poe's Theory of Unity," *Philological Quarterly*, 37 (January, 1958), 34–44, offers a view that differs from mine when he says that Poe reconciled structural unity and unity of effect through the denouement. Poe, however, consistently tried to keep the two separate.

30. Emerson, *Works*, VI, 289; Poe, *Works*, VII, xliii; XVI, 29; XIV, 207.

31. Emerson, *Works*, II, 338–39; VII, 47, 49.

32. Emerson, *Works*, VII, 53; *Early Lectures*, II, 215; Poe, *Works*, XI, 108.

33. See, for instance, two chapters of Edd Parks, "Poe on Fiction" and "Poe on Poetry," in *Edgar Allan Poe as a Literary Critic* (Athens, Georgia, 1964).

Selected Bibliography

1. General Discussions of Literary Criticism and Literary History

ABRAMS, MEYER. *The Mirror and the Lamp: Romantic Theory and the Critical Tradition*. New York: Oxford University Press, 1953. The best study of the English shift to philosophical and literary romanticism, useful as background for the similar shift in the United States.

BROWN, CLARENCE. *The Achievement of American Criticism*. New York: Norton, 1954. Excellent introductory essays documenting shifts in critical attitudes.

CHARVAT, WILLIAM. *The Origins of American Critical Thought, 1810–1835*. Philadelphia: University of Pennsylvania Press, 1936. Seminal study of the period's criticism, with emphasis on associationist influence.

CLARK, HARRY HAYDEN, ed. *Transitions in American Literary History*. Durham: Duke University Press, 1953. Authoritative studies of the rise and decline of literary movements in the United States essential to the study of American literary criticism.

CURTI, MERLE. *The Growth of American Thought*. New York: Harper, 1943. Brilliant intellectual history essential for understanding literary and critical backgrounds.

HOWARD, LEON. *Literature and the American Tradition*. New York: Doubleday, 1961. Suggestive background study that views the mid-nineteenth century as a "time of tension" between the empirical and transcendentalist visions.

JONES, HOWARD MUMFORD. *Ideas in America*. Cambridge: Harvard University Press, 1945. Collection of well-documented essays, in which the drift to liberalism and the influence of European ideas are used as contexts for nineteenth-century American literary history.

MATTHIESSEN. F. O. *American Renaissance: Art and Expression in the Age of Emerson and Whitman*. London: Oxford University Press, 1941. Explores the period 1850–1855 to establish the aesthetic attitudes of America's major writers.

MOTT, FRANK. *A History of American Magazines*. 5 vols. Cambridge: Harvard University Press, 1930–1968. Standard study of the founding and history of periodicals in the United States.

PRITCHARD, JOHN PAUL. *Criticism in America*. Norman: University of Oklahoma Press, 1956. Survey from the beginnings to the present, with a very useful bibliography.

SPILLER, ROBERT. *The Cycle of American Literature*. New York: Macmillan,

1955. Focuses on two broadly parallel eras in the nineteenth and twentieth centuries; useful for its discussion of Emerson, Hawthorne, and others.

————et al. *Literary History of the United States.* New York: Macmillan, 1948. Chapters by leading scholars on all aspects of American thought and literature.

STOVALL, FLOYD, ed. *The Development of American Literary Criticism.* Chapel Hill: University of North Carolina Press, 1955. An excellent study. Chapters by Harry Hayden Clark and Richard Fogle cover the period 1800–1860.

WELLEK, RENÉ. *A History of Modern Criticism, 1750–1950.* New Haven: Yale University Press, 1955. Devoted to English and continental critics, useful as background on scholars who influenced Americans.

2. Individual Authors and Schools of Thought

Chapter One

CLARK, HARRY HAYDEN. "Literary Criticism in the *North American Review, 1815–1835." Transactions of the Wisconsin Academy of Sciences, Arts and Letters,* 32 (1940), 299–350. Annotates critical articles and illustrates the complex nature of criticism at the time.

HUBBELL, JAY. *The South in American Literature, 1607–1900.* Durham: Duke University Press, 1954. Perceptive and balanced sectional history organized largely by author.

JONES, HOWARD MUMFORD. *The Theory of American Literature.* Ithaca: Cornell University Press, 1948. Third chapter discusses the controversy over a national literature in terms of the philosophical debate over the nature of American institutions.

MILLER, PERRY. *The Raven and the Whale.* New York: Harcourt Brace, 1956. Engaging study of the literary controversies that stirred New York during the era of Poe and Melville.

PARKS, EDD. *Ante-Bellum Southern Literary Critics.* Athens: University of Georgia Press, 1962. Chapters devoted to individual authors, with extensive documentation.

————. *William Gilmore Simms as Literary Critic.* Athens: University of Georgia Press, 1961. Study of Simms's views on novels, poetry, nationalism and sectionalism. Well documented.

PRITCHARD, JOHN PAUL. *Literary Wise Men of Gotham.* Norman: University of Oklahoma Press, 1963. Antebellum New York literary and critical theories and controversies.

RUSK, RALPH. *The Literature of the Middle Western Frontier.* New York: Columbia University Press, 1926. Standard treatment of the subject.

SPENCER, BENJAMIN. *The Quest for Nationality.* Syracuse: Syracuse University Press, 1957. Survey from the beginnings to the present by an acknowledged authority.

————. "Regionalism in American Literature." In *Regionalism in America*, edited by Merrill Jensen. Madison: University of Wisconsin Press, 1951. pp. 219–60. Intensive study of theories supporting regional literature, complemented by other chapters in the book.

SPILLER, ROBERT. *The American In England.* New York: Holt, 1926. Travels and reactions of Americans to England to 1835.

STAFFORD, JOHN. *The Literary Criticism of "Young America."* Berkeley: University of California Press, 1952. The relationship of politics, literature, and literary criticism in the period 1837–1850, primarily in New York.

STREETER, ROBERT. "Association Psychology and Literary Nationalism in the *North American Review*, 1815–1825." *American Literature* 17 (November, 1945), 243–54. How the dominant philosophy encouraged literary nationalism; the thesis can be applied to other periodicals.

Chapter Two

BRAUN, FREDERICK. *Margaret Fuller and Goethe.* New York: Holt, 1910. Documents the extent of the major influence on Fuller.

BROOKS, VAN WYCK. *The Dream of Arcadia.* New York: Dutton, 1958. Well-written study of American travel and residence in Italy.

EVERSON, IDA GERTRUDE. *George Henry Calvert, Literary Pioneer.* New York: Columbia University Press, 1944. Excellent study of Calvert's literary and critical theory and his indebtedness to the Germans.

JONES, HOWARD MUMFORD. *America and French Culture.* Chapel Hill: University of North Carolina Press, 1927. Thorough study of French culture in America through the eighteenth century, with some chapters (language, manners, art) carrying the story to 1848.

LA PIANA, ANGELINA. *Dante's American Pilgrimage.* New Haven: Yale University Press, 1948. Surveys Dante scholarship in America from 1800 to 1944.

LONG, ORIE. *Literary Pioneers: Early American Explorers of European Culture.* Cambridge: Harvard University Press, 1935. Documents the European study of men from Ticknor to Motley and its influence on them.

POCHMANN, HENRY. *German Culture in America.* Madison: University of Wisconsin Press, 1957. The standard study, thorough and well indexed.

POWERS, EDWARD. "Orestes Brownson." *Records of the American Catholic Historical Society* 62 (1951), 82–161. Study of Brownson's shifts in philosophical attitudes, including the period when he embraced French Eclecticism.

RATHBUN, JOHN. "George Bancroft on Man and History." *Transactions of*

the *Wisconsin Academy of Sciences, Arts and Letters* 43 (1954), 51–73.
The relation of Bancroft's historiography to his theory of human nature.

SCHILLING, HANNAH-BEATE. "The Role of the Brothers Schlegel in American Literary Criticism as Found in Selected Periodicals, 1812–1833."
American Literature 43 (January, 1972), 563–79. Cautious assessment of
the Schlegels' influence with the intention of correcting previous
scholarship.

VOGEL, STANLEY. *German Literary Influences on the American Transcendentalists.* New Haven: Yale University Press, 1955. A good background
study; criticism is covered through J. F. Clarke and Margaret Fuller.

WILLIAMS, STANLEY. *The Spanish Background of American Literature.*
New Haven: Yale University Press, 1955. The standard study, well
indexed.

WURFL, GEORGE. "Lowell's Debt to Goethe, A Study of Literary
Influence." *The Pennsylvania State College Bulletin* 1 (1936), 1–89.
Draws together an immense amount of material without losing perspective.

Chapter Three

BASKERVILLE, BARNET. "Emerson as a Critic of Oratory." *Southern Speech
Journal* 18 (March, 1953), 150–62. The early and continuing influence of
rhetorical theory on Emerson's attitudes toward art.

CHAMBERS, STEPHEN, AND MOHRMANN, G. P. "Rhetoric in Some American
Periodicals, 1815–1850." *Speech Monographs* 27 (1970), 111–20. The
roles of religion, freedom, and eloquence in rhetorical theory.

HERRICK, MARVIN. *The Fusion of Horatian and Aristotelian Literary Criticism, 1531–1555.* Urbana: University of Illinois Press, 1946. Background
study of a link that persisted in American rhetorical theory.

RIED, EUGENE. "The Philosophy of American Rhetoric as it Developed in
the Boylston Chair of Rhetoric and Oratory at Harvard University."
Ph.D. dissertation, Ohio State University, 1959. Examines the rhetorical theories of occupants of the chair as a means for showing shifts in
American rhetorical theory.

WALLACE, KARL, ed. *History of Speech Education in America.* New York:
Appleton-Century-Crofts, 1954. Excellent for chapters on rhetorical
theory, homiletics, and elocution in the period.

Chapter Four

CALHOUN, RICHARD JAMES. "Literary Criticism in Southern Periodicals:
1828–1860." Ph.D. dissertation, University of North Carolina, 1959.
Documents the persistence of judicial criticism in the South.

CURTI, MERLE. "The Great Mr. Locke: America's Philosopher 1783–1861."

Huntington Library Bulletin 11 (April, 1937), 106–51. The extensive influence of Locke throughout the romantic period, especially on traditionally minded critics.

GALLAWAY, FRANCIS. *Reason, Rule, and Revolt in English Classicism.* New York: Charles Scribner's Sons, 1940. The breakdown of English classicism, valuable because of parallel movements in the United States.

MULQUEEN, JAMES. "Conservatism and Criticism: The Literary Standards of American Whigs, 1845–1852." *American Literature* 44 (1969), 355–72. Explores the link between Whig political views and the literary criticism in the *American (Whig) Review.*

PRITCHARD, JOHN PAUL. *Return to the Fountains: Some Classical Sources of American Criticism.* Durham: Duke University Press, 1942. Background to some of the values of American judicial critics.

SIBLEY, AGNES. *Alexander Pope's Prestige in America, 1725–1835.* New York: King's Crown Press, 1949. Attitudes of American neoclassicists and judicial critics to the English writer.

SIMPSON, LEWIS, ed. *The Federalist Literary Mind.* Baton Rouge: Louisiana State University Press, 1963. Useful introductions to what is mainly an anthology of writings from the *Monthly Anthology.*

Chapter Five

ADAMS, RICHARD. "Romanticism and the American Renaissance." *American Literature* 23 (January, 1952), 419–32. Analysis of some representative American works according to Morse Peckham's theory of philosophical romanticism.

CLARK, HARRY HAYDEN, AND FOERSTER, NORMAN. *James Russell Lowell.* New York: American Book Company, 1947. Valuable for its study of shifts in Lowell's thought, together with Foerster's study of Lowell's literary and critical theory.

COOKE, G. W. *An Historical and Biographical Introduction to Accompany the Dial.* Cleveland: Rowfant Club, 1902. Study of the Transcendentalist periodical with identification of the authors of articles.

FROTHINGHAM, OCTAVIUS. *Transcendentalism in New-England.* New York: G. P. Putnam's Sons, 1876. Still indispensable to a knowledge of the movement.

FUER, LEWIS. "James Marsh and the Conservative Transcendentalist Philosophy." *New England Quarterly* 31 (March, 1958), 3–31. Dramatizes the differences between Vermont and Concord Transcendentalists, and points out the consequences of those differences.

HUDSON, W. P. "Archibald Alison and William Cullen Bryant." *American Literature* 12 (March, 1940), 59–68. The standard study of Bryant's indebtedness to Alison.

LOVEJOY, ARTHUR. *Essays in the History of Ideas.* Baltimore: Johns Hopkins University Press, 1948. Valuable for its essays on the nature of romanticism.

PECKHAM, MORSE. "Toward a Theory of Romanticism." *Publications of the Modern Language Association* 66 (March, 1951), 5–23. Builds on Professors Lovejoy and Wellek to formulate an excellent theory of philosophical romanticism.

SPILLER, ROBERT. "Critical Standards in the American Romantic Movement." *College English* 8 (April, 1947), 344–52. Cites factors that put the brakes to extreme romanticism.

STRAUCH, CARL, ed. "Critical Symposium on American Romanticism." *Emerson Society Quarterly*, no. 55 (1964), 2–60. Short essays by American scholars on matters of style, sympathy, time, and the like in American romanticism.

WADE, MASON. *Margaret Fuller: Whetstone of Genius.* New York: Viking Press, 1940. A good presentation of Fuller's thought and ability as literary critic.

WELLECK, RENÉ. "German and English Romanticism: a Confrontation." *Studies in Romanticism* 4 (1965), 35–56. Points up differences between England and Germany, even though romanticism was essentially similar throughout the western world.

Chapter Six

BENSON, A. B. "Henry Wheaton's Writings on Scandinavia." *Journal of English and Germanic Philology* 19 (1930), 546–61. Wheaton's pioneering effort to apply historical scholarship to ethnic literature.

FIRDA, RICHARD ARTHUR. "German Philosophy of History and Literature in *The North American Review*, 1815–1860." *Journal of the History of Ideas* 32 (1971), 133–42. Survey of German influence on the rise of romanticism in this country, with emphasis on Herder's influence.

GRIFFITH, JOHN. "Longfellow and Herder and the Sense of History." *Texas Studies in Literature and Language* 13 (1971), 249–65. How the two men viewed historical scholarship as an aid in the study of national cultures.

RATHBUN, JOHN. "The Historical Sense in American Associationist Literary Criticism." *Philological Quarterly* 40 (1962), 553–68. Identification of those elements in associationism that promoted historical scholarship.

——. "The Philosophical Setting of George Ticknor's 'History of Spanish Literature.' " *Hispania* 43 (March, 1960), 37–42. Analysis of the first full-length book published in the United States to adapt German historical criticism to the study of a national literature.

SHERZER, JANE. "American Editions of Shakespeare." *Publications of the Modern Language Association* 22 (1907), 633–96. The standard survey.

Chapter Seven

ALTERTON, MARGARET. *Origins of Poe's Critical Theory.* Iowa City: University of Iowa Press, 1925. The standard genetic study of the development of Poe's theories.

CAMPBELL, KILLIS. *The Mind of Poe and Other Studies*. Cambridge: Harvard University Press, 1933. Essential to an understanding of Poe.

CARPENTER, FREDERICK IVES. *Emerson Handbook*. New York: Hendricks House, 1953. Pulls together all the major scholarship on Emerson to that date, and includes chronology and annotated bibliographies.

DAVIDSON, EDWARD. *Poe, A Critical Study*. Cambridge: Harvard University Press, 1957. Penetrating analysis of Poe's aesthetic theory.

FLANAGAN, J. T. "Emerson as a Critic of Fiction." *Philological Quarterly* 15 (1936), 30–45. Draws together much material to show that Emerson remained abreast of contemporary developments.

FOERSTER, NORMAN. *American Criticism*. Boston: Houghton Mifflin, 1928. Fine on Emerson and Lowell, less certain on Poe.

HOPKINS, VIVIAN. *Spires of Form: a Study of Emerson's Aesthetic Theory*. Cambrdige: Harvard University Press, 1951. Authoritative study which divides Emerson's theory into three phases: creativity, organic art, and response.

KELLY, GEORGE. "Poe's Theory of Beauty." *American Literature* 27 (January, 1956), 521–36. Finds great consistency in Poe's concept of beauty and places beauty at the center of Poe's theories of poetry and literature.

LASER, MARVIN. "The Growth and Structure of Poe's Concept of Beauty." *English Literary History* 15 (March, 1948), 69–84. Traces the successive influences of Coleridge, phrenology, and Shelley.

MARKS, EMERSON R. "Poe as Literary Theorist: A Reappraisal." *American Literature* 33 (November, 1961), 296–306. Admits some limitations in Poe, but finds his theories of imitation, form, creativity, and the function of criticism are still relevant to criticism today.

METZGER, C. R. *Emerson and Greenough: Transcendental Pioneers of an American Aesthetic*. Cambridge: Harvard University Press, 1954. Comparative study of the organic theory of art.

MOSS, SIDNEY. *Poe's Literary Battles*. Durham: Duke University Press, 1963. Intensive study of Poe's conflicts with the New York literati.

O'DANIEL, THERMAN. "Emerson as a Literary Critic." *College Language Association Journal* 8 (September, December, 1964), 21–43, 157–189; (March, 1965), 246–76. Massive compilation of Emerson's statements and essays in defense of the view that Emerson was a critic of merit.

PARKS, EDD. *Edgar Allan Poe as Literary Critic*. Athens: University of Georgia Press, 1964. Balanced study of Poe as critic, with acknowledgement of his shortcomings.

PAUL, SHERMAN. *Emerson's Angle of Vision*. Cambridge: Harvard University Press, 1952. Study of Emerson's reconciliation of the real and the ideal.

RUSK, RALPH. *The Life of Ralph Waldo Emerson*. New York: Charles Scribner's Sons, 1949. The definitive study.

STOVALL, FLOYD. "An Interpretation of Poe's 'Al Aaraaf.'" *University of*

Texas Studies in English 9 (1929), 106–33. Examination of the aesthetic underlying the poem.

——. "Poe's Debt to Coleridge." *University of Texas Studies in English* 10 (1930), 70–127. Intensive study of all the data.

WAHR, F. W. *Emerson and Goethe*. Ann Arbor: G. Wahr, 1915. Scholarly study that strikes the right balance.

Index